Victorian Suicide

VICTORIAN SUICIDE

Mad Crimes and Sad Histories

Barbara T. Gates

Princeton University Press
Princeton, New Jersey

Published by Princeton University Press, 41 William Street,
Princeton, New Jersey 08540

In the United Kingdom: Princeton University Press, Guildford, Surrey

Publication of this book has been aided by a grant from the Paul Mellon Fund of
Princeton University Press

This book has been composed in Linotron Garamond

Clothbound editions of Princeton University Press books are printed
on acid-free paper, and binding materials are chosen for
strength and durability. Paperbacks, although satisfactory
for personal collections, are not usually suitable
for library rebinding

Printed in the United States of America by Princeton
University Press, Princeton, New Jersey

Library of Congress Cataloging-in-Publication Data

Gates, Barbara, 1936–
Victorian suicide.
Bibliography: p.
Includes index.
1. Suicide—Great Britain—History—19th century.
2. Suicide in literature. I. Title.
HV6548.G7G38 1988 362.2 88–15144

ISBN 0–691–09437–3 (alk. paper)

To my Australian friends,
whose love and sense of irony sustained me
through all these many suicides.

CONTENTS

ILLUSTRATIONS

PREFACE

Some ten years ago, in one of my graduate seminars, I was asked just why Matthew Arnold's haunting *Empedocles on Etna* had been suppressed by its author. As I had long been unconvinced by Arnold's own answer—that the poem failed to give joy to its readers—I suggested that another explanation might lie in Victorian attitudes toward suicide. After class I dashed off to the library to prove myself right before our next meeting. Unfortunately, my student's question long remained unanswered. There were many sources of information about Victorian death and Victorian murder, but none explaining Victorian suicide. And so a decade and many dozens of libraries later, I offer this book, which attempts to fill a gap in our knowledge of those verbose yet elusive Victorians. I also offer thanks and apologies to a one-time student.

Any work over ten years in the making incurs many debts, and this book is no exception. My primary indebtedness is to a number of student research assistants who helped me hunt down, photocopy, and digest hundreds of Victorian documents. Among them I am especially grateful to Anne Adkins, Nancy Fredericks, Anne O'Donnell, Martha Senkbeil, and Martha Zingo, as well as to Joan Bennett of the University Honors Program at the University of Delaware, who helped to get us together. Other university colleagues who have been more than supportive are Jerry Beasley and Bonnie Scott, who read and commented on this manuscript. Two kind Californians, Ann Abbott and Debra Teachman also provided much help.

Three summer research grants and two sabbatical leaves from the University of Delaware made possible two fact-finding trips to England and the time in which to write. Further research funding came from the American Philosophical Society, the American Council of Learned Societies, and the National Endowment for the Humanities. I am very grateful to these institutions and agencies. A special and heartfelt thanks I offer to the Blue Mountain Center in upstate New York, where I finally completed the writing of this book.

My final statement of gratitude I have reserved for librarians on both sides of the Atlantic who helped me search for the buried secrets of history in everything from computers to hidden-away boxes, and for Deborah Lyall, Suzanne Potts, and William Davis, whose careful work in manuscript preparation and reference-checking helped me put all my words into their final order.

INTRODUCTION

Camus reminded us that there is just one truly philosophical problem—suicide—and that judging whether life is worth living is and must always have been the fundamental question for every human being.[1] Up to now, students of Victorian culture have had little idea of how Victorians confronted the problem of suicide. We know that they openly mourned death and sensationalized murder, but they seem to have deeply feared suicide and to have concealed it whenever possible. Duplicitous Dr. Jekyll hides (as Mr. Hyde) and then fittingly dies a suicide's death to continue concealing his double identity. For most Victorians there was something subversive about suicide, something that demanded suppression and swift entombment.

My book sets out to air Victorian attitudes toward suicide, and my approach has been determined by the quality of available sources. Statistics of suicide, for example, have been of little use. They are virtually nonexistent for the first half of the nineteenth century and for the second half appear to be underestimates of actual numbers. Definitions of suicide vary, records from different parts of Britain are uneven in quality, and concealment was always widespread. Whenever possible, Victorians tended to interpret available statistics to reaffirm pre-existing ideas about suicide rather than revise their attitudes to conform with statistics. Although the incidence of suicide seems not to have risen considerably until near the end of the period, people chose to be alarmed that it had. Something other than facts or numbers determined what Victorians believed about self-destruction.

Almost from the beginning my subject led me into a world of mentalities, not facts, and this is where my book is based. From first to last, this is a study of what Victorians chose to believe about the taking of one's life—of what they felt and of what they wanted or needed to think. In penetrating what initially seemed a prevailing silence about suicide, I uncovered conflicting ideas and feelings. There are, of course, no generic Victorians. When I use the term Victorian, I use it bearing this in mind. The classes and sexes, for example, often viewed suicide very differently. Some Victorians realized that suicide can both entail the negation of the self and represent the ultimate in self-possession. But this very paradox was fearful since it either threatened the Victorian belief in willpower or suggested that such a belief was unchristian. Although not all Victorians understood these threats intellectually, many, nevertheless, acted and reacted toward suicide with personal dread. In Britain, no Durkheim or Freud emerged at the end of the nineteenth century to set the record straight and interpret this dread. By the close of what we choose to call the Victorian age, suicide was felt to be something of a universal plague.

As I burrowed through Victorian documents, more and more voices began to make themselves heard. Mainly they were those of male professionals—doctors, lawyers, essayists, novelists, and poets. Sometimes, however, they were the voices of women, or children, or the working-class, or even of freaks, like John Merrick, "the Elephant Man." Because I hoped that these voices would add a new dimension to my study, I tried to listen to and include them all. And because I sought links between social and aesthetic forms, I tried to keep in mind that I was interpreting not just a text but a culture, not just a single viewpoint but multiple points of view. For this purpose traditional literary texts—which so many of us have been trained to see as high points in a culture—often came to be no more important than letters, scientific treatises, or broadsides. All helped to tell the story of suicide, some more eloquently than others. To those literary critics who may wince at the summary treatment I have given their favorite poems and novels, I can only say that I have tried to provide a new angle of vision for those works by viewing them in the light of opinion about suicide. To those historians who mistrust literary texts as fictions, I would suggest that contemporary literary criticism has much to offer history, for it has reminded us that people fictionalize their lives every day by arranging and editing their perceptions and that not only novels, but autobiographies, newspapers, and letters are fictitious. For many of the voices I have interpreted, I have attempted to read beyond the text, to decode attitudes toward the mystery that is suicide. As often as possible, however, I have let the Victorians speak in their own words and thus reveal a nineteenth- more than a twentieth-century bias.

I had set out to use traditional chronology and to bind myself to the reign of Queen Victoria (1837–1901). But again, my materials dictated a different narrative, even as to beginning and ending. Suicide law was significantly revised in 1823, where I now open my account, and suicide remained illegal in England until 1961. I have ended my book somewhat arbitrarily in the late 1890s, with the close of the Victorian century, a time when many foresaw what Hardy called "the coming universal wish not to live." As we all know, the generations succeeding Hardy did not wish themselves out of existence and drift willingly toward death. Hardy and his contemporaries simply held one more set of attitudes toward self-destruction; theirs was a way of talking about the perniciousness of despair, an attempt at making desperate sense of a senseless world. Despite dire late-Victorian fears and prophecies, more than the fittest survived the cities, the fall of the empire, and even two world wars. Selves did not atomize, and divided selves were sometimes made whole. Soon after the turn of the century, the subconscious self became the side to listen to. It could even help one become freer and seem more integrated. And so my book might have gone on. We still seek to define suicide and despair.

As it stands, this study begins with the death of Castlereagh and the end of Old Europe and concludes with the death of Eleanor Marx and the dawn of the twentieth century. In each chapter I look at a set of attitudes and then follow them through time. In Chapter I, I describe how folklore about suicide flourished alongside legal verdicts and medical knowledge. Chapter II reveals how, through powerful spokespeople like Carlyle, Mill, and Nightingale, willpower became the Victorians' number one defense against self-destruction. Shifting focus, I then indicate how open discussion of suicide was unusual except in the case of the impoverished, the ill-famed, or the self-sacrificial. Otherwise, except by the medical community, suicide was dealt with mainly through displacement. The more powerful liked to think of self-destruction as the appropriate refuge or punishment for the seemingly weaker, even when evidence suggested the contrary. Middle-class men, in particular, tended to make suicide the province of other selves—of men belonging to other times or places, of make-believe monsters, or of women.

The chapters record an important drift that I believe would have been detectable by intelligent persons living in the years 1822–1898. In a recent study of death and culture, Philippe Ariès argues that changes in human attitudes toward death happen very slowly or else take place between what he calls "periods of immobility" that "span several generations and thus exceed the capacity of collective memory."[2] Contemporaries, he suggests, do not notice such changes. I would counterargue that an English person living during the time span I have delimited could have known revolutionary changes in attitudes toward suicide. For every social class, moral and theological stands against self-destruction would weaken, while existential and social interpretations of suicide would increase. In every decade of the period, however, persistent questions about suicide would be posed: was suicide illegal? was it immoral? what kind of person committed suicide? and was the suicidal individual insane? These questions, which plagued the coroner's jurymen after Castlereagh's death in 1822, could still trouble the jury at Eleanor Marx's inquest in 1898. Answers to them were offered by men and women of every cast of mind. This book tells the story of some of those answers.

ABBREVIATIONS

A	*Autobiography*, John Stuart Mill, ed. Currin V. Shields.
AL	*Aurora Leigh*, Elizabeth Barrett Browning, ed. Gardner B. Taplin.
BB	*The Bab Ballads*, W. S. Gilbert, ed. James Ellis.
CB	*The Christmas Books*, Charles Dickens, ed. Michael Slater.
CPW	*The Complete Poetical Works of Browning*, Riverside Edition.
GS	*Ghost Stories and Tales of Mystery*, Joseph Sheridan Le Fanu, intro. Devendra P. Varma.
HB	*Helbeck of Bannisdale*, Mary Augusta Ward, intro. Brian Worthington.
IGD	*In a Glass Darkly*, Joseph Sheridan Le Fanu.
IP	*Imaginary Portraits*, Walter Pater, ed. Eugene J. Brzenk.
JO	*Jude the Obscure*, Thomas Hardy, ed. C. H. Sisson.
LD	*Little Dorrit*, Charles Dickens, ed. R. D. McMaster.
LJ	*Lord Jim*, Joseph Conrad, ed. Cedric Watts and Robert Hampson.
NGS	*New Grub Street*, George Gissing, ed. Bernard Bergonzi.
NP	The Florence Nightingale Papers, British Library.
OCS	*The Old Curiosity Shop*, Charles Dickens, ed. Angus Easson.
PDG	*The Picture of Dorian Gray*, Oscar Wilde, ed. Peter Ackroyd.
PMA	*The Poems of Matthew Arnold*, ed. Kenneth Allott.
PP	*The Purcell Papers*, Joseph Sheridan Le Fanu.
PS	*The Purgatory of Suicides: A Prison Rhyme*, Thomas Cooper.
PT	*The Poems of Tennyson*, ed. Christopher Ricks.
PW	*The Poetical Works of James Thomson*, ed. Bertram Dobell.
SC	*The Strange Case of Dr. Jekyll and Mr. Hyde and Other Stories*, Robert Louis Stevenson, ed. Jenni Calder.
SP	*Selected Poems of Thomas Hood*, ed. John Clubbe.
SR	*Sartor Resartus*, Thomas Carlyle, ed. C. F. Harrold.
TTC	*A Tale of Two Cities*, Charles Dickens, ed. George Woodlock.
US	*Uncle Silas: A Tale of Bertram-Haugh*, Joseph Sheridan Le Fanu.
UTF	*Under Two Flags*, Louise De la Ramée.
WPRK	*The Writings in Prose of Rudyard Kipling.*
WGM	*The Works of George Meredith.*
WH	*Wuthering Heights*, Emily Brontë, ed. William M. Sale, Jr.
WWLN	*The Way We Live Now*, Anthony Trollope, ed. Robert Tracey.

Victorian Suicide

I

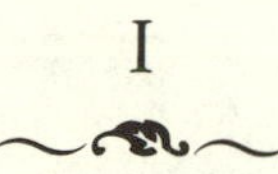

Verdicts

Consider the dilemma of a coroner's juryman in North Cray, Kent, on the afternoon of 13 August 1822. The previous morning, Lord Londonderry, Viscount Castlereagh—architect of the Grand Alliance, shaper of post-Napoleonic Europe, Foreign Secretary, and leader of the House of Commons—got up from his bed, complained of his breakfast, walked to his dressing room, summoned his physician, and then slashed deeply into his own neck with a pen knife. The doctor arrived only in time to catch the sinking lord, who had severed his carotid artery, and to hear him murmur, "Bankhead let me fall upon your arm. 'Tis all over."[1] What our juryman and eleven others had to decide was whether his lordship was insane at the time of his death or was *felo-de-se*, a self-murderer. These were the choices for the legal verdicts in 1822, but to dub such an eminent man insane was to help label British power at its highest level as mad, and to pronounce Castlereagh *felo-de-se* was still worse. A sane and deliberate suicide in 1822 was subject to even greater ignominy: he or she could be buried at a cross-roads with a stake through the heart. As Lady Londonderry still had hope of a state funeral and interment in Westminster Abbey for her lord, a verdict of *felo-de-se* seemed unthinkable. In deference to her, our juryman suggested that he and his fellows take off their shoes and tiptoe past the grieving lady's bed-chamber to view the ill-fated dressing room and corpse. All were deeply affected. In yet further deference to Lady Londonderry, the coroner uncharacteristically led his jury. First he delivered the usual formal charge, then added a qualifying "I think." Next, evidence was heard, and finally, the verdict was given

> that an inquest taken at the house of the late most noble Robert, Marquis of Londonderry, at North Cray, in the county of Kent, on Tuesday the 13th August, on view of the body of the said Marquis, we, the jurors, on our oaths, say that the said Marquis of Londonderry, on the 12th of August, and for some time previously, under a grievous disease of mind, did labour and languish, and by reason of the said disease, became delirious and not of sound mind; and that on the said 12th of August, in the said parish, while labouring under such disease, did, with a certain knife of iron or steel, upon himself make an assault and did strike and cut and stab himself on the carotid artery; and gave himself one mortal wound of the length of one inch and the depth of two inches; of

Death of the Marquis of Londonderry (1822), print after a drawing by George Cruikshank.

which said wound he did then and there instantly die; and being under a state of mental delusion in manner aforesaid, and by the means aforesaid, did kill and destroy himself, and did not come by his death through the means of any other person or persons whatsoever.[2]

Our juryman signed the legal document that carried the verdict, was thanked by the coroner, and then heard a letter from the Duke of Wellington attesting to Castlereagh's recent delusions. His moral dilemma resolved, the juror could head home with his job completed, his charge met.

What followed was public outrage. Placards were raised insisting that no suicide could be buried in the great Abbey. Crowds congregated outside Lord Londonderry's house in St. James Square. Byron would neatly but cruelly summarize radical sentiment at the time in his preface to cantos VI–VIII of *Don Juan*:

Of the manner of his death little need be said, except that if a poor radical . . . had cut his throat, he would have been buried in a cross-road, with the usual appurtenances of the stake and mallet. But the minister was an elegant lunatic—a sentimental suicide—he merely cut the "carotid artery," (blessings on their learning!) and lo! the pageant, and the Abbey! and "the syllables of dolour yelled forth" by the newspapers—and the harangue of the Coroner in the eulogy over the bleeding body of the deceased—(an Anthony worthy of such a Caesar)—and the nauseous and atrocious cant of a degraded crew of conspirators against all that is sincere and honourable. In his death he was necessarily one of two things by the law—a felon or a madman—and in either case no great subject for panegyric.[3]

Actually the pageant on August 20 was curtailed. Because of the protests, the funeral procession was limited to friends and relatives. When the pallbearers bore the body into the Abbey to be placed between those of Pitt and Fox, members of the crowd that had gathered there cheered Castlereagh's death and had to be hushed by the Duke of Wellington. And John Cam Hobhouse discreetly wrote in his journal for 1822 that "many sober persons thought that, considering the manner of his death, it would have been more judicious to give him a private funeral at Cray."[4]

Clearly, much of the hostility toward Castlereagh's funeral and burial was political. For many, Lord Londonderry had become a symbol of privilege, rigidity, conservatism, and collaboration with the *ancien régime*. He was an emblem of the Old Europe. But some of the hostility was moral and marked contemporary feeling about injustice in ignominious disposal of suicides. In June of 1823, less than a year after Castlereagh's death, there was another, sorrier burial of a suicide in

London. Abel Griffiths, a twenty-two-year-old law student, clad only in drawers, socks and a winding sheet, was interred at the cross-roads formed by Eaton Street, Grosvenor Place and the King's Road. Wrapped in a piece of Russian matting, his bloodied, unwashed body was quickly dropped into a hole about five feet deep. The *Annual Register* for that year reports that "the disgusting part of the ceremony of throwing lime over the body and driving a stake through it was dispensed with."[5] Griffiths had killed himself after having murdered his father. A chemist with personal knowledge of Griffiths, presumably a reliable witness, told the coroner's jury that Griffiths had had a "depression in the brain" and had inquired about leeching; he was certain that Griffiths was suffering from mental disease. But Griffiths's jury consulted for two hours and pronounced that Abel Griffiths "killed himself in a sound state of mind."[6] Resistance to this seemingly unfair verdict was expected but did not develop. Nevertheless, on the morning of the interment, constables and watchmen were stationed about the neighborhood of the deceased to keep an eye out for protestors.

They would be the last such watchdogs ever needed, for Griffiths was the last London suicide known to have been buried at a cross-roads. Glaring legal inequities, like those apparent in the Londonderry and Griffiths cases, were to come to an end in mid-1823, with the passage of 4 George IV.c 52. This law made it illegal for coroners to issue a warrant for burial of a *felo-de-se* in a public highway. Within twenty-four hours of the inquest, the suicide was to be interred in a churchyard or public burial place. Superstitions and the desire to punish self-murderers remained, however. Suicides had been buried at cross-roads because these were signs of the cross; because steady traffic over the suicide's grave could help keep the person's ghost down; and because ancient sacrificial victims had been slain at such sites. Since they were considered the ultimate sinners, suicides had been staked to prevent their restless wanderings as lost souls. If life was a gift from God, the taking of it was God's prerogative only. This latter belief died hard, and the 1823 law contained punitive clauses. A *felo-de-se* must still be buried without Christian rites and at night, between the hours of nine and midnight, and his/her goods and chattels must still be turned over to the Crown.

Ambivalence in this law mirrored the ambivalence of English public opinion from the late eighteenth century throughout much of the nineteenth. Forfeiture was generally waived by the Crown in cases in which a suicide was not committed in order to avoid conviction for another felony, and temporary insanity was returned as a verdict far more often than *felo-de-se*. It became an aphorism to say that in England you must avoid suicide on pain of being regarded as a criminal if you failed and a lunatic if you succeeded. Thus by the 1820s there was considerable support for liberalizing an antiquated law dating from the tenth century. In 1820, a letter writer to the *London Times* felt it necessary to contend that "a jury is fully warranted in bringing in a verdict of insanity in such cases, unless there be clear and decided proof to the contrary; and that to err on that side, if we are to err, is more just than on the other."[7] Yet this view, like that of Castlereagh's coroner, was countered by its opposite. Two years before publication of the letter to the *Times*, in a sermon entitled "Suicide: An Atrocious Offence against God and Man," the Reverend Henry George Watkins railed uncharitably that verdicts of insanity "*rather palliate the crime than prevent its increase*."[8]

Religious sanctions against suicide would remain strong throughout the nineteenth century, but by 1823 many legal authorities, moralists, and parliamentarians did support reform. Most of them realized that earlier laws governing the punishment of *felonia-de-se* were developed by medieval judges to enrich the royal treasury. Thomas De Quincey refined contemporary thinking by arguing that it was necessary to distinguish between justifiable self-homicide and culpable self-murder. The first should apply whenever interests of others were involved, the second when simple personal interest was the motivating factor.[9] Then, on 26 May 1823, Sir James MacKintosh, an impassioned parliamentarian, rose to the floor of the House of Commons. He labeled those who could approve of impaling bodies of other human beings, "Cannibals," and then called for an end to forfeiture. Not for a moment did he think that the penal laws against suicide were representative of current public conscience. Nor was there fairness in verdicts:

> Verdicts of insanity were almost always found in the cases of persons in the higher stations of life: where self-slayers were humble and defenceless, there *felo-de-se* was usually returned. This might perhaps be accounted for, without any imputations upon the impartiality of juries. First, because persons in high life had usually better means of establishing the excuse for the criminal act. Secondly, because suicide was rarely the crime of the poorer classes occupied with their daily labours. It was the effect of wounded shame; the result of false pride, and the fear of some imaginary degradation. Thirdly, the very barbarity of the law rendered it impotent; for juries would not consent that the remains of the dead should be thus outraged if they could find any colour for a verdict of insanity.[10]

Cheers went up from the House as MacKintosh seated himself after this speech. On 4 July, the new law passed, replacing a custom that the *Annual Register* termed "revolting to every natural feeling."[11]

Even though Westminster moved to lay them to rest, ghosts and atrocities at cross-roads would continue to haunt fiction and the British popular imagination. Published just a year after the passage of the new English law and capitalizing on public interest throughout Britain,[12] James Hogg's *The Private Memoirs and Confessions of a Justified Sinner* contains a macabre, fictional letter recounting the exhumation of a suicide. Purportedly from *Blackwood's* in August of 1823, it describes the perfectly preserved body of a supposedly devil-assisted suicide, dead for over one hundred years and interred at a cross-roads. Hogg concludes his imaginative book by noting that "in this day, and with the present generation, it will not go down that a man should be daily tempted by the Devil, in the semblance of a fellow-creature; and at length lured to self-destruction."[13] Yet some twenty years later, in Emily Brontë's day, devils, crossroads, and suicides continued to spellbind readers.

Brontë's *Wuthering Heights*, set in 1771–1803 but published in 1847, alludes both to pre-1823 burial customs and to those of 1823. Brontë seems to have felt free to use both the laws in effect during the time of her story and those governing early Victorian times.[14] In narrating the details surrounding Hindley Earnshaw's death (1784), for example, she draws upon the earlier statutes. Although the exact cause of Hindley's death is never determined, all who saw him at the end claim that he died in a state of drunkenness. Mr. Kenneth, who tells Nelly about the death, says that he "died true to his character, drunk as a lord."[15] And Heathcliff, when Nelly asks if she may proceed with suitable arrangements for Hindley's funeral, retorts that "correctly . . . that fool's body should be buried at the cross-roads, without ceremony of any kind. I happened to leave him ten minutes, yesterday afternoon; and, in that interval, he fastened the two doors of the house against me, and he has spent the night in drinking himself to death deliberately!" (*WH*, 153).

The precise circumstances of Hindley's death, which are reported in considerable detail, have important implications for the course of Brontë's novel. For if Hindley did die drunk and debauched, as both Kenneth and Heathcliff indicate he did, in the eighteenth century he would automatically have been considered a suicide, exactly as Heathcliff suggests.[16] Even more importantly, in that case his property could legally have been forfeited to the Crown, with nothing left for Hareton and hence nothing left for Heathcliff to employ as a tool in his revenge. It is probably for this reason that Heathcliff allows Nelly to perform proper burial rights for Hindley, thus relinquishing a more immediate revenge upon Hindley's dead body while gaining a long-term hold on the entire Earnshaw family.

Earlier, just before coming to the Heights, Nelly had consulted with Linton's lawyer about Hindley's death and had requested that the lawyer come to the Heights with her. His refusal is telling, for he advises that "Heathcliff be let alone, affirming that if the truth were known, Hareton would be found little else than a beggar"(*WH*, 153). The "truth" here may be that Heathcliff is Hareton's only hope because he is Hindley's creditor; or that the lawyer, probably Mr. Green, is already under Heathcliff's influence. But it may also be that Hindley's death as a suicide is better left ignored, primarily because of the possibility of forfeiture.

Catherine Earnshaw's death precedes her brother's by only half a year, and it too can be considered suicidal. There is little doubt that Catherine knows how to induce her own ill health, even though she does not intend suicide when she first embarks upon her fast in Chapter 11. At this point, totally breaking her own body and heart is, for Catherine, still "a deed to be reserved for a forlorn hope" (*WH*, 101). What happens, however, is that Catherine's body only partially cooperates with her will, and Nelly's assumption that Catherine is in total control of her situation is a tragic miscalculation. After only three days' fast, Catherine is already past saving. When she realizes that neither Linton nor Heathcliff has become genuinely alarmed and then chooses not to die, she cannot reverse her headlong journey toward destruction.

The important scene before her mirror (*WH*, 106) already spells this doom for Catherine, as Q. D. Leavis has realized.[17] Catherine is shocked when she sees her own reflection because she seems to understand what Yorkshire folklore dictates: that sick people should never look at themselves in a mirror. If they do, their souls may take flight from their weak bodies by being projected into the mirror, and this can cause their death. In accordance with this belief, immediately after she sees her reflection in the mirror, Catherine is convinced that she really will die. Leavis suggests that this realization replaces Catherine's fear of ghosts, anxiously expressed just before: "I hope it will not come out when you are gone! Oh! Nelly, the room is haunted!" (*WH*, 106). I believe, however, that the realization and the fear are even more closely related. For Catherine actually seems to consider herself to be the ghost once she recognizes that the face in the mirror is her own. " 'Myself,' she gasped, 'and the clock is striking twelve! It's true then; that's dreadful!' " (*WH*, 106). Catherine's utter horror here stems from her superstitious belief that suicides become restless ghosts.[18] She now assumes herself to be a suicide, and it is this aspect of Catherine's unnerving realization before the mirror that incites her subsequent raving about the ghosts at Gimmerton Kirkyard.

After this scene, there is only one more meeting between Catherine and Heathcliff before her actual death. On that occasion their dialogue is filled with allusions to Catherine's suicide and her would-be haunting of Heathcliff. Catherine now feels that she will never be at peace; while Heathcliff repeatedly expresses regret over what he feels is Catherine's self-murder and his relationship to it. In desperation, Heathcliff can forgive Catherine her murder of him but not her own willed death, which she in turn blames on him. All this seemingly metaphorical talk of murder reflects suicide law. Any accomplice of a suicide was legally considered his/her murderer,[19] so that, ironically, the protagonists' accusations of one another could, were they true, carry the weight of law, as well as of guilt.

Catherine is not, however, buried as a suicide. Nelly wonders "after the wayward and impatient existence she had led, whether she merited a haven of peace at last" (*WH* 137–38), but after looking at her in death, decides that she probably does. Instead, Catherine is interred in the corner of the Kirkyard under the wall, "to the surprise of the villagers" (*WH*, 140). Because the local people did not know of the means of Catherine's death, they might have expected that she would lie either in the chapel with the Lintons or by the tombs of the Earnshaws. Their wonderment is understandable when one recalls another folk belief about suicides. Particularly after the 1823 law, when suicides could legally be buried in churchyards, it became customary in parts of northern Britain for their bodies to be laid below the churchyard wall, so that no one would be likely to walk over their graves.[20] The place of Catherine's burial would thus have had particular significance for the folk of Gimmerton, who would no doubt have inferred the nature of her death from the location of her grave.

Unquestionably the place of Catherine's burial determines Heathcliff's own choice of a burial site and consequently his own need not to become discovered as a suicide. Because of his reputation and his doubtful place in the Gimmerton community, it is far less likely that Heathcliff would be extended the kind of pity that had allowed for the churchyard burials of Hindley and Catherine. He knows this and knows too of the possibility of interment in the public highway and is therefore scrupulous about not appearing suicidal. This accounts for the long delay of his own death, which continues to trouble the novel's critics.[21] Unfortunately for Heathcliff's union with Catherine, Linton dies before Heathcliff does and is the one to be buried in the grave next to hers. Lawyer Green, now the tool of Heathcliff, does suggest that Linton be buried appropriately in the chapel. Linton's death is of natural causes and his family all lie there. But Green, though under Heathcliff's influence, must abide by the stipulations of Linton's will, which states Linton's desire to be buried with Catherine. Nelly, for one, issues "loud protestations against any infringement of its directions" (*WH*, 226).

Less than a year elapses between Linton's death and Heathcliff's, the year in which Heathcliff and Wuthering Heights are so intensely haunted by Catherine that even the prosaic Lockwood is influenced to dream of her. Toward the end of this time, Nelly observes how isolated and peculiar Heathcliff has become and warns him against taking his own life. As she notes, he undergoes his most dramatic set of changes from the time of his curious hunting accident, when "his gun burst" while he was "out on the hills by himself" (*WH*, 246). Finding himself still alive after the accident, Heathcliff forces himself to reach home, despite a heavy loss of blood. Detained by this accident, he is brought into closer contact with Cathy and Hareton. Now, however, as his tormentings of them only serve to remind him of Catherine, he becomes affected by the strange *tedium vitae* that was considered the cause of so many nineteenth-century suicides.[22] "I cannot continue in this condition," he tells Nelly. "I have to remind myself to breathe—almost to remind my heart to beat!" (*WH*, 256). He also forgets to eat but makes the attempt when Nelly urges him and then takes great care to tell her that "It is not my fault, that I cannot eat or rest. . . . I assure you it is through no settled designs" (*WH*, 262).

As he begins to fail, the one thing uppermost in Heathcliff's mind is his burial. To Nelly he gives detailed instructions for its procedures: ". . . you remind me of the manner that I desire to be buried in. It is to be carried to the churchyard, in the evening. . . . No minister need come; nor need anything be said over me" (*WH*, 263). Each of Heathcliff's requests is in accord with the 1823 statute governing the burial of suicides: the hour, the place, and the lack of a Christian burial service. Nelly seems to realize their significance. In a moment of insight she brings up the fear that has haunted Heathcliff ever since the day of Catherine's death: "And supposing you persevered in your obstinate fast, and died by that means, and they refused to bury you in the precinct of the Kirk?" (*WH*, 263).

Heathcliff's only means of recourse now are to charge Nelly with the business of moving his body, so that he can be with Catherine, and directly to threaten Nelly with haunting should she fail to comply. The threat seems sufficient to frighten the superstitious servant, and the next evening when Heathcliff does die, Nelly conceals her suspicions about his death from Kenneth: "Kenneth was perplexed to pronounce of what disorder the master died. I concealed the fact of his having swallowed nothing for four days, fearing it might lead to trouble, and then, I am persuaded he did not abstain on purpose; it was the consequence of his strange illness, not the cause" (*WH*, 264). Her actions now free Nelly to carry out Heathcliff's instructions to the letter and "to the scandal of the whole neighbourhood" (WH, 265). Shocked by Heathcliff's interment side by side with the married Lintons, the people also appear to know the meaning of Heathcliff's burial without Christian rites. It is not long afterward that under the Nab the local shepherd boy sees the ghosts of what he must now consider as two suicides, Heathcliff and Catherine. In the end, Lockwood's much-discussed final words in *Wuthering Heights* take on added irony in light of the folklore of suicide. Referring to the gravesites of Catherine, Linton, and Heathcliff, Lockwood wonders "how anyone could ever imagine unquiet slumbers for the sleepers in that quiet earth" (*WH*, 266). But anyone knowing the customs surrounding suicide in eighteenth- and nineteenth-century Britain—as Emily Brontë did—could, on the contrary, hardly imagine quiet slumbers for them.

I have lingered over Brontë's great mid-century novel to show that a Victorian reader aware of suicide law and lore might have judged its first generation of characters quite differently from the way we regard them now. The legal and moral implications of suicide and the folklore they generated took deep hold in Victorian Britain. As late as 1886, suicides and cross-roads continued to sell stories. *Tinsley's Magazine* of that year published an awkward one by Philippa Prittie Jephson, called "The Cross Roads." In this story, mares shy and mysterious lights appear and vanish in an Irish glen when two men approach a cross-roads. From a local cottager they later hear that a suicide walks in that haunted spot:

> "There was an inquest, and great searching to find out who he was, and where he came from, but no one ever found out, from that day to this. I think there was a halfpenny in his pocket and an old knife, but whatever it was the polis' took it, and Father Doyle said he should not be buried in consecrated ground, seeing he made away with himself. So the boys took his body up to the cross roads in a barrow, and buried him there, and that's why he walks. Sure there was never a prayer said over him at all, poor wretch; I would not tell you a lie. And to think you saw him—well, well!"[23]

In the outposts of Britain—in Hogg's Scotland, Brontë's Yorkshire, and Jephson's Ireland—fascination with ignominious burial did not fade with the passage of 4 George IV. c. 52 in London.

Nor did the nineteenth-century controversy over the question of temporary insanity end in 1823. Rather, it intensified. As the century progressed, physicians were increasingly called upon to define insanity in cases of suicide. Their definitions became the focus of debate throughout the Victorian era, and their community can serve as a microcosm of educated, scientific opinion about suicide. Medical views form both a contrast and a complement to superstitions about crossroads. Take for example the discussion of "moral insanity," an idea first suggested by the Bristol physician James Cowles Prichard in 1835. In his *Treatise on Insanity and Other Disorders Affecting the Mind*,[24] Prichard called for a redefinition of the characteristics of mental illness. Until the *Treatise* and its follow-up study *On the Different Forms of Insanity in Relation to Jurisprudence*,[25] mental illness was considered an impairment of the intellect and judgment, a twofold classification that had held from the time of the Greeks to the eighteenth century in England.[26] But Prichard posited the equivalent possibility of impairment of the emotions, what he called "moral insanity" and defined as

> a morbid perversion of the natural feelings, affections, inclinations, temper, habits, moral dispositions, and natural impulses, without any remarkable disorder or defect of the intellect or knowing and reasoning faculties, and particularly without any insane illusion or hallucination. . . . The individual is found to be incapable, not of talking or reasoning upon any subject proposed to him, for this he will often do with great shrewdness and volubility, but of conducting himself with decency and propriety in the business of life.[27]

This concept, which influenced Esquirol in his famous book *Des Maladies Mentales*,[28] revolutionized thinking about criminal insanity in cases of suicide as well as of murder. For if an individual suffering from moral insanity in cases of suicide were liable to instinctive and involuntary impulses that would determine his or her behavior of a moment (and it was Prichard who coined the term "irresistible impulse"), nearly any criminal act could be labeled as insane. This possibility Prichard admitted: "Homicides, infanticides, suicides of the most fearful description have been committed under its influence."[29] Crime, then, could be directly linked with mental illness, and the acceptance of moral insanity as a legal category threatened to shift the burden of judicial responsibility from legal to medical practitioners.[30]

If the Victorian pronounced *felo-de-se* in the 1830s and 1840s could be seen as suffering from "moral insanity," he or she nonetheless remained the most miserable of sinners, at least according to Forbes Winslow of the Royal College of Surgeons in London, the preeminent expert on suicide during those years. In 1840 Winslow deliberately set out to produce the initial book-length Victorian consideration of self-murder, *The Anatomy of Suicide*, "the first in England that has been exclusively devoted to this important and interesting branch of inquiry."[31] Ranking suicide morally among the "black catalogue of human offences" and branding it as "a crime against God and man,"[32] Winslow nonetheless attributed it to medical causes such as depression, physical pain, and insanity. Winslow's dual perspective—as the righteous moral condemner of suicide while at the same time the physician most concerned with its meaning, history, and even prevention—seriously flaws his book, rendering it full of contradictions. Yet Winslow's study reveals the two minds that so many educated Victorians brought to this subject. They wanted to know more about suicide, to understand its causes and "cures," but they felt a moral aversion toward the act that was still deeply rooted in their religious and legal history.

Winslow's name arises in another significant context in the history of Victorian attitudes toward both murder and self-murder, this time as the two related to the plea of insanity. Winslow was also one of the examining physicians in the famous case of Daniel McNaughton (1843). McNaughton was the convicted murderer of Edward Drummond (secretary to Prime Minister Sir Robert Peel), whom McNaughton had slain, mistaking Drummond for Peel. Winslow testified that he had "not the slightest hesitation in saying that [McNaughton was] insane, and that he committed the offence whilst afflicted with a delusion, under which he appears to have been labouring for a considerable length of time."[33] Because of the testimony of the doctors in this case, McNaughton was committed to an asylum rather than executed. But the public hue and cry that arose from the lack of severity in the sentence prompted the House of Lords to ask the fifteen judges of the common law courts for the famous clarification of grounds for legal insanity known as the McNaughton Rules. In these rules, which dominated criminal and therefore suicide law with respect to insanity until the 1960s, the Lords asked the judges to respond to five questions about the nature of the knowledge of right and wrong: (1) To define the law pertaining to crimes committed by persons suffering from "insane delusion," (2) To offer what would be the appropriate questions to put to the jury in such cases, (3) To state in what terms the questions ought to be left to the jury, (4) To decide whether a person suffering from insane delusion should be executed, and (5) To determine whether a medical practitioner was qualified to judge such insane delusion if he had never previously seen the accused. The judges' answers to these questions indicated that a person would be punishable under the law if he or she knew at the time of committing a crime that he or she was acting contrary to law; that the jury has ultimate responsibility in adjudging a person insane or not; and that medical practitioners could give scientific evidence but that, again, the jury had to make the ultimate decision.

Thus the McNaughton Rules did not allow the burden of judicial responsibility to pass from legal to medical practitioners in cases of criminal insanity. Regardless of Prichard's influence in the 1840s, there was no mention of an irresistible impulse in the Rules. English law refused to recognize this plea if the criteria for unsoundness of mind spelled out in the McNaughton Rules were absent. Nonetheless, by the late 1840s Prichard's idea had taken firm hold of the minds of practitioners of psychological medicine and of the popular and literary mind as well. When in 1846 Elizabeth Barrett heard of the death of her friend, the painter Benjamin Haydon, she was convinced that he had succumbed to a "sudden" suicidal impulse. "For he was mad if he killed himself! of that I am as sure as if I knew it," she exclaimed to a friend. "If he killed himself, he was mad first."[34]

Haydon's macabre suicide raises another question about suicide in the England of the 1840s: that of the relationship of the physical brain to the act of self-destruction. Haydon was morbidly interested in this relationship, which had been of concern to materialist psychiatry throughout the thirties and forties. Winslow's *Anatomy*, for example, included a chapter entitled "Appearances Presented After Death in Those Who Have Committed Suicide" in which the condition of the brain was discussed, and coroners' inquests carefully recorded reports of physicians on the physical appearance of the brain. In Haydon's own case, the doctors' post-mortem discovered "innumerable bloody points through the brain," clearly felt to be indicators of "brain disease," although the doctors differed as to the duration of this so-called disease.[35] Ironically, Haydon had studied such diagnoses before he took his own life by both shooting himself and slitting his throat, and had considered that he himself was a victim of too much pressure on the brain. The throat-slitting was to have eliminated just those bloody points discovered in the post-mortem. In his diary Haydon confessed, "It may be laid down that self destruction is the physical mode of relieving a diseased brain, because the first impression on a brain diseased, or diseased for a Time, is the necessity of this horrid crime."[36] In contemplating reports of the suicides of Castlereagh and Sir Samuel Romilly, he inferred that the two must have achieved relief when they cut their throats and the blood began to flow, removing the pressure built up in their brains.

During the 1850s interest in the close connection between mind and matter reached its zenith in the work of George R. Drysdale, "a doctor of medicine" whose *Elements of Social Science* (1854) became a popular success and went through innumerable editions. Drysdale hypothesized that moral transgression was in fact disease, "but that men, in general, do not recognize moral disease, they do not allow sorrow, fear, &c., to be diseases."[37] He was eager for his contemporaries to understand that the spirit belongs to the brain and that all moral diseases are the result of our ignorance of natural laws. If only we were to realize this, we should be able to live more in accordance with those laws, whenever possible shunning moral disease as we do physical disease, since the two are of a piece. To us today this may seem an odd way to solve the philosophical question of the duality of mind and body, but to many Victorians, Drysdale's work became a kind of Bible. The implications of the work for the study of suicide were clear enough: understand the disease that underlies the act of suicide, live in accordance with the natural law that makes self-preservation so important, and thus eliminate suicide altogether.

In general, however, the 1850s saw more discussion of suicide and moral insanity than suicide and empirical morality, and Prichard's ideas came under careful review. Popular magazines like *Hogg's Instructor* offered articles on suicide in which the notion of "sudden impulse" was accepted as a valid category, and the *Irish Quarterly Review* of 1857 showed concern that a "great difference of opinion exists among high medical authorities on the question, whether the mere act of self-destruction is in itself a proof of insanity."[38] One event that illustrates the difference of opinion and that triggered reevaluation of Prichard's work was the publication of Dr. Thomas Mayo's *Croonian Lectures on Medical Testimony and Evidence in Cases of Lunacy* (1853).[39] According to Mayo, Prichard's ideas were undercutting the effectiveness of the McNaughton Rules. Mayo thought that this was true to the extent that all criminal actions, including suicide, were in danger of being adjudged the results of insanity. *Fraser's Magazine* (March 1855) championed Mayo's point of view, while the *London Journal of Psychological Medicine* printed an article entitled "On Suicide" (1858) which asserted that "suicide can never be committed when the mind is perfectly healthy."[40] So the controversy raged on, although the trend was certainly toward considering suicides insane rather than criminal.

In another interesting development of the 1850s, physicians began commenting upon suicide and insanity in literary works, while literary figures increasingly based their viewpoints upon medical knowledge. As Henry Maudsley would later say, imagination hastens "to fill the voids of knowledge with fictions,"[41] and alienists were coming to value such fictions. In 1855, Sir John Charles Bucknill, who later became president of the Medico-Psychological Association and the editor of the

Asylum Journal of Mental Science, reviewed Tennyson's *Maud* from the physician's point of view. Bucknill examined the hero of the poem in an effort to show that poets were superior psychologists. Tennyson, he felt, was in line with contemporary psychological understanding when he showed his narrator's hereditary tendency toward instability and stressed the shock to his emotions caused by the suicide of his father. Four years later, in 1859, Bucknill analyzed the psychology of Shakespeare in a lengthy volume,[42] again showing how literary work complemented medical knowledge of mental illness. In the same year, the writer Harriet Martineau offered a detailed consideration of self-murder in *Once a Week* and drew heavily upon contemporary medical opinion about suicidal insanity, including coroners' reports. Her essay was in part a plea for the early acknowledgment of any form of insanity that might lead to suicide. Her hope was that in some cases the insanity might be cured and suicide prevented. Martineau was clearly influenced by the Victorian concept of brain disease, and she deplored the stigma attached to madness by families. She argued that if brain disease were seen as potentially curable like any other disease, families would learn to have it treated. Eventually they would shed their ancient prejudices against it, since such prejudices were, to her mind, merely outdated notions of possession and fears of a wrathful God.[43]

But Prichard's morality died hard, and the 1870s saw further reinterpretation of his still vital concepts of the sudden impulse and moral insanity. William Carpenter in *Principles of Mental Physiology* (1874) found that the "insane impulse" was often "the expression of a dominant idea," capable of controlling an individual so forcefully that he would think of himself as driven by necessity.[44] It was, however, Henry Maudsley's influential *Pathology of Mind* (1879) that most carefully refined Prichard's arguments. Maudsley deplored the legal "justice" that tried to measure the "lunatic's responsibility by his knowledge of right and wrong" and agreed with Prichard and Carpenter that insane impulses did exist. He posited that such impulses were secondary to what he called "morbid perversion of feeling."[45] In his chapter "The Symptomatology of Insanity," Maudsley counseled that "what we have to fix in the mind is that the *mode of affection* of the individual by events is entirely changed by the disordered state of the nerve-element: that is the fundamental fact, from which flow as secondary facts the insane impulses, whether mischievous, erotic, homicidal, or suicidal."[46] Suicides in particular could seem "quite rational" but could apply their cunning to frequent suicide attempts. Thus Maudsley encouraged practitioners to become alert to the "whole manner of feeling" in their patients. He went much further in exploring similar territory than did

Prichard, finding heredity and epilepsy at the base of much moral insanity and discussing the hallucinations associated with this form of derangement. Most significantly, he stressed the social importance of understanding moral insanity: all of society is threatened by the potential for destruction evident in those who are morally insane. For this reason above all he wished to make certain that Prichard and Esquirol were not forgotten.

Maudsley's work showed a compassion for the victim and a social dimension that were to become increasingly evident in British medical writing on suicide. In an 1878 article, "On Suicide, in Its Social Relations,"[47] James Davey, another Bristol physician, evinced both of these concerns when he pleaded for further change in suicide law. Like Maudsley, Davey thought that emotions, rather than the reflective mind, were involved in cases of insanity leading to suicide, and he advocated less severity in legal dealings with the act. Denial of the rites of a Christian burial to the suicide was particularly distasteful to Davey.

Despite consistent interest in suicide throughout the mid-Victorian decades, there was no full-length study of self-destruction from the time of Winslow's *Anatomy of Suicide* in 1840 until the 1880s. Then, in 1881, came a highly influential book, Henry Morselli's *Suicide: An Essay on Comparative Moral Statistics*, an Italian work translated into English and published in London. Morselli, a professor of psychological medicine at the Royal University, Turin, provided the most comprehensive set of statistics on suicide available in England. Tuke, for example, in his section on suicide in the *Dictionary of Psychological Medicine*,[48] would need only to summarize Morselli's data for page after page. In Morselli's *Suicide*, we have the culmination of a trend that had been developing in England since the 1860s—the increased use of statistics coupled with an interest in the social dimension of suicide. It took an Italian to carry this trend to its ultimate extent because in England suicide statistics were still suspect. There was no accurate, consistent system of classification for cause of death until 1858, when William Farr, the Registrar-General, began to tabulate suicides separately from other deaths. Even then there was widespread skepticism about statistics of suicide because concealment was presumed to be common and definitions of suicide varied. Moreover, the British seemed disinclined to bring positivism to bear on the study of suicide or to take the lead in establishing the science of sociology. Thus, as Olive Anderson so persuasively argues, "Victorian ideas about the incidence of suicide were illustrated by statistics rather than founded upon them."[49] Comparing and interpreting British statistics, Morselli gratefully filled the gap left by the British themselves. In the preface to his *Essay*, he nodded in thanks to Darwin, Buckle, Spencer, and Wallace and claimed to be carrying their scientific example over into his new and original inquiry into self-destruction. Because he believed that the "old philosophy of individualism" was dead, Morselli thought suicide should no longer be studied in terms of individual cases but rather as "a social phenomenon."[50] Although he believed that statistics were invaluable in understanding human behavior, he realized that they could not be presumed to reveal the true mental states preceding an act of suicide. Thus it was wisest to use them to study the whole of society in "its wants and tendencies, that is in the functions of its complicated organism," a variation of the myth of the body politic. When one does so, "the most fatal and at the same time apparently most arbitrary human actions, suicide and crime, show themselves to us in their similarity subject to numerous influences, which the examination of every single case would not suffice to reveal to us, and which collectively are universal, perpetual, and intense, and such as the most positive mode of psychological study would fail to discover in the individual."[51]

Morselli also thought that his statistics would "trace the indications of the prophylactics and therapeutics of suicide against which laws and philosophy show themselves powerless."[52] This latter claim he failed to prove, but the conclusions to his study form an interesting chapter in the history of social Darwinism. For Morselli's statistics led him to one grand conclusion: "*suicide is an effect of the struggle for existence and of human selection, which works according to the laws of evolution among civilized people*."[53] Weaker individuals who cannot cope with the stresses of civilized life are the ones who commit suicide. A neo-Malthusian, Morselli found that a "sad law of necessity" was weeding out these weaker types in order to maintain the population of the civilized world at a subsistence level. The only way to prevent suicide was somehow to diminish the struggle for existence among large numbers of the populace, "establishing a balance between individual needs and social utility."[54] We can only begin to do this by developing our moral character, Morselli concluded, yet he gave no clue as to how to go about this difficult task.

Contemporary British reviews of Morselli's work were divided. *Nature* (vol. 25) noted the power of the statistical method as exhibited in *Suicide*, while *The Dial* (March 1882) found the statistics "dry" and the necessitarianism "false," although it too praised the thoroughness of the compilation. William Wynn Westcott, deputy coroner for central Middlesex, found Morselli's work of considerable use in his own full-length book, *Suicide: Its History, Literature, Jurisprudence, Causation, and Prevention* (1885).[55] Like Morselli, Westcott prefaced his study by considering suicide as "one of our social problems" and cited the prevention of suicide as one of his aims in writing the treatise. He also relied heavily upon Morselli's statistics and gave nodding acceptance to the notion of the social Darwinism involved in suicide. Nevertheless he was worried about the increasing reliance upon statistics in the study of suicide; in his estimation, a return to a closer look at mental states and emotions was in order. Westcott also insisted that it was time, once and for all, to cease thinking of suicide as a crime. He maintained that suicide was not an equivalent to murder: we cannot estimate its injury to the victim; it creates no terrible public alarm; and it cannot be repeated. He believed that Forbes Winslow had been wrong in making the connection between suicide and madness, and too many had followed suit. What was now needed was attention to melancholia, despair, and misery in an effort to diminish the number of deaths by suicide.[56] Such emphasis upon prevention was also a chief concern of the prominent alienist G. H. Savage. In a paper read at the quarterly meeting of the Medico-Psychological Association in February 1884,[57] Savage offered a practical approach to prevention. The paper largely applied to patients in mental institutions like Bethlehem Royal Mental Hospital (Bethlem), where "constant watching" was practiced. Although he agreed that watching might be one way of coping with suicidal behavior, from experience he was convinced that it often "dared" the patients to attempt suicide. His remedy was to encourage self-reliance among potential suicides, since he presumed that this, if anything, might allow them the exercise of self-control essential to their survival.

Savage, Tuke's co-editor of the *Journal of Mental Science*, was quite as interested in arriving at a definition of suicide in relation to insanity as he was in preventing suicide. Both Tuke and Savage were also instrumental in the revalidation of Prichard's idea of "moral insanity" that occurred toward the century's end. In his *Chapters on the History of the Insane in the British Isles* (1882), Tuke commended the clinically oriented Savage for "recognizing the abstract metaphysical difficulty of conceiving moral as distinct from intellectual insanity" and yet for admitting "as a clinical fact the form of mental disease for which Prichard contended."[58] Tuke also felt himself bound to admit, as "an impartial historian," that Prichard's "views are still by no means unanimously adopted, and that I am only expressing my own sentiments when I avow that what Latham says of Prichard's 'Researches into the Physical History of Mankind'—'Let those who doubt its value try to do without it'—applies to the teaching contained in the remarkable treatise entitled 'Different Forms of Insanity in Relation to Jurisprudence.' "[59] Tuke and Savage also collaborated on the section of Tuke's *Dictionary* devoted to suicide, with Savage writing the section entitled "Suicide and Insanity." Here the double classification of sane and insane suicides was upheld, and a table was offered that represented medical orthodoxy on the divisions of insane suicides at this time (1892). Table 1 illustrates Savage's own schema, in which Prichard's impulsive behavior is given five aspects, and deliberate suicide given an even more extensive subdivision.

The end of the century also encouraged a review of thinking about suicide, a phenomenon clearly visible in S.A.K. Strahan's *Suicide and Insanity* (1893).[60] For Strahan, a barrister who was also a member of the Medico-Psychological Association and a fellow of the Royal Statistical Society, physiology and sociology were of equal interest. Strahan accepted the twofold classification of rational and irrational suicide, and under irrational suicide carefully reviewed the general subject of suicide and insanity. Here he too took issue with the analysis of Forbes Winslow. How, he questioned, could Winslow contend that all suicides are insane at the same time that he saw suicide as morally culpable, "High up in the black catalogue of human offences"? Are all madmen then immoral? Suicide, according to Strahan, was quite as often associated with idiocy and drunkenness as with insanity. Other aspects of Strahan's study tallied with the work of Tuke, Westcott, and Morselli. Strahan would, however, disagree with those who felt that a suicide necessarily inflicted harm upon society by leaving it. Often quite the reverse was true, for a suicide might remove an intolerable social burden. And

Impulsive suicide may be	Neurotic. Hysterical. Maniacal. Alcoholic. Epileptic.	
Deliberate suicide may depend on	Egotistical feelings	Pain. Worry. Sleeplessness. Ruin. Shame.
		To avoid persecution, &c.
	Altruistic feelings	To save others from suffering. To benefit others.
	or be	
	Indifferent to these	As result of "voices." As a result of fixed delusion. As result of weak mind.

INTENTIONAL SUICIDE

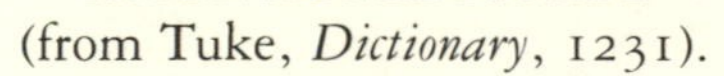

(from Tuke, *Dictionary*, 1231).

since the contract between a society and its members was supposed to be one of mutual benefit, such a contract could be broken by either side—the individual's or the society's. The truth of this view with respect to society he thought was obvious. But the individual should have the same option, even though it gave him or her the right to self-destruction.[61]

In general, Strahan's book is sympathetic to the right to die as well as to the suffering of many potential suicides, and his compassion was largely shared by his fellow members of the Medico-Psychological Association. In a paper entitled "Suicide in Simple Melancholy," Maudsley, for example, addressed the problem of prolonged depression. He took care to distinguish between *melancholia*, a form of insanity, and melancholy, prolonged and morbid depression "due to internal failure of the springs of re-action, without external cause";[62] but he gave no advice as to how to overcome such melancholy. Instead he concluded his paper with some philosophical thoughts on the question of suicide:

> Considered objectively, as a physical event, suicide is a natural event of the human dispensation, just a necessary incident from time to time of the course of its organic evolutions and dissolutions, and no more out of keeping then than any other mode of death. It seems unnatural, because mankind, thinking the universe made for it and not it for the universe, has never yet sincerely reconciled itself to accept death as a fit event, and deems it nothing better than madness for anyone to do that in quiet consciousness so long as he can avoid it.[63]

In view of Maudsley's care for the patient suffering from morbid melancholy, these words are anything but callous. What they indicate is a far different attitude from those typifying the earlier decades of the century. Suicide is certainly not a sin; still less is it a crime. Many of those who consider it a sign of insanity do so only out of a basic fear of dying. Here Maudsley takes the biologist's, almost the ecologist's, broader view, ignoring both legalists and moralists except in stressing humankind's relative smallness in the universe. This kind of Darwinism rather than Morselli's social Darwinism marked the later writing of the foremost British psychiatrist of his day. A far cry from Prichard and even from Maudsley's earlier revisions of Prichard, this naturalism was the final verdict of the Victorian medical community on the human act of suicide. Typifying educated scientific thinking at the end of the century, it would stand alongside the McNaughton rules, which remained the verdict of the legal community at the century's close.

II

Willing to Be

"*The English* have been accused by foreigners of being the *beau-ideal* of a suicidal people. The charge is almost too ridiculous to merit serious refutation. It has clearly been established that where there is one suicide in London, there are five in Paris."[1] Forbes Winslow's words typify Victorian defensiveness over England's seemingly undeserved reputation as "*la terre classique du suicide*." England's fogs, her earnestness, her graveyard school and poetry of melancholy had given rise to a French myth that was difficult to dispel. By 1800, England had become known as the European center of suicide: home of Edward Young who had cried "O Britain, infamous for suicide";[2] home of Robert Blair who had exclaimed "Self-murder! name it not: Our island's shame/ That makes her the reproach of neighbouring states";[3] and home of Chatterton, boy wonder and romantic suicide *par excellence*, whose celebrated early death seemed a glorious martyrdom to Europe's artists. It was a land of black, dark Novembers, dripping with mists of self-destruction. On the continent this myth persisted, provoking an angry English response throughout the nineteenth century. As late as 1878, Thomas Hardy was continuing Winslow's battle by undercutting the French. In *The Return of the Native* he says of Clym Yeobright: "He had reached the stage in a young man's life when the grimness of the general human situation first becomes clear; and the realization of this causes ambition to halt awhile. In France it is not uncustomary to commit suicide at this stage; in England we do much better, or much worse, as the case may be."[4]

The French were not alone in advancing England's reputation as the classic land of suicide. In *Dichtung und Wahrheit* Goethe recalled the story of an Englishman who had hanged himself to be rid of the trouble of dressing and undressing each day. This was possible, he said, because the English took hanging lightly, observing it so frequently as a form of public punishment.[5] Yet according to Goethe, English poetical literature was characterized by an "earnest melancholy" that deeply marked the English character as suicidal. He convinced himself that England and English literature had prepared the way for the craze that followed the publication of his *Sorrows of Young Werther* in 1774—the epidemic of Wertherism that swept Europe in the late eighteenth and early nineteenth centuries. Werther's love-lornness, his clothes, his sensibility, and even his death were imitated. Thus, through Goethe's Werther, suicide became fashionable in Germany, just as through Vigny's *Chatterton* (1835) it would in France some half a century later. One young man committed suicide while watching Vigny's play; another killed himself with his hand resting on the last page of *Chatterton*.[6]

Ironically, at no time did the English embrace Wertherism or fashionable suicide as wholeheartedly as did the Continentals. Quite the contrary, people like the Reverend Solomon Piggott abhorred such dangerous fads. "I would," said Piggott in 1824,

> most strongly reprobate the sickly notions, the sentimental nonsense, the false morality, the infidel opinions, the immoral precepts, contained in many of our popular novels, romances and plays, which the idle and dissipated waste their hours in persuing [*sic*]. There is not a book of a more dangerous tendency in many of these respects than the undeservedly admired "Sorrows of Werther," a book which should be forbidden and proscribed, as having largely contributed to diffuse licentiousness, to encourage effeminacy, and to seduce the weak and the agitated to suicide.[7]

Less vehement critics also had doubts about Werther and the kind of suicide he represented. In romantic suicide the individual hopes that consciousness will be absorbed by the infinite, but few British ever fully accepted this romantic illusion. English romantics like Wordsworth instead tried to expand and transcend the self through acts of imagination, not self-murder. By the transforming power of mind, mountains, mists, and sea might appear to merge for a moment, yielding intimations of immortality and a respite from entrapment in self. But by Byron's day both Werther's suicide and Wordsworth's imaginative transcendence were all but *passé* in England.

According to Thomas Carlyle, Byron himself was the most Werther-like of the English romantics, their "Sentimentalist and Power Man, the strongest of his kind in Europe."[8] Certainly Byron's characters wanted to lay aside the claims of human identity. Childe Harold yearns to belong to mountains and sea. Nevertheless his creator can neither wholly recapture the Wordsworthian vision nor kill Harold as Goethe killed Werther. Like Lord Byron himself, most of Byron's heroes live on in existential exile. For all his romantic posturing, Byron led the English into the Victorian period, disdainfully branding Castlereagh "the Werther of politics." Byron was on the way to realizing that to create all things, including death, out of the self is neither to transcend

Henry Wallis, *Chatterton* (1855–56).

the human lot nor to confront death. It is only to know the time of dying. Ruefully, his Manfred and Cain front their painful destinies.

Byron's successors in Victorian England also felt that self-created death could not control the fact of death and, far from perpetuating Wertherism, they actually took the lead in drawing Europe out of the era of romantic suicide. In part theirs was a bourgeois reaction to dashing anti-bourgeois figures like Werther and the mythological version of Chatterton. When Henry Wallis painted his dramatic *Chatterton* in 1855–56, with George Meredith posing as the dead boy-wonder, reactions to the painting were mixed. It was praised by Ruskin and others for its artistic realism, color and drama, and it catapulted Wallis to instant fame. But it was also viewed as an example of how not to die. The *Saturday Review* thought the painting represented a "mad deed," the sorry end to the "sad history of Chatterton's misdirected genius and boyish vanity,"[9] and the *Handbook to the Gallery of British Paintings* in 1857 concurred: "never was the moral of a wasted life better pointed in painting."[10] When Robert Browning wrote his "Essay on Chatterton" (1842),[11] he focused upon Chatterton's pride, which allowed the boy-wonder the illusion of leaving no alternative but to die. Browning found both this pride and this illusion tragic, but his own tone and perspective are those of an older, wiser poet. Browning kept a compassionate distance from Chatterton.

Thus as the Victorians set about reviewing romantic notions about men like Chatterton and Goethe's hero, they took a closer look at themselves. In an 1861 essay in *The Psychological Journal,* aptly called "The Classic Land of Suicide," the writer first castigates the British for collaboration in their reputation for suicide: "With the happy facility for parading our short-comings which is so incomprehensible to other nations, we, before the era of statistics, succeeded in imposing as well upon our neighbors as ourselves the belief that suicide was in an especial manner a bane of this kingdom."[12] He then works his way back to Goethe's view of English literature to see whether it is just. Melancholy the national literature may be, but not suicidal, he decides. Hamlet did not beget Werther; Werther was the first of his kind, a confirmation that the Victorians would make over and over again. Goethe misperceived the British and misconceived his own arguments. Fortunately Wertherism "was comparatively short-lived in England, and at the present day, perhaps, only to be found in France where it still flourishes with considerable vigour."[13] Winslow's war wages on in the pages of this essay, which is also firmly against suicide. The writer wants to destroy the image of England as suicidal because suicide is "revolting," caused by "self-cultivated self-indulged life-weariness."[14]

This view was typical of those Victorians who strongly believed suicide to be immoral even after the laws against *felonia-de-se* were modified. If both religious and non-religious people condemned suicide, their condemnation was tied to the Victorian question of the will. Romantics like Wordsworth and the fictional Werther in one way or another used willpower to destroy the boundary of self and other—whether that other was nature, a lover, or an idea of God. The Victorians, on the other hand, employed will for self-discipline. Again and again the personae in Emily Brontë's poetry move toward release from selfhood through union with earth and sky or with a beloved person, or through short-lived flights of fancy and mystical moments. Each flight is, however, met with a corresponding return to a self still caught in a world of flux. This entrapment is as much Catherine's and Heathcliff's problem in *Wuthering Heights* as it is the problem of the personae of Brontë's poems. But in the poems, Brontë offers a solution other than suicide or Byronic desperation: the Victorian solution of endurance. In the later poems the central narrator of the non-Gondal poems realizes that she has no cowardly soul and wills to live on to a natural death: "Then did I learn how existence could be cherished, / Strengthened, and fed without the aid of joy."[15]

Thus if the romantics and the romantic side of the Victorians favored expanding the self into infinity, a more typically Victorian stance was self-defensive.[16] The Victorians imagined the self as something like a fortified castle and prepared themselves to endure a siege. The chains the romantics wished to break became the necessary walls of a well-protected self, safeguards to be tended, kept up, and repaired. In this stalwart frame of mind, suicide looked less like release than defeat. Self-murder became externalized, like murder, an alien force to be feared and resisted. Against this force, the human will became the first and last line of defense, but fractured selves, fabricated enemies, and visions of Armageddon were part of the outcome of battle.

The Victorian revision of Goethe put him in the vanguard of the battle, the captain of willpower. The favored Goethe was the author of *Wilhelm Meister's Apprenticeship*, the man who "became king over himself."[17] George Henry Lewes took great pains to point out that Werther was not Goethe: Werther perishes because of weakness, whereas Goethe saw Werther's failings, wrenched himself from the woman he loved, and lived on. Volition mastered desire, for "Goethe was one of those who are wavering because impressionable, but whose wavering is not weakness; they oscillate, but they return to the direct path which their wills have prescribed."[18] Lewes was writing in 1855, looking back at the Werther craze and confirming that *Werther* was no longer much read, especially in England where it suffered both from a bad name and a bad translation. Less far removed from Wertherism in time and temperament, Carlyle had written his essay on Goethe in 1828 and felt called upon not only to prove Goethe the master of willpower but to show him free from suicidal taint. In his essay he quotes extensively from *Dichtung und Wahrheit*, here focusing on a passage revealing Goethe's resistance to suicide:

> I saved myself from the purpose, or indeed more properly speaking, from the whim, of suicide, which in those fair peaceful times had insinuated self into the mind of indolent youth. Among a considerable collection of arms, I possessed a costly well-ground dagger. This I laid down tightly beside my bed; and before extinguishing the light, I tried whether I could succeed in sending the sharp point an inch or two deep into my breast. But as I truly never could succeed, I at last took to laughing at myself; threw away all these hypochondriacal crotchets, and determined to live.[19]

Carlyle was fascinated by Goethe's abandonment of "hypochondriacal crotchets" because he had such crotchets himself. Goethe became an exemplar for him, a kind of benign father-figure who had purged his childish thoughts of suicide by writing about them in *Werther*. This prepared him for a second and "sounder" period in his life when the despair of *Werther* gave way to the "peace" of *Meister*. Carlyle too would try to write away despair while writing his own way into maturity.

In the early 1820s, about the time of Castlereagh's death and the passage of the new suicide law, Carlyle reached the stage that Hardy attributes to Clym Yeobright. "Grimness of the general human situation" had become all too clear, but being British, Carlyle was ready to do "much better, or much worse" than commit suicide. He would become the first eminent Victorian to pose a cure for Wertherism. In the early twenties, however, he was still in the throes of depression, a kind of alien in the universe. His letters show a young man rife with contradictions: he wants a vocation and feels worthy of one, but is "full of inquietude and chagrin"; he wants independence, yet is afraid to lose the love of his parents; he is "timid yet not humble, weak yet enthusiastic." Most of all he feels unwell to the point that

> the gloom of external things seemed to extend itself to the very centre of the mind, till I could remember nothing, observe nothing! All this magnificent nature appeared as if blotted out, and a grey, dirty, dismal vapour filled the immensity of space; I stood alone in the universe—alone, and as it were a circle of burning iron enveloped the soul—excluding from it every feeling but a stony-hearted, dead obduracy, more befitting a demon in its place of woe than a man in the land of the living![20]

In 1821 Carlyle is already a victim of the Victorian view of will—encircled in iron walls, well defended but trapped in himself. By 1822 things begin to open up. Then on Leith Walk he encounters his famous moment of illumination. He will use volition to spring the trap and write a work that both creates and demonstrates a new self. Yet the notebooks of 1823 show him blocked on this course, self-consciously asking about suicide: " 'Then why don't you kill yourself Sir? Is there not arsenic? Is there not ratsbane of various kinds, and hemp and steel?' Most true, Sathanas, all these things *are*: but it will be time enough to use them when I have *lost* the game, which I am as yet but losing."[21] Carlyle persisted, bid farewell to poisonous 1823 in a scathing poem, and eventually got on to 1830 and *Sartor Resartus*, retailoring himself as he wrote. What he did write was "an inner history of the will," as Wilhelm Dilthey so clearly discerned from his own perspective in the nineteenth century.[22] It is another paean to endurance, an affront to ratsbane, hemp and steel.

Thoughts of self-destruction enter *Sartor Resartus* with Chapter 6, "Sorrows of Teufelsdröckh." Like Werther, Teufelsdröckh has been miserably disappointed in love and feels himself an alien in a ruined universe. Carlyle's fictional editor brashly declares that Teufelsdröckh has but three courses open to him, "Establish himself in Bedlam; begin writing Satanic Poetry; or blow-out his brains."[23] The last two were once fashionable courses but will not be those of Carlyle's hero. In the language of Victorian self-defensiveness, Carlyle describes Teufelsdröckh's stance, which is very like his own in 1823. "Thus, if his sudden bereavement, in this matter of the Flower-goddess, is talked of as a real Doomsday and Dissolution of Nature, in which light doubtless it partly appeared to himself, his own nature is nowise dissolved there by; but rather is compressed closer" (*SR*, 147). Teufelsdröckh internalizes his woe, consumes his choler, and keeps his own Satanic School spouting "inaudibly." He thus becomes the archetypal Victorian male: not a voluble Byronic hero but a stoical person who can control himself, if not outward circumstance. Whereas "worldlings puke up their sick existence by suicide" (*SR*, 159), Teufelsdröckh, the Carlylean hero, endures and moves into the dark world of "The Everlasting No."

There he simmers away like a pressure cooker, existing but not living, eventually becoming limp and sodden—impotent. Already nearly dead within, he nonetheless fears death and refuses suicide.

> From Suicide a certain aftershine (*Nachschein*) of Christianity withheld me: perhaps also a certain indolence of character; for, was not that a remedy I had at anytime within reach? Often, however, was there a question present to me: Should some one now, at the turning of that corner, blow thee suddenly out of Space, into the other World, or other No-world, by pistol-shot,—how were it? On which ground, too, I often, in seastorms and sieged cities and other death-scenes, exhibited an imperturbability, which passed, falsely enough, for courage. (*SR*, 165)

Such imperturbability could not mask dread. Teufelsdröckh still feels passive, an unwilling victim of outside forces: "I lived in a continual, indefinite, pining fear; tremulous, pusillanimous, apprehensive of I knew not what; it seemed as if all things in the Heavens above and the Earth beneath would hurt me; as if the Heavens and the Earth were but boundless jaws of a devouring monster, wherein I, palpitating, waited to be devoured" (*SR*, 166). Only when he acknowledges that death is his chief fear and then confronts it, not through succumbing to it by suicide but through defiance, does he feel free to become a man. Growing up for this first-generation Victorian involves putting aside childish wishes both for the happiness of perfect love and for death.

Armed with these insights, Teufelsdröckh passes through his "centre of indifference." He turns outward, looks toward, and wanders through the world. What he finds are spectres, with his own spectral self a part of this ghostliness. What is wanted, however, is substance both in self and other so that there can be conflict or warfare, a testing of the embattled self. Weary with world-wandering, he becomes indifferent alike to life and death. For Carlyle's editor, as for Carlyle himself, this indifference constitutes the "first preliminary moral Act, Annihilation of Self (*Selbst-todtung*)" (*SR*, 186) and leads to relief. The universe now becomes not spectral but "godlike and my Father's." Here, then, is the legitimate form of Victorian suicide; not literal death but renunciation of self. Carlyle's hero gives up his "whims" of personal happiness and frees himself by self-imposing his very chains. Paradoxically he wills the death of self: ". . . the Self in thee needed to be annihilated. By benignant fever-paroxysms is Life rooting out the deep-seated chronic Disease, and triumphs over Death" (*SR*, 192). Teufelsdröckh is now at liberty to work and most of all to work just where he is. With selfish needs annihilated, the duty nearest to hand serves as sufficient reason for being.

Through the mental and physical peregrinations of Teufelsdröckh, Carlyle clarifies, structures, and fictionalizes his own journey toward suicide and back. This fabrication becomes Carlyle's "work," his own *raison d'être*. His will and imagination have fashioned a parable of self-defense, self-repression and self-renunciation that will in turn become a paradigm of Victorian thinking. Teufelsdröckh's reflections are certainly representative of Victorian views of self-destruction. The Christian sanctions against suicide that lingered in the mind of the once-Calvinistic Carlyle and are projected into Teufelsdröckh remained powerful in Britain up through the 1880s; and Teufelsdröckh's imperturbability in the face of death would pass for courage throughout the era. Like Teufelsdröckh, Carlyle had closed his Byron and opened the Goethe of *Wilhelm Meister*, had killed the devil despair, and had found a father in the bargain. Whereas for Goethe in *Meister* renunciation had been a part of *Bildung*, self-development, and a form of integration, for Carlyle and for many Victorians renunciation would instead become a dying to the self. Carlyle had toward Goethe "the feeling of a Disciple to his Master, nay of a son to his Spiritual Father,"[24] but Carlyle was no clone. With his own British version of renunciation, Carlyle himself became a kind of spiritual father to his age. Thus for R. H. Hutton, writing in 1887, "Carlyle was to England what his great hero, Goethe, long was to Germany,—the aged seer."[25] *Sartor* functioned as a sermon for eminent later Victorians like Froude; it became a work of salvation, like *In Memoriam*.[26] In both of these influential works, Victorian will-power and the will to write about personal anguish come to the aid of mystery and stage a momentary defeat of death. In orchestrating this defeat, Carlyle projected a message that his own doubting and death-haunted successors wanted to hear.

If Carlyle in many ways typifies the first generation of eminent Victorians, so does John Stuart Mill, whom Emery Neff saw as its other major representative.[27] Carlyle was a spokesman for religion—not for orthodoxy, surely, but for mystery and submission. His savior was Goethe. Mill, on the other hand, was the voice of reason, of utilitarianism made palatable, of liberty made tame. Yet from his very different perspective Mill, too, had undergone a conversion experience preceded by a wish not to be. His savior would be Wordsworth. Clinically and seemingly unselfconsciously, Mill relates the crisis "in his mental history" in the famous fifth chapter of his *Autobiography*. From an early age he had "an object in life: to be a reformer of the world." Nevertheless in 1826, in a "dull state of nerves," he asked himself whether he would be happy if all his social aims were fulfilled, if all the institutional changes and changes of opinion he hoped for were effected. "An irrepressible self-consciousness distinctly answered, "No!", and Mill's "heart sank." "Dry, heavy dejection" and melancholy followed in the winter of 1826–27.[28] Mill walked through that winter in a daze, deadened and mechanical, until life became unbearable. "I frequently asked myself," he says, "if I could, or if I was bound to go on living, when life must be passed in this manner. I generally answered to myself, that I did not think I could possibly bear it beyond a year" (*A*, 91).

Mill makes it clear that he could not consult his father in his crisis because his father's famous education—designed to make him a prodigy, a rationalist, and a Benthamite—did not allow for such a state of nerves. Instead, Mill found succor in two men of letters. Marmontel's *Mémoires* moved him to tears of relief when he read of the death of the father. This much-discussed gesture of Mill's is usually seen as a Freudian death-wish toward the repressive James Mill, a wish so undetected by the younger Mill that he was free to write openly about it. Yet it was also a move out of the entrapment of a limiting system of thought, quite as Mill says it was. Interestingly, the relief afforded by Marmontel leads Mill to the Carlylean realization that happiness is not to be found through searching for it; it appears along the way as one pursues some other end. Mill would later term this realization Carlyle's theory of "anti-selfconsciousness." Thus Mill rejects the self-destructive constrictions of Benthamism but, Victorian that he is, discovers a way of stilling yearnings without killing self. Wordsworth's poetry completes Mill's cure, convincing him that the cultivation of feelings can be coupled with concern for the "common destiny of human beings" (*A*, 96). Byron, on the contrary, had only exacerbated his depression, being of a state of mind too like his own.

Exactly why Mill reaches the impasse of 1826 is never really made clear in the *Autobiography*. A. W. Levi[29] is convinced that guilt over a death-wish for his father is the reason, and Gertrude Himmelfarb's insights into the "other John Stuart Mill" substantiate Levi's theory.[30] Himmelfarb refers to a second mental crisis in 1835 when Mill suffers pain in the stomach and head, infection, and severe muscular twitches of the face. All these symptoms occurred after James Mill himself fell ill, and all of them disappeared when the elder Mill died. John Stuart Mill's second breakdown is not discussed in his *Autobiography*, which may indicate that youthful crises like those of Carlyle and Mill were more acceptable to the Victorians than were those of later life. The Victorians did not want to believe that conversion experiences did not solve life's crises once and for all.

Like Carlyle, Mill refers to the will in his discussion of dejection in the *Autobiography*. After recalling how his character seemed to have been formed by "antecedent circumstances" that crushed and smothered him, Mill says that he pondered

> painfully on the subject, till gradually I saw light through it. I perceived, that the word Necessity, as a name for the doctrine of Cause and Effect applied to human action, carried with it a misleading association; and that this association was the operative force in the depressing and paralysing influence which I had experienced: I saw that though our character is formed by circumstances, our own desires can do much to shape those circumstances; and that what is really inspiriting and ennobling in the doctrine of free-will, is the conviction that we have real power over the formation of our own character; that our will, by influencing some of our circumstances, can modify our future habits or capabilities of willing. (*A*, 109)

The theory of necessity now ceased to oppress him, and he learned the difficult Victorian art of adhering faithfully to no single system. Like Carlyle, Mill went on to offer his insights to others through his writing. As he said, "the train of thought which had extricated me from this dilemma, seemed to me, in after years, fitted to render a similar service to others; and it now forms the chapter on Liberty and Necessity in the concluding Book of my 'System of Logic' " (*A*, 110). Suicide never became the subject of Mill's other writings. In *On Liberty* he totally avoided the issue of the ultimate freedom to take one's own life. Arguing that one legitimately can do whatever does not harm another individual or the public, he carried his argument as far as to slavery. Since individual liberty is to be desired, Mill insists that if one were to sell oneself into slavery, one would be moving contrary to basic human desires. "The principle of freedom cannot require that he should be free not to be free."[31] Although he could logically have extended his argument to self-murder, Mill did not. He did, however, return to the question of happiness in his 1861 essay *Utilitarianism* and there gave an indication of why suicide was not a fitting subject for his essays. Even this later, revised version of utilitarianism is based on the pursuit of happiness, a happiness now conditioned by "anti-selfconsciousness." He points out that even if it were not so, utilitarianism would at the least espouse the "prevention or mitigation of unhappiness," greatly needed by humankind "so long at least as mankind think fit to live, and do not take refuge in the simultaneous act of suicide recommended under certain conditions by Novalis."[32] Suicide, then, undermines utilitarianism, and Mill would remain a modified utilitarian to the end.

Mill and Carlyle both found in work—writing, reforming, and teaching—ways to overcome "the stage in a young man's life when the grimness of the human situation first comes clear." A young woman's life offered few such outlets. Half a generation later than Mill, Florence Nightingale would confront depression and suicide from a female vantage point. A mother, not a father, was her *bête noire*, and enforced idleness, not purposeful work, seemed her future. As a lady and member of a wealthy, upper-class family, Nightingale was expected to marry, to visit, and to entertain. She was accorded a role to play, not a vocation for which to live; and, detesting that role, she tried for years to break free from it. Throughout the 1840s, the decade of her twenties, she suffered intolerable frustration. By 1844 she had already settled on a metier—nursing—but she was barred access to it. Gentlewomen were not to put themselves in the way of dangers like exposure to dirt and disease, let alone warfare, nor were they to put aside Victorian modesty with regard to the human body. Nursing was a job for lower-class women or dedicated nuns. Nightingale's family strongly objected to her choice of nursing on such grounds and on the grounds that Florence might also be exposed to the flirtations and lechery of doctors. Nightingale's mother, Fanny, said as much and counselled marriage and travel as antidotes for Florence's "nursing fever."

Fanny's effect on her daughter was profound. Caught between her sense of duty to family and her desire for work, Nightingale fell victim to severe bouts of depression. Even recreational trips to the Continent inflamed her thwarted need to work. Throughout 1850 and 1851 she experienced her worst frustration. An unpublished diary for 1850 and an "autobiography" and memoranda for 1850–51 self-document two years of awesome hopelessness and yearning for death.[33] In May of 1850 Nightingale read Cowper and identified with his "deep despondency." In Greece by 7 June, she determined to go to the Eumenides cave to exorcise her Furies. Unlike Carlyle's devils, her demons resembled the women in her family. Nightingale felt guilty and sinful toward her mother and conformist sister, Parthe, and angry at what felt like their vengeful fury-like pursuit of her. Unfortunately, the cave was of no help to her. Alone inside, she still felt pursued and wondered "who shall deliver me from the body of this death?" No Wordsworth, no Goethe came to her aid, only Richard Monkton Milnes, intellectual and philanthropist, who would ask for her hand in marriage in 1850. Much to her family's dismay, Nightingale refused. She thought her "active moral nature" would have been compromised even by this match. By Christmas eve, she lamented that "in my thirty first year, I can see nothing desirable but death. . . . I cannot understand it. I am ashamed to understand it" (NP, leaf f. 53).

For a year and a half, Nightingale had tried to suppress her daydreams and prepare for a life of action but had failed. What she did not realize was that those dreams were in fact her salvation, since her life was already like death. She had confused the literal with the symbolic: she really wanted metaphorically to kill her old life in order to assume a new one, but she thought she simply wanted to die. Her diary entries are full of such confusion: "voluntarily to put it out of my power ever to be able to seize the chance of forming myself a . . . rich life would seem to me like suicide. And yet my present life is suicide" (NP, leaf f. 54).

Eventually the diaries focus on a metaphor that more clearly expresses Nightingale's state. Florence Nightingale is starving to death for want of work. Her suppressed rebellion against her family has left her a kind of emotional anorexic. She sees in her current state an equivalent to murder: she is being starved by others' expectations. "I am perishing," she says, "for want of food. And what prospect have I of better? While I am in this position, I can expect nothing else. Therefore I spend my day in dreams of other situations which will afford me food" (NP, leaf f. 55). Hers, then, is a death-in-life; but she does not really want to die, only to die to idleness and live through work:

Starvation does not lead a man to action—it only weakens him. Oh weary days—oh evenings that seem never to end—for how many years I have watched that drawing room clock . . . it is not the misery, the unhappiness that I feel is so insupportable, but I feel this habit, this disease gaining ground upon me and no hope, no help. This is the sting of death.

Why do I wish to leave this world? God knows I do not suspect a heaven beyond—but that He will set me down in St. Giles, at a Kaiserswerth, there to find my work. (NP, leaf f. 55)

Once Nightingale really understands the nature of her problem, her diary entries alter. She has converted herself, although she is not yet fully aware of this. A kind of religious meditation follows on an overleaf of the last letter of 1850. In it she opens a casement and feels the night wind blow over her. Unlike the early English romantics for whom such wind was beneficial, a corresponding breeze answering the breaths of their voices, Nightingale experiences several winds from different directions. If some are benign, others are hostile. They indicate conflicting but invigorating movements in her life and thought by the end of 1850.

After this meditation come a new form of self-discipline and a new form of self-address in Nightingale's papers. She begins to command herself; her voice is imperative: "Let me not try to disguise these two facts from myself, Spirit of Truth, but let me honestly and with simplicity of purpose set to work not to complain, but to find the means to live" (NP, leaf f. 67). She asks to do God's will but determines to regiment her own. She must place intercourse with her family on a new footing; she must grow up; she must refuse to be treated as a child; she must give over the thoughts of real death; she must quit trying to be understood by her parents. She must also "take" the food she has been perishing for, "a nourishing life—that is happiness." Nightingale must feed herself in order not to become like the suicidal self-starvers of George Burrows's classic nineteenth-century work on insanity.[34] Such people show either a disgust for food or an obstinate rejection of it, whereas Nightingale wants to relieve her starvation.

By 1851, Nightingale turns more directly to the question of happiness. Once in her life she had been happy, at Kaiserswerth in Germany, where in 1848 she spent a fortnight at a model hospital staffed by a Protestant religious order. In the summer of 1851 she would return there and experience similar happiness. To Fanny she wrote: "I find the deepest interest in everything here and am so well in body and mind. . . . I really should be sorry now to leave life. I know you will be glad to hear, dearest mother, this" (NP, leaf f. 137). Nightingale did not live happily ever after, however. Her depressions recurred, and her troubles with Fanny and Parthe were never really resolved until her mother's and sister's final illnesses when Florence gained absolute control over her two weakened Furies. Maybe by then she realized that she herself was a Fury in their eyes, that they were all three the avengers.

Throughout her life Nightingale would continue to long for death. To Mary Clarke Mohl in 1881 she wrote: "I cannot remember the time when I have not longed for death. After Sidney Herbert's death and Clough's death in 1861, 20 years ago, for years and years I used to watch for death as no sick man ever watched for the morning. It is strange that now bereft of all, I crave for it less."[35] Throughout her life, too, she put herself in the way of death and disease merely by exercising her profession. And when she was not directly in touch with danger, she underwent or contrived prolonged periods of invalidism when she controlled her mother, sister, and male associates by letter and directive sent out from her bedroom. These illnesses were both forms of self-destruction and a means of survival. Yet Nightingale, like Carlyle and Mill, had one major suicidal crisis. When it passed she, too, wrote, offering others directives on how not to die. Still in her thirty-first year, she received a call from God to be a "saviour" and produced *Suggestions for Thought to Searchers After Religious Truth*. A ponderous work in three volumes, *Suggestions* aims at an audience of artisans, purporting to give them a theology to live by. Newly in contact with the working classes, Nightingale was appalled at their lack of religion. Her message for them would be her diary's message to herself: individuals must use their own wills for human betterment and thus help to accomplish God's will on earth. "Many," she would say, "long intensely to die, to go to another world, which could not be worse and might be better than this. But is there any better world there to go into?"[36]

Mill would be amused by Nightingale's missionary zeal in exhorting the working class to live and work on in God's service.[37] Nightingale, however, was utterly serious about her mission. In the notes for *Suggestions* she asks herself, "Can I will what I wish? Can I do what I will?"[38] What she would will in 1852 was to rewrite her diary in the service of humanity, careful to include not just working-class but also female humanity. In this light, the section of Volume II called "Cassandra" bears reexamination. Like Nightingale, middle-class women are starving for work. They sit down daily to large meals of food but lack spiritual and mental sustenance. Idleness and marriage stifle them to the point that "some are only deterred from suicide because it is the most distinct manner to say to an indifferent God: 'I will not, I will not do as Thou wouldst have me,' and because it is 'no use.' "[39] And yet these women continue to wait for a palpable deliverer. Nightingale concludes this section of *Suggestions* with symbols and ambivalences. "The next Christ will perhaps be a female Christ," she hopes, and yet she asks, "Do we see one woman who looks like a female Christ? or even like the messenger before her 'face,' to go before her and prepare the hearts and minds for her?"[40] Her answer to these questions is only implied: no, there is no such Christ unless she herself is to be one. There is only Cassandra, the dying and unheeded prophetess whose real death has already taken place in the thwarting of her talent, not in her ultimate physical end.

Suggestions was revised in 1859 and privately printed in 1860, after Florence Nightingale's return from Crimea. By then, Nightingale's personal and vocational crises had passed, and she had become less dedicated to philosophical and literary pursuit. Her mission lay elsewhere, in physically ministering to other lives. In doing so, she became both a literal saviour and a legendary figure: the "Lady with the Lamp," a living female counterpart of Holman Hunt's portrait of Christ as *Light of the World*.[41] With no Goethes, nor Wordsworths, nor even James Mills to show her the way, she transformed herself into her own and others' source of salvation from death—if not a kind of female Christ, then surely a kind of Virgin Florence. Unlike Carlyle and Mill and the women who left fathers only to marry, Nightingale did not want a change of masters. Instead she became one of the first Victorian women to point the way toward self-mastery as a road to female salvation.

Despite differences in temperament and sex, the sage of Ecclefechan, the great utilitarian and apostle of liberty, and the Lady of the Lamp all warred with suicidal despair in similar ways. Each had to metamorphose: to convert him- or herself from youthful despair and desire for death to useful adulthood. All three had to grow up. For Carlyle, self-denial, itself a kind of suicide, paradoxically offered the way. For Mill and Nightingale self-denial was hardly liberating but rather a kind of self-starvation. Yet each of these three eminent Victorians had metaphorically to kill a parent or bogey—a former self of sorts—in order to emerge rather than die. And because each had a mission, each had to write and then rewrite his or her story, shifting from the private world of letters, notebooks, and journals to a public voice in more formal prose. Thus personal crisis became public narrative for the greater good of community, so that their literature is strongly marked by morality and didacticism. All three girded themselves in perseverance, willpower, and work and battled their own suicidal despair. In doing so they became apostles of self-transformation and endurance, evidence that upper- and middle-class Victorian Britain seemed determined not to be a "classic land of suicide." They laid legal issues and implications of insecurity aside, confronting suicide as a personal moral choice. Hard as it might seem, it was simply better to be than not to be.

III

Cases and Classes: Sensational Suicides and Their Interpreters

In the autumn of 1838, not long after Florence Nightingale had returned to Embley from a busy if unfulfilling London season, another young woman mounted the stairs of London's Monument, hoisted herself to the top of the rail, and swiftly dropped to a bloody death below. Margaret Moyes's human predicament was nearly the opposite of Florence Nightingale's: her mother was dead and her father lay dying. Because her own sensational death became a favored subject of broadsides and newspaper accounts, "authentic particulars" of Miss Moyes's "extraordinary suicide" abound. Just before ten on Wednesday morning, 11 September, Margaret Moyes, twenty-three, arrived at the Monument from Charing Cross, said she was to meet friends there, waited for them for about twenty minutes while she chatted with the porter of the Monument, paid her sixpence, and then ascended alone. Her fall ended miserably. On its way down, her body hit a bird cage and a potted lilac, and her arm was severed by the railing at the foot of the Monument. Moments later, when the first looker-on arrived at her side, she was dead.

Margaret Moyes's was one of the few suicides to achieve a notoriety akin to that of Victorian murder cases. For the most part, Victorians feared suicide far more than they did murder. Certainly both acts were subversive, contrary to the Ten Commandments and to Victorian secular notions of self-help and the judicious exercise of willpower, but suicide was more easily internalized than murder. A writer for *Temple Bar* observed of murder and murderers that "there is always something agreeable to us in the misfortunes of our neighbours. It would certainly seem as though a record of their vices is eminently pleasing."[1] Self-murder, on the other hand, could lead survivors toward a painful self-examination in the search for motives. Murder might satisfy the Victorian sense of justice, since murderers could be caught and imprisoned or in turn be killed for their crimes—an eye for an eye—but self-murder, was a personal challenge to the will of God in which human justice could never really intervene. Thus if murder caused sensation among the Victorians, suicide was more often a source of anxiety and disgrace.

Middle-class families took pains to conceal self-destruction, not only because suicide was illegal and considered immoral but also because the insanity plea was the only way of preventing the property of a proven suicide from reverting to the Crown. They faced the awful dilemma of choosing the lesser of two evils: hereditary insanity as a future stigma, or poverty as an immediate prospect, that is, if the suicide were a breadwinner. These alternatives—little better than Dickens's choice of a slow death in the workhouse or a quick one out of it for the poor—were to be avoided at all costs. Even clergymen were enlisted in cover-ups since, until the 1880s, proven suicides could not be buried in consecrated ground.

But Margaret Moyes's suicide was an open statement of despair, committed in the most public of places, and drawing the attention of those who loved hangings and murder trials. A person walking toward the Monument on the day after her death would have been blocked by the crowds—mostly women—spilling into every street leading to the Monument Yard, or by police trying to keep order. A person attempting to gain admission to the Monument itself would in all likelihood have been thwarted. The Yard was crammed with people trying to gain access to the staircase and heights. A person desiring to attend the inquest on Friday might similarly have been balked. Many who begged admission that day to the Swan Tavern, Fish-street Hill, were flatly refused. So the press enthusiastically took on the job of interpreting the event for those not present. Customers for every London newspaper craved knowledge of the particulars of such an audacious act. What they wanted most of all were detailed descriptions of the fall and attempted explanations for such bitter desperation. Every type of coverage featured these two aspects of the case, and each paper reflected the language and mores of its readers when presenting its details.

The *Times*, for example, fully described the gory details of the appearance of the body but used Latinate terms like "cranium" and "integument" to sound clinical rather than sensational:

> Upon examination of the body, it was found that the spine was fractured as also the back of the cranium, but the features are in no way disfigured, save by the appearance of coagulated blood forced from the nostrils, eyes, and mouth by the sudden concussion; the left arm is severed just above the elbow, and is only retained in its place by the integuments and the sleeve of the dress.[2]

The *Observer*, though an upper-middle to upper-class paper, offered its Sunday readers something far more dramatic than such dissecting-room language:

Her left arm, near the shoulder, came in contact with the bar, and was so violently severed that the part cut off flew over the iron railings several yards into the square. After striking the bar, the body fell on a tub containing a lilac plant, which it broke in pieces, as well as several flower pots, placed on the right side of the door. Not a sign of life, except some contortions of the muscles of the legs and arms, was discernible on the body when it was picked up.[3]

Sunday editions of *The Weekly Dispatch* and Bell's *Life in London* relayed the *Observer's* accounts to a less well-to-do readership. So did a street pamphlet printed by Goode in Clerkenwell, while *The Wednesday Standard* contained both the Latinate and dramatic accounts. And two broadsides entitled a "Copy of Verses on the Melancholy Death of Margaret Moyes" gave a far cruder version of the fall and of the severed left arm. The verses were the product of a literary hack in London's Seven Dials area, whose well-off publishers like James Catnach were known for purveying lurid sensationalism and getting it out to the streets as quickly as possible. For them, concern over stylistic awkwardness came second to the many thousands of pennies gained by providing the first broadside about a bloody case like Moyes's:

> From strangers oh! What awful shrieks,
> When she let go her hold,
> Like lightning she descended.
> 'Twas dreadful to behold;
> With a heavy crash upon the rails,
> The shock was most severe,
> Which cut off her arm and it was found,
> Near the centre of the square.[4]

Descriptions of the ugliness of Moyes's death came easier than explanations for it. Most Victorians, whatever their class or education, had stock assumptions about suicide: it was committed by the unhappy, the lonely, the lovelorn, the mad, the ruined—all poor unfortunates at the end of an emotional tether. Most coroners' inquests looked for such motives. In murder cases, there was always the hope of confession, but in suicide cases there was usually no one able to disprove customary assumptions. They were endlessly perpetuated unless a note or other concrete evidence happened to be available. Moyes left such a note on her father's mantel shelf, but it too was inconclusive: "You need not expect to see me back again, for I have made up my mind to make away with———Margaret Moyes."[5] With the reflexive pronoun "myself" missing here, Moyes's signature dramatically represents the object to be "made away with"—quite simply Margaret Moyes. Yet Moyes's note offers no reasons for her action.

What would cause an attractive young woman to choose such a hideous exit from life? This question intrigued the Victorian public. Moyes's father was a master-baker, a position he may well have bought, and his daughter had pretensions to the upper-middle class. She was probably educated to desire the very idleness that Nightingale detested and to expect a suitable and financially comfortable marriage. But as one of four sisters of a dying father, she was suddenly confronted with the prospect of working for a living. Unexposed to anything other than the baking business, she had contracted to work in a confectioner's shop. As a shop girl, she might have been subject to harassment and taunts about her father's station. This prospect, coupled with grief over the father whose side she rarely left, might well have made her desperate.

The coroner's inquest explored these aspects of the case with several witnesses, all of whom attested to Moyes's fear of "going out into the world." Most of the daily and Sunday papers read by the middle classes reported the inquest verbatim, but accounts in the *Times* and *Standard* conjectured further about Moyes's station. Her "dress denoted that the unfortunate wearer had moved in a circle above the middle class of life. It consists of a good black silk dress, undergarments of fine linen, silk stockings, and a worked habit-shirt; on the fore-finger of the left hand there was a gold signet ring."[6] Readers of the *Times* could empathize with such a person and would find her fall—financial and literal—very "unfortunate" indeed. Broadside readers of the working class, on the other hand, got a different version with which to identify:

> The maiden's mother had been dead,
> Two years we have been told,
> Her father, with sickness long confin'd,
> Besides he's very old;
> Which plunged the family in distress,
> That to service she must go,
> That so afflicted her youthful mind,
> Caus'd this dreadful scene of woe.[7]

No mention of "service" was ever made during the inquest. That was simply a fiction offered to lower-class readers by the presses of Seven Dials.

Lessons to be drawn by middle-class readers were inherent in the inquest itself. Underlying many of the questions was the basic suspicion that the unfortunate Margaret Moyes might have been lovesick or, worse, seduced and abandoned. The ring mentioned was suspect but was found only to be a gift of a sister. An army captain, a lodger with the Moyes family, was rumored to have been a sweetheart but proved simply an acquaintance. The doctor examining the body was asked whether Moyes was pregnant, and her sisters were expected to reveal whether there had been any love letters to Margaret Moyes. Yet Miss Moyes had no known lovers, was not pregnant, and received no love letters. Thus "dullness of mind" and "depression of spirits" over being forced to go out in the world became the official causes of Moyes's "temporary insanity," and the inquest into her death concluded with a recommendation to put a guard rail at the top of the Monument to prevent further tragedies.

Graphic accounts of "extraordinary suicides" like the extensive reporting of the Moyes case would come under heavy censure in nineteenth-century England. As early as 1828, George Burrows's *Commentaries* on insanity had blamed the "cheap press" for increases in suicide. "Nothing," Burrows cautioned, "is found so attractive as tales of wonder and horror, and every coroner's inquest on an unhappy being who has destroyed himself is read with extraordinary avidity."[8] Suicide by imitation was Burrows's chief fear. He felt that the daily papers were at fault for providing details of the means of successful suicide: "No sooner is the mind disturbed by any moral causes, than the thoughts are at once directed, through these channels [the newspapers], to mediate an act, which otherwise neither predisposition, despair, nor the nature of their insanity, would have suggested."[9] According to Forbes Winslow in 1840, even those whose minds were not deeply disturbed could be affected by imitation. He told of a friend of a friend who "had the curiosity to visit the spot, and on looking down the awful height from which this poor unfortunate girl had precipitated herself . . . felt suddenly an attack of giddiness, which was succeeded in a moment by one of the most pleasurable sensations he had ever experienced, accompanied with a desire to jump off."[10] By 1843, concern over imitation had increased, and William Farr, the Registrar-General, called for "some plan for discontinuing, by common consent, the detailed dramatic tales of murder, suicide, and bloodshed in the newspapers."[11] In 1868, a writer for the *Bookseller* took this recommendation a step further. Newspapers were bad, but only contained the written word. "Glaring woodcuts" like those of Miss Moyes, were still worse, with "murders, hangings, suicides, &c. all pictorially described in detail, with a degree of unctuous horror quite impossible to be conveyed to the uninitiated."[12]

Unfortunately, Farr's recommendations were not implemented by October of 1839, when a fifteen-year-old boy mounted the stairs of the Monument and reenacted Margaret Moyes's suicidal plunge to the

Monument Yard. Young Richard Hawes's suicide was certainly imitative. He frequently talked of Moyes's death to the other servants at the home of the surgeon where he was employed. Hawes had told them that one probably would not feel pain in a death like Moyes's. At his inquest, these servants reported that Hawes had previously threatened suicide from a height. While cleaning windows he would deliberately "stand recklessly on one leg." On the very morning of his death, he had been dismissed from his job both for lethargy and for threatening to jump out of a window. Hawes also read murder stories. Here was just the sort of impressionable person that Burrows had been worrying about.

As in the Moyes case, newspapers focused on the details of Hawes's bloody death and then on possible reasons for a second such suicide. Hawes clearly had not been seduced and abandoned; nor, as a poor boy, had he known financial reversal. This time the Victorian press and the coroner's jury sought elsewhere for causes of death: in hereditary insanity leading to suicide, in Hawes's melancholia, and in his reading habits. Hawes was the son of a laundress and of a father who had killed himself, a fact that the inquest drew out in hushed tones. At the inquest, the chaplain of St. Anne's, Brixton, where Hawes had been a pupil, brought forth a St. Anne's Society register that listed "Robert Donaldson Hawes—father a coachman of good character—mother a widow, father having died insane." Then the coroner queried, "is this correct that the father of the deceased died insane?" A witness replied (in a low tone): "His father destroyed himself."[13] Whatever his origins, Hawes himself became an enigma. Impressions of him were at odds. Most witnesses at the inquest had found him a quiet and tractable lad, but fellow servants and several others reported him unpredictable and violent. He often withdrew to read books, but these, too, varied from *Jack Sheppard* to the Holy Bible. Some weeks before his death, he had sent to his mother's place for the Bible that he had been awarded for good conduct at St. Anne's. He had the Bible with him when he ascended the Monument and left it in the gallery with several pages carefully turned down.

Twentieth-century psychology might consider Hawes an attention-seeker. He had been dismissed from two jobs as lazy or derelict in duty, but when behaving well, was a person who was generally ignored. Conjecture might continue that he sought attention by creating disturbances like teasing the kitchen help, or threatening to kill the housemaid or, finally, imitating his father and the widely publicized Miss Moyes. His avid reading no doubt fed his fantasies. He too could act like Jack Sheppard and Margaret Moyes and attract public attention for notorious, sensational behavior. The Victorians, however, chose to see him somewhat differently from this. If the question that was raised at Margaret Moyes's death was if she was a fallen woman, the question that arose at Richard Hawes's was if he was indeed a good boy. "The deceased was of a quiet and steady disposition, but very melancholy and fond of reading religious and serious works, which he invariably did in some retired spot," reported *The Weekly Dispatch*.[14] Thus clues to Hawes's death were sought in the leaf-turned Bible he left behind. It was read as a kind of suicide note:

> Proverbs, chap. 29 v. 1.—"He that, being often reproved, hardeneth his neck, shall be suddenly destroyed, and that without remedy." Verse 2.—"When the righteous are in authority the people rejoice, but when the wicked beareth rule the people mourn." St. Luke, v. 53.—"The father shall be divided against the son, and the son against the father; the mother against the daughter and the daughter against the mother; the mother-in-law against her daughter-in-law and the daughter-in-law against her mother-in-law." Chapter 14, v. 11.—"For whosoever exalteth himself shall be abased; and he that humbleth himself shall be exalted." St. Mark, chap. 13 v. 32—"But of that day and that hour knoweth no man. No, not the angels which are in heaven; neither the son nor the father." Verse 33.—"Take ye heed, watch and pray, for ye know not when the time is."[15]

Although these passages deal with punishment and death and certainly could show guilt or vindictiveness on Hawes's part, ultimately they only served the Victorian jury as proof of the boy's melancholia. Both his mother and his school had testified that he was often depressed. And so Hawes was judged of unsound mind, but not of weak intellect. Impressionable and misguided, he was "temporarily insane" when he leapt from the Monument, a good boy seized by an unfortunate fit of madness.

Unlike most suicides that could be covered up or ignored except by those near at hand, these two widely publicized plunges from the Monument—and others that followed them in the 1840s—awakened public interest in suicide prevention. There was further outcry against cheap literature and the graphic reporting of suicides, and eventually the Monument was caged to prevent more deaths. Although stock motives were still relied upon in verdicts of suicide, physicians' testimony was now leading to deeper questioning of the causes of suicide. By 1857 there was an audience for articles like "Suicide: Its Motives and Mysteries," which appeared in the *Irish Quarterly Review*. This essay attempted to explain Moyes's death and the subsequent loss of Hawes and others. "Excited curiosity" could lead people to the sites of such deaths, empathetic imagination could then begin to discern the motives and sensations of the suicides, and what was called "visionary" power could finally drive a new victim on to his or her death.[16]

If abundant cheap literature was helping to excite such curiosity, it was certainly not discontinued as a result. A struggle to control the lucrative media that appealed to the working classes yielded both sensational and moral accounts of suicide. Until well after mid-century, the most widely available forms of literature for the masses were the broadsides and broadsheets. Broadsides, which were hawked on the streets and in the public houses of Victorian cities, were single unfolded sheets of paper with printing on one side; broadsheets had the printing on both sides. They functioned as poor people's newspapers until newspaper taxes were removed in 1855. Since many were written as songs, they also continued the ballad tradition into the nineteenth century. Most popular among them were "gallows literature" recounting crimes and punishments. Like traditional oral ballads, broadsides attempted to comment upon aspects of the human predicament, often concluding with admonishments or prayers for forgiveness.

Margaret Moyes's suicide generated a full complement of such literature. In addition to the "Authentic Particulars" offered in the form of a pamphlet, there was a broadsheet of "Particulars of the coroner's inquest held on the body of Margaret Moyes who met her death by throwing herself off the monument."[17] The sheet offered readers who could not afford newspapers an account of the suicide and a very abbreviated version of the inquest. More spectacular was the woodcut at the head of the text, which showed a wasp-waisted young woman hurtling through the air beneath the Monument. Woodcuts also adorned the two different broadsheets carrying the "Copy of Verses on the Melancholy Death of Margaret Moyes Who Committed Suicide by Throwing Herself off the Monument on Wednesday, September 11, 1839." One of these depicts a pensive Victorian woman with tear-drop earrings in a portrait profile; the other is yet another view of Monument and body, this time with the church spire of St. Magnus the Martyr in the background, just on a level with the plummeting body. The verses conclude:

> Now may God in his great mercy,
> This maid's rash act forgive
> And her dreadful fate a warning be,
> To others while they live;
> In their station for to be content,
> Tho' reduc'd to poverty,
> And not while in the prime of life,
> Plunge themselves into eternity.[18]

"Self Destruction of a Female by Throwing Herself off the Monument" (1839).

"Particulars of the Coroner's Inquest Held on the Body of Magaret [*sic*] Moyes" (1839).

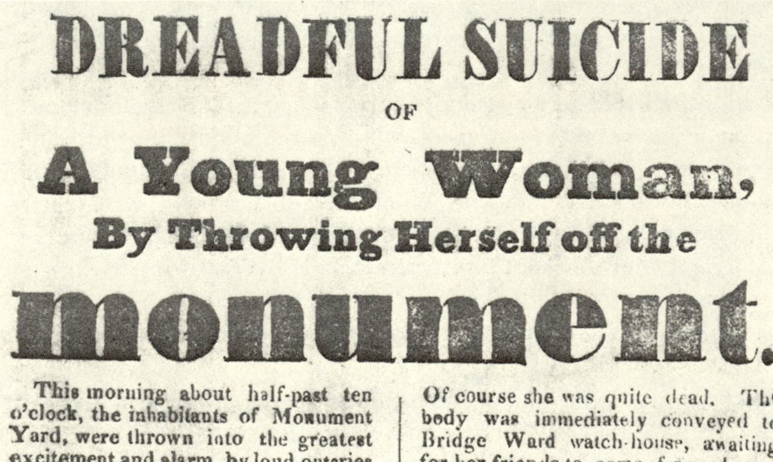

DREADFUL SUICIDE

OF

A Young Woman,

By Throwing Herself off the

monument.

This morning about half-past ten o'clock, the inhabitants of Monument Yard, were thrown into the greatest excitement and alarm, by loud outcries from several persons. & upon inquiring the cause; they were horror-struck to find that another rash and unfortunate being had committed suicide by precipitating herself from the gallery of the Monument. So great was the sensation that this created. and such was the feeling of horror excited, that it was

Of course she was quite dead. The body was immediately conveyed to Bridge Ward watch-house, awaiting for her friends to come forward and own the body.

The news of the awful tragedy was quickly tpread; and a great crowd of persons assembled on the spot, who appeared completely paralysed at the awful occurance. We cannot of course at the present time give any particulars that might explain the motives that

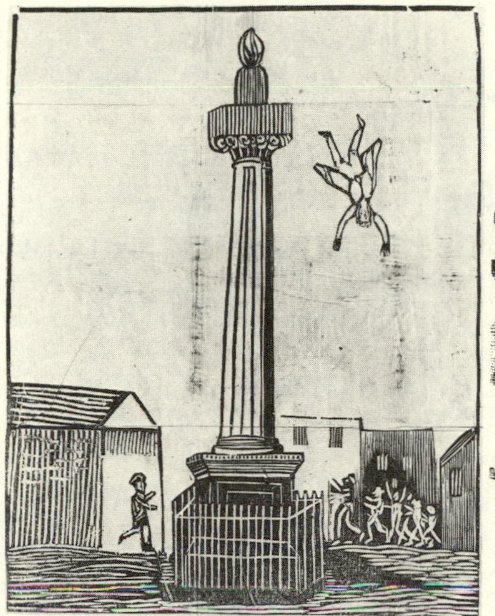

The suicide of Robert Hawes, broadside woodcut (1839).

"Another Dreadful Suicide at the Monument, by a Young Woman" (1842).

Again, the Seven Dials's morality was in effect, giving the working classes sensation but keeping them in place by affirming the virtue of accepting poverty.

Since successful *felonia-de-se* is self-punished, there was no real "gallows" literature for suicides, but there were many Victorian broadsides about murderers who escape the gallows only through suicide. Some are bent on vengeance, some on gain, but all are felt to get their just deserts when they in turn die. A popular variation on this theme was the domestic tragedy. Broadside after broadside recounted the details of families murdered by parents who then turned on themselves to complete the destruction of the group. "Shocking murder of a wife and six children"[19] is one such. The upper half of this sheet is devoted to a detailed prose account of a certain Duggin of Hosier-lane, City, who had been dismissed from his employment and had received an eviction notice from his lodgings. Presumably Duggin sent a note to the police saying he had murdered seven persons and was about to poison himself. When the constables arrived, they found the entire family dead. The lower half of the broadside about Duggin displays a crude ballad that concludes with a request for forgiveness of "sinful souls." If the prose account of the Duggin incident was based in fact, the ballad was em-

COPY OF VERSES

ON THE MELANCHOLY DEATH OF

Margaret Moyes

Who committed Suicide by throwing herself off the Monument on Wednesday, September 11, 1839.

YOU heedless youths of either sex,
  I pray you will attend,
And to this melancholy tale,
  A serious ear now lend ;
Of Margaret Moyes a blooming maid,
  Her death I will unfold,
And when the same you come to hear,
  'Twill make your blood run cold.

On Wednesday last in the prime of life,
  To the Monument did go,
She said her friends had not arriv'd,
  So she asked to sit down ;
Soon after for admission paid,
  To the top she did ascend,
But little did the keeper think,
  Her life was so near its end.

Scarce twenty minutes had elaps'd,
  Before she reach'd the top,
When many persons in the yard,
  To see her they did stop ;
Upon the cornice she did stand,
  Outside the iron rail.
In that dreadful situation,
  Many did her fate bewail.

From strangers oh ! what awful shrieks,
  When she let go her hold,
Like lightning she descended.
  'Twas dreadful to behold ;
With a heavy crash upon the rails,
  The shock was most severe,
Which cut off her arm & it was found,
  Near the centre of the square.

This maiden's mother had been dead,
  Two years we have been told,
Her father with sickness long confin'd,
  Beside he's very old ;
Which plung'd the family in distress,
  That to service she must go,
That so afflicted her youthful mind,
  Caus'd this dreadful scene of woe.

Now may God in his great mercy,
  This maid's rash act forgive
And her dreadful fate a warning be,
  To others while they live ;
In their station for to be content,
  Tho' reduced to poverty,
And not while in the prime of life,
  Plunge themselves into eternity.

JUST PUBLISHED!

THE

AUTHENTIC PARTICULARS

OF THE MOST

Determined and Frightful

SUICIDE,

OF

MISS MOYES,

By throwing herself from

The Monument,

Also a Correct

COPY OF A LETTER

Which was found after she left her home.

LONDON

Published by G. GILBERT, 2, Green-arbour Court, Old Bailey.
Printed by T. Goode, 12, Wilderness Row, Clerkenwell.

(*Above*) "Just Published! Authentic Particulars of the Most Determined and Frightful Suicide . . ." (1839).

(*At left*) "Copy of Verses on the Melancholy Death of Margaret Moyes" (1839).

bellished with conjecture as well as with warnings to other parents. On the other hand, the "Esher Tragedy, six children murdered by their mother" contained only a thread of fact: Mary Brough slit the throats of her six children on the 9th of June, 1854, and afterwards tried to cut her own throat but failed. The top half of this sheet displays elaborate verses, including fictional pleas from the children ("Mother, dear, don't murder me") and a final word about motives:

Oh! what must be the woman's motive,
  Did she think she'd done amiss,
Or did she think of death and judgment
  To perpetrate a deed like this?
But now the wretch she is committed,
  To a prison's gloomy cell,

Where midnight dreams to her will whisper
And her deeds of blood will tell.[20]

The bottom half of the sheet is pure "cock," a wholly fictitious confession, supposedly by Mary herself and sold as a true account.

"Cocks" were as popular as genuine reportings of inquests. For all their horror, they still seemed plausible to the people of the streets. Those who read Victorian broadsides were no strangers to unemployment, frustration, poverty, fury, and violent death. Nor were these troubles unknown to readers of "hungry forties" novels like Elizabeth Gaskell's. In Gaskell's *North and South* (1854), working-class John Boucher is forced to join a trade union against his will. When the union goes on strike, Boucher's employer imports workers from Ireland, causing the starving Boucher and other desperate workers to riot, and after the strike, Boucher is unemployable. Following many futile attempts to get work, Boucher drowns himself in a shallow stream rather than go home to face his querulous wife and eight hungry children. His is a touching story, and people could empathize with Boucher—and with Walter Duggin and Mary Brough—as well as be warned by their brand of violence. Yet not all literature of domestic murder and suicide was serious. The Crampton collection in the British Library contains a "Horrible Tale!" that spoofs the broadsides of suicide. The tale tells of a highly respectable family that

. . . grew sadder and sadder,
And each was affrighted by the other's shadow.
They pull'd down the blinds to keep out the light,
Till everything was as dark as night,
And as they were bent on suiciding,
I'll tell you the manner they respectively died in.

One day as the father, in the garden did walk,
He cut his throat with a piece of chalk:
The mother an end to her life did put,
By hanging herself in the water butt.

The youngest daughter on bended knees,
She poisoned herself with toasted cheese:
The youngest son, a determined young fellow,
Blew out his brains with an old umbrella.

The gard'ner came in and saw the blood,
He run himself through with a stick of Rhubarb;
His wife saw the sight and it turned her savage,
So she burnt herself to death with red pickled cabbage.

The old tom cat as he sat by the fire,
Bit a piece off the fender and then did expire:
The flies on the ceiling, their case was the wors'n,
For they blew themselves up with spontaneous combustion.

The old cow in the old cow shed,
Took up the pitchfork and knock'd off her head:
The little donkey hearing the row,
Knocked out its brains with the head of the cow.[21]

It is difficult to say whether this ballad reveals working-class animosity toward foolish respectability or a free-wheeling moment of a Seven Dials hack on a dull day for sensational stories. Certainly it shows that straight-laced admonitions were not the only purpose of the Victorian broadsides of suicide. The people needed a good laugh as well as reminders to persevere.

That the working classes could chuckle even at the darkest aspects of their lot, including their alleged propensity to suicide, is also evident from "The New Intended Reform Bill," a tongue-in-cheek broadside with twenty clauses to be made operative "as soon as the Lords and Commons think fit." The bill sounds like a poor-man's *Punch*, with bleak-humored references to workhouses, drunkenness, and skirt-chasing policemen. Clause 19, the suicide clause, reads, "all persons contemplating suicide, are earnestly requested not to drown themselves, as bodies lying too long in the Thames cause the water to become very unwholesome."[22] Absurd as it is, this "request" was a feasible reaction to mid-Victorian strictures on suicide and opinions on the worth of the poor. Dickens reacted with kindred irony in his *Chimes* (1844), where Toby Veck, a ticket porter who has fallen on hard times, wonders whether he has either the right to live or the right to die. Says Toby: "I can't make out whether [the poor] have any business on the face of the earth, or not. Sometimes I think we must have—a little; and sometimes I think we must be intruding. I get so puzzled sometimes that I am not even able to make up my mind whether there is any good at all in us, or whether we are born bad. We seem to be dreadful things; we seem to give a deal of trouble; we are always being complained of and guarded against. One way or other, we fill the papers."[23] Later when he reads the newspaper account of a woman who killed both herself and her child, he exclaims to his daughter Meg that he now has proof that poor people like themselves are indeed "bad" (*CB*, I: 196). Here Dickens posits that loss of self-esteem is the final conviction of the down-and-out. To his mind this loss is what allows the poor to commit suicide; it is the one conviction that they must shun at all costs. "Toby," notes

Dickens, "was very poor, and couldn't well afford to part with a delight—that he was worth his salt" (*CB*, I: 153–54).

Through Toby, Meg, and their oppressors, Dickens was directly responding to a sensational domestic tragedy of 1844. Early that year, a young woman named Mary Furley left a workhouse where her infant was mistreated and tried to make a living by sewing shirts. When she failed to eke out even the meagerest existence on her own, she desperately decided to drown both her child and herself. Her attempt miscarried when she was saved but the baby was not, and Mary Furley was tried, convicted of child-murder, and condemned to death. Public opinion was outraged. *The London Times* denounced the New Poor Law for having "brought this poor creature to the verge of madness,"[24] while *Lloyd's Weekly* called for petitions to the throne to commute the sentence. In response to this sort of pressure, the Home Secretary, Sir James Graham, gave a stay of execution and then commuted the sentence to seven-years' transportation. Dickens, among others, found even this new sentence unfair and in response wrote a bitterly ironic piece for *Hood's Magazine*.[25] There he mocked dutiful officials for their wise severity in quelling such "revolutionary" females, and in *The Chimes* he gave Toby a dreadful vision of his Meg headed "To The River": "To that portal of Eternity, her desperate footsteps tended with the swiftness of its rapid waters running to the sea" (*CB*, I: 239).

Dickens continued his commentary on severe public officials in his portrait of Alderman Cute in *The Chimes*. Cute wants to end suicide by imposing sentences like the one for Mary Furley:

> "And if you attempt, desperately, and ungratefully, and impiously, and fraudulently attempt to drown yourself, or hang yourself, I'll have no pity on you, for I have made up my mind to put all suicide down. If there is one thing," said the Alderman, with his self-satisfied smile, "on which I can be said to have made up my mind more than on another, it is to Put Suicide Down. So don't try it on." (*CB*, I: 172)

This delineation of Cute is a thinly disguised indictment of Sir Peter Laurie, a Middlesex Magistrate and one-time Lord Mayor of London. In the 1840s Laurie was frequently quoted in the press for his relentless campaign against suicide and was notorious for this kind of sentencing: "Suicides and attempts, or apparent attempts, to commit suicide very much increase, I regret to say. I know that a morbid humanity exists, and does much mischief, as regards the practice. I shall not encourage attempts of the kind, but shall punish them; and I sentence you to the treadmill for a month, as a rogue and vagabond. I shall look very narrowly at the cases of persons brought before me on such charges."[26]

Charles Dickens's was not the only witty pen poised to take action against Laurie. *Punch* too dealt a blow in calling Laurie "The City Solon"; and Thomas Hood penned the following nasty quotation:

> When would-be suicides in purpose fail—
> Who could not find a morsel though they needed—
> If Peter sends them for attempts to jail,
> What would he do if they succeeded?[27]

Sir Peter's severity was part of a conservative backlash of the 1840s, yet his intentions were very like those of the physicians and Registrar General: suicide prevention. Dickens and Hood, on the other hand, were focusing on the possible causes of suicide: poverty and desperation. All of these men, conservative and nonconservative alike, succeeded in arousing further Victorian interest in the liberalizing of suicide law and in the "motives and mysteries" of self-destruction.

Such motives and mysteries were further probed in the 1840s by G.W.M. Reynolds. Reynolds took full advantage of the fact that sensational suicides like those from the Monument lingered in Victorian public memory. In 1844–46 he issued the first series of his immensely popular *Mysteries of London*. An upper middle-class writer with a lower middle-class and working-class audience, Reynolds knew his audience well. The *Mysteries*, patterned after Eugene Sue's *Mysteries of Paris*, sold nearly 40,000 copies a week and was in all probability the most widely circulated fictional work of its decade. Mysteries literature of this sort viewed the great nineteenth-century cities of Paris and London as tropes for life, as dark mazes of secrecy and corruption, menacingly unpredictable and ultimately unknowable. "Haply," teases Reynolds, "the reader may begin to imagine that our subject is well-nigh exhausted—that the mysteries of London are nearly all unveiled?"[28] Unquestionably Reynolds's reader would then be wrong. Like the intrigues of life, the intrigues of London defied total exposure.

Reynolds no doubt achieved his popularity because many of his readers were dispossessed. To them the corridors of power must indeed have seemed like labyrinths. Reynolds fed their mistrust by painting the upper classes as deceitful and responsible for the mysteries of London. Characters like Reginald Tracy and Lady Cecilia Harborough, who both commit suicide, live wholly hypocritical lives. Wealthy and outwardly respectable, under the surface they are cruel and debauched. Tracy begins as a repressed clergyman seduced by Lady Cecilia. Once his lusts for women are aroused, however, he becomes obsessed with sexual fantasies and dreams, and even with spying on women in the bath. Eventually Tracy and Lady Cecilia are caught in bed together by Mrs. Kenrick, the loyal housekeeper. Subsequently Mrs. Kenrick is poisoned and ultimately Tracy's part in her murder is uncovered. Locked in Newgate prison, Tracy bribes Lady Cecilia to bring him suicidal poison and promises his fortune in return. Actually Tracy is framing Lady Cecilia through this action; he sets her up in revenge for her part in his original fall into sin. After he receives the poison, Tracy paces his cell "like a wild beast" and then downs his draught and dies. The next day when Lady Cecilia looks through the morning paper, she finds an account very like the ones on Moyes and Hawes, "Suicide of the Rev. Reginald Tracy." Eager for her inheritance, she goes to Tracy's lawyer and finds herself to be not an heiress but a woman implicated in abetting a suicide. Under mid-Victorian law, she can be tried for murder.

Like Tracy, however, Lady Cecilia prefers to take her own life:

> "The river—or the Monument," she said, as she continued her rapid way: "the river is near—but the Monument is nearer. Drowning must be slow and painful—the other will be instantaneous. From the river I might be rescued; but no human power can snatch me from death during a fall from that dizzy height."
>
> And she glanced upwards to the colossal pillar whose base she had now reached.[29]

Reynolds exploits every aspect of the sensational suicides from the Monument in his next paragraphs. Lady Cecilia makes her way to the Monument, and a porter, very like the one in the accounts of Moyes's and Hawes's deaths, takes her sixpence. Reynolds then pulls out all the stops: Lady Cecilia thinks of her "poor mother" as she ascends; she stares at the labyrinth of London from the top, stares at the "quicksilver" serpentine Thames, stares at the contrasting expanse of sky above, and loves the beauty. Then she prays. Finally, as if on "sudden impulse," she leaps, and

> Terrific screams burst from her lips as she rolled over and over in her precipitate whirl.
>
> Down she fell!
>
> Her head dashed against the pavement, at a distance of three yards from the base of the Monument.
>
> Her brains were scattered upon the stones.
>
> She never moved from the moment she touched the ground:—the once gay, sprightly, beautiful patrician lady was no more!
>
> A crowd instantaneously collected around her and horror was depicted on every countenance, save one, that gazed upon the sad spectacle.[30]

Clearly Reynolds read his own newspapers and knew his readers. He gave them accounts of suicide like the ones they had come to know, but often substituted callous aristocrats for "unfortunates" like Moyes and Hawes and Mary Furley. Yet Reynolds himself was not really a revolutionary. He offered no hope that the deserving poor would one day control London and make it a better place to live. And unlike Dickens's Toby and Meg, many of his lower-class characters are no more moral than the upper classes whom they serve. The hag who helps Lady Cecilia get the poison is the very person who uncaringly offers her a choice of the Thames or the Monument as the solution to her dilemma. Why, then, was Reynolds so popular with his lower-class readers? Possibly because he, a man of means, showed them what they already suspected—that violence, corruption and misery were not class-based but were everyone's lot. Or possibly because of his skillful use of social melodrama—[31] his juxtaposition of dark, realistic appraisals of human nature in the city with plot resolutions that punish evil-doers and reward the good. Reynolds's readers were shown the consequences of moral laxity and offered the choice of goodness, just as were the readers of broadsides dealing with murder and suicide. Like Carlyle and Nightingale, eminent Victorians who agonized over self-destruction in middle-class studies or in private corners of great houses like Embley, the working classes too could exercise willpower in not choosing not to be. They loved Reynolds because he showed them this without lecturing or condescension.

Domestic melodrama, like social melodrama, appealed to the working class, and since it centered on the powerless in the family unit, it also appealed to women.[32] All melodrama tries to show how the pain and unfairness of the world are a part of a moral order that is ultimately just. It fulfills the personal fantasy that the world will eventually answer our heart's needs. Domestic melodrama posits that family life too works to one's ultimate advantage. The fictional Mary Furleys and Margaret Moyeses of the world are rescued and swept into the safety of domestic bliss much as is Dickens's Meg in the dreamlike ending of *The Chimes*. Into such a world of Victorian domestic melodrama walked visitors to the Princess Theatre in London on 12 August 1868. Dion Boucicault's *After Dark* was playing that summer day, its plot exhibiting the heightened emotional situations of all melodrama: Young George, threatened with exposure as a forger, will inherit his father's estate and thereby avoid prosecution only if he will marry his cousin, Rose. A villain, Bellingham, who is an escaped convict, convinces him to send his current young wife Eliza abroad and to keep their marriage secret. Apparently betrayed, Eliza attempts suicide by jumping from Blackfriar's Bridge. Miraculously she is saved and the couple eventually are reunited, whereas Bellingham is apprehended.

Eliza has suffered terribly as a result of her rejection and has tried to kill herself not because of desperation, but because she is consciously, willingly sacrificing herself for George. She would have been happy to share adversity with him but will not "help him to commit a new crime"—bigamy. For his part George is taken with her strength of character in parting with him. All this points to a reason why such drama was popular with women: in a world like Eliza's that conspires to defeat women, women characters prove themselves morally superior to social conspiracies. Whether or not Eliza were rescued, George would have been the real loser in this human drama. Yet neither George nor Eliza is forced to suffer forever. The benign universe of melodrama fosters their ultimate reunion and final happiness. Chastened George and vindicated Eliza survive separation and suicide attempts to live on in wedded union. As a result of her jump from Blackfriars, Eliza even finds her long-lost father. The family is complete.

Sensational suicides were included in melodrama because they were a means of punishing evil or, in the case of the unsuccessful Eliza, of rewarding good. In "mysteries fiction" of the sort written by Sue and Reynolds, they had served a similar function. Later mystery stories were more concerned with the triumph of the rational over the irrational or with the exposure of secrecy, and were directed more toward the middle class, which had been so careful to conceal suicide in its midst. Thus one might expect the "sensation school" of mystery novelists to have invented countless self-murders. Their aims included revealing hidden bourgeois secrets like incest, bigamy, and murder; they introduced into fiction what Henry James called "those most mysterious of mysteries, the mysteries which are at our own doors."[33] Yet the secrecy and mystery of suicide were not subjects that most sensation novelists wanted to reveal. Despite general interest in newspaper accounts of suicide, most novelists still did not seem to believe that suicide was a subject that middle-class readers wanted to have probed. Only one sensationalist, Wilkie Collins, moved deeply enough into what Ulrich Knoepflmacher calls "the counterworld of Victorian fiction"—a world of amorality and darkness, "opposed to the lawful, ordered Victorian values to which novelist and reader tacitly agreed to subscribe"[34]—to plumb the depths of suicide. From *Antonina* in 1850 at the beginning of his career to *Blind Love* in 1890 at its end, Collins painted a whole gallery of self-destructives, ranging from Roman nobles to lonely, isolated wives and mothers, amoral heroines, crazed vivisectionists, and discredited barons.

To the distraction of Dickens and others of Collins's immediate contemporaries and literary friends, Collins also never shed a desire to shock the bourgeoisie. In large part drawing upon the same middle-class readership as did Dickens and Trollope, he resented its pretensions far more than did Dickens, who always wished to belong to the class whose follies so often irked and dismayed him. Collins's prefaces and essays characteristically lectured this middle-class public, warning it to set aside narrow-minded notions of what was or was not acceptable in fiction:

Readers in particular will, I have some reason to suppose, be here and there disturbed, perhaps even offended, by finding that "Armadale" over-steps, in more than one direction, the narrow limits within which they are disposed to restrict the development of modern fiction—if they can. Nothing that I could say to these persons here would help me with them as Time will help me if my work lasts. I am not afraid of my design being permanently misunderstood, provided the execution has done it any sort of justice. Estimated by the clap-trap morality of the present day, this may be a very daring book. Judged by the Christian morality which is of all time, it is only a book that is daring enough to speak the truth.[35]

Phrases like "clap-trap morality" worried Dickens who, a few years before this preface to *Armadale*, warned his sub-editor for *Household Words* to "look well to Wilkie's article . . . and not to leave anything in it that may be sweeping, and unnecessarily offensive to the middle class. He always has a tendency to overdo that."[36] All the same, the illegal, the immoral, and the shocking continued to fascinate Collins, who thought the middle class needed to think about such things and was not afraid to use fiction to portray life's offenses. He wanted to give "the truth as it is in Nature,"[37] not to exclude the violence, obsession, or despair he saw as basic to human nature, itself red in tooth and claw. Thus in the preface to *The Law and the Lady* (1875), Collins warned his readers that "characters which may not have appeared, events which may not have taken place, within the limits of our own individual experience, may nevertheless be perfectly natural Characters and perfectly probable Events for all that."[38] Earlier, in his essays for *Household Words* in the late 1850s, he had envied Balzac the free choice of subjects that made Balzac unfit reading for lovers of English novels. In these essays, Collins had also shown interest in reaching and educating an "Unknown Public" of three million English readers who devoured penny-novel journals. And later, in the preface to *Jezebel's Daughter* (1880), he would complain that "there are certain important social topics which are held to be forbidden to the English novelist . . . by a narrow-minded minority of readers, and . . . critics who flatter their prejudices."[39]

Certainly one of those topics was suicide, a subject that appealed to Collins both because it was subversive and because it was an ultimate test of character. As Collins discovered in the 1870s, the secrecy surrounding suicides made them fitting subjects for the detective novel. Both *The Law and the Lady* and the later *I Say "No"* (1884) are unraveled through the discovery of suicide. The suicides in this detective fiction have taken place long before the openings of the novels and are discovered only as the action unfolds, but character is still of the utmost concern. In murder stories the reader wants to find the murderer: who did it? what was his or her motive? In these detective novels of suicide, the question becomes not who killed the dead person but why he or she should want to die. Motivation is the key to truth, but all judgments must be based upon historical record or partial knowledge, since the self-murderer has passed from the scene. Suspense is heightened as we search for absolute truth and can only find partial truths. Drama is increased as we ourselves become the detectives.

The Law and the Lady emphasizes all this by offering as its detective/protagonist/first-person narrator a woman who stands most to gain by discovering the story's secret. Valeria Macallan is second wife to a man with a past. He has married Valeria under an assumed name, Eustace Macallan, to cover the fact that he has been tried for allegedly poisoning his first wife, Sara. At the time of Sara's death in Scotland, a jury could return a verdict of "Not Proven," allowing a person like Macallan his freedom, but condemning him to shame. When Valeria eventually learns Macallan's story after her marriage to him, her humiliated husband wants to leave her for her own sake. To keep him she is determined to exonerate him, and so turns detective. What she uncovers is a concealment of suicide that has been so successful that even Macallan himself has been unaware of it. Sara, who had originally tricked him into marriage, had become so distraught over Macallan's indifference to her that she had poisoned herself with the arsenic initially and pathetically purchased to clear her complexion and make her more attractive to her husband.

The true "secret" of this dramatic story is that rejection in love followed by suicide is a verdict more terrible than "Murder Not Proven." Sara's self-destruction—and it is that from start to finish—will never be revealed to the world. Valeria uncovers a suicide letter indicating in Sara a misery so deep that life no longer held any interest for her, and a love so obsessive that a mere smile from Macallan might have saved her. Concealment had begun immediately, through an eccentric admirer of Sara's, abetted by a physician, but it is carefully continued by Valeria, the woman who wanted truth at all costs: "There, on the table before me, lay the triumphant vindication of my husband's innocence; and, in mercy to him, in mercy to the memory of his dead wife, my one hope was that he might never see it! My one desire was to hide it from the public view."[40] Valeria is "sickened" and "horrified" by this letter but ultimately feels she must at least offer it to Macallan. She leaves to him the decision to read or not to read:

"Let me be sure that I know exactly what it is I have to decide," he proceeds. "Suppose I insist on reading the letter—?"

There I interrupt him. I know it is my duty to restrain myself. But I cannot do my duty.

"My darling, don't talk of reading the letter! Pray, pray spare yourself—."

He holds up his hands for silence.

"I am not thinking of myself," he says. "I am thinking of my dead wife. If I give up the public vindication of my innocence, in my own lifetime—if I leave the seal of the letter unbroken—do you say, as Mr. Playmore says, that I shall be acting mercifully and tenderly toward the memory of the wife?"

"Oh, Eustace, there cannot be the shadow of a doubt to it!"

"Shall I be making some little atonement to any pain that I may have thoughtlessly caused her to suffer in her lifetime?"

"Yes! yes!"[41]

Macallan foregoes the reading, and the verdict of "Not Proven" stands, but the Macallans are spared the further taint of a suicide revealed in their past.

By the 1880s, just after the suicide of Collins's old and close artist friend, Edward Mathew Ward, there are still more significant changes in Collins's fictional presentations of suicides. They tend to be males, not females, and their deaths are very violent. In *I Say "No,"* the second of Collins's detective novels involving a suicide, the self-murder is described in the manner of the *Times*, with a graphic, seemingly dispassionate style that fails to blanket the underlying horror: "The internal jugular vein had been cut through, with such violence, judging by the appearances, that the wound could not have been inflicted, in the act of suicide, by the hand of the deceased person."[42] The bloody secret of this act of self-violence is kept through a cover-up quite true to life in Victorian England. Concealment here is instigated by a friend of the family, Sir Richard, a "great London surgeon" whose efforts are carefully described:

"He went with Miss Letitia to the inquest; he won over the coroner and the newspaper men to his will; he kept your aunt's name out of the papers; he took charge of the coffin; he hired the undertaker and his men, strangers from London; he wrote the certificate—who but he! Everybody was cap in hand to the famous man!"[43]

This suicide is discovered only years later. James Brown, the victim, was a man who, like Sara Macallan, suffered from unrequited love. Again his means of death have been unknown to his beloved, who finds out about her lover from his now grown daughter and responds with a stock Victorian reaction and no little remorse for once having said "no" to poor Brown: " 'Do you suppose I could for a moment anticipate that he would destroy himself, when I wrote my reply? He was a truly religious man. If he had been in his right mind, he would have shrunk from the idea of suicide as from the idea of a crime.' "[44] One reason why Brown's lover deduces that Brown must have been insane at the time of his death is that she knows a deliberate suicide would quite literally be guilty of crime.

So a conventional Victorian might have thought. Collins thought differently. For him, cruelty was crime. His James Brown's sane despair becomes clear enough as the story unfolds, though he is never seen in so pitiful a light as Sara Macallan. There is daring in Collins's portrayal of Brown and realism in in his choice of the means for Brown's suicide. Victorian statistical tables and court proceedings show a higher incidence of the use of sharp instruments in male suicides and of poisons in female self-destruction.[45] Collins kept his suicides true to the trends, consulting actuarial tables of suicide. He also kept his suicides true to his sense of human nature. What is sensational in his work is not only descriptions of death throes and jugular veins but exposure of concealment in pitiful middle-class suicide cases. Collins's self-destructives are less extraordinary cases than lost and saddened people. Wilkie Collins was sensational because he pointed out to the bourgeoisie that suicide among them was more pervasive than they cared to believe.

By 1875, the year of *The Law and the Lady*, the famous suicides from the Monument had passed into history. The Monument itself had now long since been "bird-caged" and further mishaps thus prevented. Some memory of those suicides lingered, but their bloody, authentic particulars were forgotten. In *The Way We Live Now* (1874–75) Anthony Trollope would say of one of his characters, "No man in England could be less likely to throw himself off the Monument."[46] Monument suicides had passed into cliché. By the 1870s, too, the broadsides that helped publicize these suicides had become less available; tax-free after 1855, newspapers had taken over the function of reporting sensational crime. Charles Hindley was now out on the streets collecting broadsides so that those remaining would be preserved for posterity. And the *Annual Register* had quit indexing suicide as an item of special note.

Interest in self-destruction itself had, however, not really declined, only the interest in sensationalizing it. Collins's work reflects this point of view, whereas Reynolds and the newspapers and broadsides of an earlier day had been out to expose outrageous or extreme behavior and to warn against deviation. From the 1860s on, suicide had been discussed more openly by social critics, lawmakers, and physicians, and it therefore seemed more pervasive. Suicides were not only special cases; suicide was a social problem, quite as Dickens had suspected. An 1861 editorial in the *London Times* posited that a generation of crime had given way to a generation of remorse, followed by a generation of reflection—of reasoning about human affairs.[47] Into that generation came men like Collins and the statistician J. N. Radcliffe, who searched for the causes of suicide. In studying "The Relevance of Suicide in England" in 1861, Radcliffe could find no positive correlation between crime or poverty and suicide, nor any alarming increase in its incidence. Reflection on these tasks instead brought him to what he would call "the great principle with the commission of self-murder": that "the suicide, truly, believes death to be an evil of less magnitude than the ill from which he seeks to escape."[48] Far from being immoral or the act of a lunatic, after mid-century, suicide could seem a very sane retreat for the down-and-out Victorian Briton.

IV

Bad and Far Better Things

If poverty was disgraceful to many Victorians and associated with suicide, so was an excess of money, even when generated by hard work and frugality. John Wesley had already warned the English of the dangers of wealth: "religion must necessarily produce both industry and capitalism, and these cannot but produce riches. But as riches increase, so will pride, anger and love of the world in all its branches."[1] Such vices deeply troubled Victorians like John Henry Newman, who claimed not to "know any thing more dreadful than . . . that low ambition which sets every one on the look-out to succeed and to rise in life, to amass money, to gain power to depress his rivals, to triumph over his hitherto superiors, to affect a consequence and a gentility which he had not before."[2] And such ambition, so well-defined by Newman in 1836, was still with the Victorians in 1860 when Ruskin reminded them that "there is no wealth but Life."[3] For as Victorian society became ostensibly wealthier, the accumulation of money came to be seen as more pernicious, even sinful. "The wages of sin is death," recalled many Victorians—death to those exploited by others' gain, or death by moral atrophy to those involved in the pride, anger, or excessive love of the world that Wesley had cautioned about.

Preventives for such shriveling of the soul were clearly and zealously announced by Victorian moralists and always included a strong dose of social conscience. Even Samuel Smiles, who counselled that "comfort in worldly circumstances is a condition which every man is justified in striving to attain by all worthy means,"[4] also warned that "money is power of a sort, it is true; but intelligence, public spirit and moral virtue are powers, too, and far nobler ones."[5] Nonetheless, historical records and Victorian literature show countless transgressions against such public spirit, with greed and nonchalance substituted for time-honored virtues like benevolence and charity.

Newspaper writers and essayists exposed greed, while writers of fiction and poetry time and again brought fictional golden calves face to face with the dead-end of finance—killing off either their characters, those characters' fortunes, or both. Numbers of these immoral rich die by suicide, a mode of death that seemed especially appropriate to the

Victorians. Because of its illegality and its association with forfeiture, suicide was linked with godlessness and general indifference to the lives of others. In 1880 a writer for *Blackwood's* observed of self-destroyers that "the God who was said to prohibit suicide has ceased to be a God for them, and that suicide being no longer interdicted by any power they respect, has become once more, in their eyes, a permissible solution for the difficulties of life."[6] Similarly, Mammon was felt to be increasingly substituted for the God who had interdicted the misuse of money, so that many Victorians came to think of suicide as the fitting end for those in the spell of this false god, and many Victorian writers sought to confirm this association. In literature, as in Victorian society when characterized by a writer for *Chambers's*, "very few instances of self-destruction occur among hard-working heads of families who have insured their lives."[7]

Early in the era, in 1840, Thomas Hood described a more decadent family in a trenchant spoof called "Miss Kilmansegg and Her Precious Leg: A Golden Legend." Miss Kilmansegg's name alone would give away Hood's purpose: children of a gold-happy father, her family are capable of destroying the eggs of others in pursuit of their own nest egg. In fact, the whole family are goldbugs and Miss Kilmansegg, educated to be like the rest, develops an insufferable hauteur and prizes gold above all else. One day when this haughty young woman is out riding, her "very rich bay called Banker"[8] shies at the sight of a beggar and runs away with her. Miss Kilmansegg heads for a fall, this time only a literal one. Her leg is destroyed in the accident, yet she triumphs over adversity by acquiring her precious golden leg:

> So a Leg was made in a comely mould,
> Of Gold, fine virgin glittering gold,
> As solid as man could make it—
> Solid in foot, and calf, and shank,
> A prodigious sum of money it sank;
> In fact 'twas a Branch of the family Bank,
> And no easy matter to break it. (*SP*, 803-09)

Pride, vanity, ostentation, insensibility—these are Miss Kilmansegg's sins; but if punishment for them is due, it is slow in coming. Miss Kilmansegg dreams on, especially of the god-like veneration she feels she deserves for her goldenness. And her sins compound:

> Gold, still gold—and true to the mould!
> In the very scheme of her dream it told;
> For, by magical transmutation,
> From her Leg through her body it seem'd to go,

Till, gold above, and gold below,
She was gold, all gold, from her little gold toe
To her organ of Veneration! (*SP*, 1378–84)

But Miss Kilmansegg rides for a second and fatal fall when she foolishly marries a money-seeking count who depletes her fortune and then asks to raise more money on the golden leg. Miserable in marriage, Miss Kilmansegg now spends her nights dreaming of her past with its "golden treasures and golden toys" (*SP*, 2319). One night as she sleeps, her leg laid to one side, the count seizes the leg, beats his wife to death, and makes off with the precious limb. The ensuing inquest over her body yields a surprising verdict:

Gold—still gold! it haunted her yet—
At the Golden Lion the Inquest met—
Its foreman, a carver and gilder—
And the Jury debated from twelve till three
What the Verdict ought to be,
And they brought it in as Felo de Se,
"Because her own Leg had killed her!" (*SP*, 2367–73)

Hood bathetically depicts Miss Kilmansegg's death as a suicide because her own vanity and tenacity are really what have dispatched her. She has chosen to become gold—in thought, in dream, and even in body, and when her gold goes, so does she.

Real-life coroner's juries also tended to deal harshly with the greedy, especially with shady financiers and embezzlers as was the case with John Sadleir in 1856. Sadleir, a member of Parliament and Junior Lord of the Treasury, fraudulently oversold 150,000 pounds of shares in the Royal Swedish Railway, overdrew more than 200,000 pounds from a Tipperary bank, which he managed, represented certain assets of that bank at 100,000 pounds when in fact they were 30,000, and in the end tried to raise money to cover his enormous debts by means of a forged deed. When he realized that he could not hide his fraudulent activities, he repaired to Hampstead Heath on a cold, February night, carrying prussic acid and a case of razors. The poison proved sufficient to kill him without the razors, and the next morning he was discovered stiff and cold on the Heath. The inquest into his death went on through four sessions before the verdict of *felo-de-se* was reached. It was found that Sadleir had left intensely remorseful suicide notes reproving himself for the ruin of others:

I cannot live—I have ruined too many—I could not live and see their agony—I have committed diabolical crimes unknown to any human being. They will now appear, bringing my family and others to distress—causing to all shame and grief that they should have ever known me.

I blame no one, but attribute all to my own infamous villainy. . . . I could go through any torture as a punishment for my crimes. No torture could be too much for such crimes, but I cannot live to see the tortures I inflict upon others.[9]

Hidden at first by friends who had hoped for a verdict of temporary insanity, the notes ultimately convinced the coroner's jury that Sadleir was sane. No one, their thinking went, could so clearly realize the harm that he had done to others and be intellectually impaired.

This verdict may seem harsh to us today. Sadleir's notes are touching in their sincerity and seem to call out for some sort of leniency. Yet many middle-class Victorians thought differently. As an 1852 essay on "Chagrin and Suicide" in *Hogg's Instructor* reveals, deep disapproval of the unrepentable act of suicide could outweigh compassionate understanding of the motive power of chagrin:

The love of approbation, which is closely connected with the love of society, is generally the strongest of our passions, and is that by which the lower passions are restrained within the limits of common decorum. It is the disappointment of this passion, or chagrin, which most frequently disposes to suicide. Man's hell is the feeling of solitude, or the dread of being despised; and, if his associates cast him out of their pale, or appear completely to excommunicate him from their sympathies, he seems as if at once possessed by Satan. Should his wounding of his proud desire deprive him of all hope of restoration to the heart of at least some one being who can love him in spite of his faults, he will rush unbidden into the darkness of another world, the apprehension of which is less terrible to him than the loneliness in which he suffers. So common is that catastrophe that it appears like the result of a natural law of the guilty mind, when unacquainted with divine truth, and unsustained by the hopeful consciousness of spiritual and eternal life. Hence heathenism and infidelity have always approved self-murder as the proper remedy for extreme vexation.[10]

With Sadleir's remedy for such vexation the Victorian sense of justice seemed well-satisfied. The *Standard* called him the "deep, unscrupulous, scheming, intriguing John Sadleir,"[11] and this kind of harsh judgment would continue in subsequent assessments of his character. In 1857 the *Irish Quarterly Review* opened its article on "Suicide: Its Motives and Mysteries" with these thoughts about the Sadleir case:

The most cautious never dreamed that the apparent favourite of fortune, whose name was considered a guarantee for the success of any project, would involve establishments, undertakings, and a host of individuals, in irretrievable ruin. In almost every suicide, however abhorrent the act, there is something to elicit a touch of sympathy—'the scowl of an unpitying world,' may have driven a youthful aspirant to desperation—broken vows may have bereft a trusting husband of self-control, or a sudden bereavement quite upset reason—but in Sadleir's case, we can trace no higher feeling than an inordinate thirst of gain, which stopped at nothing for its gratification.[12]

In the same year the *Annual Register* concluded that Sadleir was "indeed a swindler on the very grandest scale, and kept up the game to the last: when his last game was played and dejection was inevitable, he committed suicide under circumstances of the utmost deliberation."[13]

Sadleir's suicide did not escape the notice of two major Victorian novelists in search of objective correlatives for the dead-end of finance. Dickens's introduction to *Little Dorrit* (1855–57) connects the novel's Mr. Merdle with the times of "a certain Irish bank," while Trollope, in *The Way We Live Now* (1874–75), patterned Melmotte in part after Sadleir. Trollope altered his original intention to have Melmotte stand trial for forgery and substituted instead Melmotte's suicide. P. D. Edwards believes that the novelist did so because three of his last four novels had included trial scenes, because he needed more space to tie up loose ends that did not include Melmotte, and because in so doing he could better preserve the ambiguity that surrounds Melmotte's character.[14] More significantly, I think, Trollope saw the symbolic importance of suicide to the theme of *The Way We Live Now.* Melmotte is a swindler of vast proportions, but he is not Trollope's only character engaged in fraud or living on scrip. Lady Carbury's books are in their own way frauds, and the members of the Beargarden club use worthless I.O.U.s as the basis for endless gambling. Melmotte is simply fraud on its grandest and most unrepentant scale and becomes an example to others in his world. His self-murder through an overdose of prussic acid serves as the climax to Trollope's novel, for it indicates the inherent self-destructiveness in the way we live now. The chapter-long inquest that replaces the once-projected trial scene stresses the deliberateness of Melmotte's actions and reinforces an earlier passage in which Melmotte "told himself over and over again that the fault had been not in circumstances,—not in that which men call Fortune—but in his own incapacity to bear his position."[15] In Trollope's final version of the novel, Melmotte is self-tried, self-condemned, self-executed, and subsequently pronounced by others to have been *felo-de-se*:

But let a Melmotte be found dead, with a bottle of prussic acid by his side—a man who has become horrid to the world because of his late iniquities, a man who has so well pretended to be rich that he has been able to buy and to sell properties without paying for them, a wretch who has made himself odious by his ruin to friends who had taken him up as a pillar of strength in regard to wealth, a brute who had got into the House of Commons by false pretences, and had disgraced the House by being drunk there,—and, of course, he will not be saved by a verdict of insanity from the cross roads, or whatever scornful grave may be allowed to those who have killed themselves with their wits about them. Just at this moment there was a very strong feeling against Melmotte . . . and the virtue of the day vindicated itself by declaring him to have been responsible for his actions when he took the poison. He was *felo-de-se*, and therefore carried away to the cross roads—or elsewhere. (*WWLN*, 710)

After Melmotte dies, the world of *The Way We Live Now* alters. The Beargarden folds, Lady Carbury gives up writing and remarries, and Ruby Ruggles and honest John Crumb, who themselves have each threatened suicide when blindly in love, now find reality in each other. In one character's estimation, Melmotte is reduced to the dimensions of the proverbial exploded frog, " 'E bursted himself, Mr. Frisker. 'E vas a great man but the greater he grew he vas always less and less vise" (*WWLN*, 789). It is as though a pernicious growth has ruptured and then wholly disappeared from the vitals of a society now free quickly to repair its surrounding cells.

Mr. Merdle's suicide in *Little Dorrit* has quite a different effect on the unravelling of Dickens's novel. Like Melmotte, Merdle is of unknown origin, is courted and even idolized by members of his society, and perpetrates fraud on the grandest scale. But there is no inquest depicted in Dickens's story because Merdle is self-condemned not only in the end of the novel but from the very beginning. He is a retiring man, almost afraid of the society that courts him because of his reputed wealth. He tucks his hands inside his coat cuffs, trying to withdraw into his clothes, and sometimes clasps his wrists as though taking himself into custody for a crime only he knows. He also suffers from some unknown "complaint" that early in the story merits an entire chapter. It is, Merdle's doctor tells us, "a deep-seated recondite complaint"[16] that does not ease from day to day. Dickens further hints of suicidal tendencies in his physical descriptions of Merdle, including a hand-to-head gesture that recalls Sadleir's last days and "black traces on his lips where they met, as if a little train of gunpowder had been fired there" (*LD*, 577).

These descriptions occur when Mr. Dorrit, newly possessed of a fortune after years of debtorship, is about to invest with Mr. Merdle. For Dorrit, however, as for Merdle and indeed for all the characters of the novel, money becomes associated with death. Wealthy but entirely out of place, Dorrit will eventually die in Italy, babbling of the lost days when he was king of debtors, "Father of the Marshalsea." In yet another important scene, Arthur Clennam goes to visit his mother, who embodies puritanical zeal and grim money-grubbing at its worst, and finds only emblems of death and suicide. On his way to her fallen-down house he passes "silent warehouses and wharves, and here and there a narrow alley leading to the river, where a wretched little bill, FOUND DROWNED, was weeping on the wet wall" (*LD*, 29). In the house itself are Mrs. Clennam, like Life-in-Death, and her partner, Flintwinch, who has "a weird appearance of having hanged himself at one time or other, and of having gone about ever since, halter and all, exactly as some timely hand had cut him down" (*LD*, 34). Both Mrs. Clennam and Flintwinch have given up life for money, as Clennam himself will have to give up money for life.

And here too is where Dickens's denouement differs from Trollope's. Merdle, like Melmotte, proves to have been a man of no substance; like Sadleir's, his complaint is related to fraud and forgery. But whereas an almost illusory Melmotte vanishes when his bubble is burst, and departs from a world that subsequently rights itself, Mr. Merdle leaves a long trail of very perceptible destruction in his wake:

> The inquest was over, the letter was public, the Bank was broken, the other model structures of straw had taken fire and were turned to smoke. The admired piratical ship had blown up, in the midst of a vast fleet of ships of all rates, and boats of all sizes; and on the deep was nothing but ruin: nothing but burning hulls, bursting magazines, great guns self-exploded tearing friends and neighbours to pieces, drowning men clinging to unseaworthy spars and going down every minute, spent swimmers, floating dead, and sharks. (*LD*, 671)

Clennam also is swamped and will suffer deeply, becoming ill in both body and spirit, almost as Merdle did. Only the love of Little Dorrit restores Dickens's hero to health, sanity, and relative unconcern over money. Amy Dorrit is, however, unique in Dickens's novel, the only character "unspoiled by Fortune" (*LD*, 713). The whole of *Little Dorrit* gives the sense of a far bleaker world than does *The Way We Live Now*, for all of Trollope's worldly wisdom in that book. Near the end of *Little Dorrit*, a minor character warns Clennam and us that the next man after Merdle "who has as large a capacity and as genuine a taste for swindling will succeed as well" (*LD*, 697). Greed, fraud and idolatry, Dickens implies, will continue to reap a grim harvest of death.

A different slant on the Victorian association of money with suicide occurs in the *Bab Ballads*, where W. S. Gilbert reprints an amusing little poem about a wealthy sugar broker who meets a sorry end. This bloated figure of fun is allied to what the Victorians called "balloon kings," people like Melmotte and the real-life George Hudson, the railway baron. Such men were considered so overinflated that their fall from fortune was often metaphorically and pictorially represented as deflation followed by a rapid plunge to earth. The Victorians were of several minds about these men. Though a cartoon in *Diogenes* in 1853 depicts and derides a corpulent Hudson plummeting downward like a great Humpty Dumpty, Hudson's eventual obituary years afterward in the *Times* of 1871 would still admire his pluck, long after he had been discovered in profiteering and brought to ruin and exile. Still later, Carlyle would side with the illustrator for *Diogenes* and rail at those who would dare think to erect a monument to this "gambler swollen *big*."[17] Gilbert's broker, on the other hand, is a benign little "balloon king," miserable with his fat. His friends look on in amazement and comment on his frantically unsuccessful attempts to dance the fat away:

"Your riches know no kind of pause,
Your trade is fast advancing,
You dance—but not for joy, because
You weep as you are dancing.
To dance implies that man is glad,
To weep implies that man is sad.
But here are you
Who do the two—
You weep as you are dancing!"[18]

The fat, of course, signifies his wealth, but the broker himself never realizes that he cannot shed the fat without shedding riches.

This lachrymose, fast-paced broker suffers from two related diseases of the Victorian world: he is discontented with his lot, and he is obsessed with ceaseless activity. In the late nineteenth century, both of these maladies were thought to lead to suicide. S.A.K. Strahan, author of *Suicide and Insanity*, directly linked self-destruction to the Victorian pace of life.[19] And Emile Durkheim's famous work, *Le Suicide*, described how compulsive activity could derive from unfulfilled or unquenchable desires and cause one type of "anomic" suicide:

> . . . demands make fulfillment impossible. Overweening ambition always exceeds the results obtained, great as they may be, since there is no warning to pause here. Nothing gives out appeasement. Above all, since this race for an unattainable goal can give no other pleasure but that of the race itself . . . once it is interrupted the participants are left empty-handed. . . . Effort grows, just when it becomes less productive. How could the desire to live not be weakened under such conditions?[20]

Like an anomic suicide, Gilbert's broker is involved in a dance of death. Eventually his mania for dancing runs away with him until at last:

Upon his shapeless back he lay
  And kicked away like winking.
    Instead of seeing in his state
    The finger of unswerving Fate,
    He laboured still
    To work his will,
And kicked away like winking. (*BB*, 133)

The poor little broker, fattened perhaps by his own sugar and surely by his riches, winds up a kind of inverted turtle. In Gilbert's accompanying sketch, he certainly looks a very dead one as well. Here Gilbert confronts not so much greed or dishonesty, but excess, self-delusion, futile reliance on willpower, and the tendency to overdo that marked so many of his contemporaries.

The broker's probable death is absurd and amusing, whereas Merdle's death is both pathetic and dangerous to others. But none of the suicides that I have so far discussed in this chapter is in any way tragic. Their stories are admonitory, Sadleir's true-life tale as reported by the Victorian press as much as the four wholly fictive accounts. The morals of the stories overshadow the fates of the people involved. They warn of the excesses of the rich—their enormous potential for ostentation, their hollowness and callousness, their pointless obsessions. They signal the dangers of a society whose members become indifferent to immorality through idolatry. They deplore a world that has forgotten *noblesse oblige*. Merdle's "chief Butler" remarks of his employer's suicide that since Merdle was no gentleman, "no ungentlemanly act on his part" (*LD*, 667) surprises him. And they warn, finally, of the godlessness of those wealthy who operate unhampered by social conscience. One of Sadleir's suicide notes shows that even he saw himself as so "wicked" that his prayers must be of no avail. Thus all of these people reach the dead end of finance by failing to acknowledge that "there is no wealth but Life." Their deaths would have seemed especially just to their contemporaries. Lawless, ruthless, or immoderate, all these once-monied ruins would, in being self-murdered, have seemed suitably self-judged.

Men like Sadleir attempted to lessen dishonor by doing what seemed to them the honorable thing, but their lives and deaths remained disgraceful. Victorian society was harsh in its judgments of men who were pronounced *felo-de-se*, placing them among its least redeemable members. Strahan quotes *Richard II* (1 i.), "Mine honour is my life, both grow in one: Take honour from me and my life is done," as a sentiment applying only to an initially virtuous person. Conscientious Victorians, he insists, "inquire into the facts of a case, which proceeding too often robs the dishonoured one of all right to pose as a martyr, and shows some gravely immoral or illegal course deliberately entered upon is the real cause of the disaster."[21] On the other hand, there was such a phenomenon as "the honourable thing" in Victorian England, and it corresponded to what both Savage and Durkheim would call "altruistic" suicide.[22] Knowingly to die for others—because of military, religious, political or personal commitment—could be a pathway to heroism. Strahan refers to this type of death as the highest form of what he calls "rational, or quasi suicide," and makes it the polar opposite of a death like Sadleir's:

> To give up life is the greatest sacrifice man can make, and when that sacrifice is made without hope of gain or reward, in order that others may escape some terrible calamity which nothing else can avert, then, if the sacrifice be at all justifiable, the act is the grandest and noblest of which fallen man is capable.[23]

In 1885 physician William Wynn Westcott summarized public opinion on ignoble and noble suicide by observing that "in some cases self-destruction is contemptible and cowardly; in some it is venial; in some cases death is distinctly the lesser evil, in a few it has been honourable, and as such should escape all condemnation, and merit the approval of men of development and refinement."[24] Earlier, Charlotte Brontë had discriminated similarly in *Jane Eyre*. Jane's cousin, John Reed, is a cruel dissolute who wantonly takes his own life; while her other male cousin, St. John Rivers, works himself to death for the sake of others, dying as a martyred missionary in India. For this Brontë rewards him both with a final call from Jesus and the closure of her novel. Today our sympathies probably lie rather with the heroism of the scrappy, living Jane than with the martyrdom of St. John, but Victorians responded with empathy toward St. John. If for them the more typical use of willpower was to defend the self and maintain the integrity of one's own life, there were occasions when exercising the will to lose life was utterly praiseworthy. Heroic self-sacrifice was the one form of romantic suicide still acceptable to most Victorians.

Ever popular and always discerning when it came to the moral judgments of his readers, Dickens humored this Victorian predilection toward self-sacrifice in his *Tale of Two Cities* (1859). There is little doubt that Sydney Carton does a "far better thing" at the end of that novel than he had ever done before. Nor was contemporary response to Carton ambivalent. The daily papers, which saw flaws in the novel's plot and in its comic characters, praised the characterization of Carton. The *Morning Post* (21 December 1859) found Carton "the finest and most finished portrait which Dickens had ever executed," and the *Morning Star* (24 December) called him "one of the finest conceptions in the whole range of fiction."[25] Here one finds no note of condemnation for suicide as there had been in the papers following Sadleir's true-life suicide three years earlier. In Victorian eyes, Carton's death seemed to redeem a misspent and virtually wasted life, and Dickens's characterization seemed artfully to offer that redemption. Carton, hardly a Christ-like figure in life, dies a Christ-like death for the sake of others.

Carton's life up until his decision to die is in many ways more suicidal than his actual death. He drinks heavily and pities himself yet more heavily. "I am a disappointed drudge. I care for no man on earth, and no man on earth cares for me,"[26] he tells Charles Darnay, his look-alike and rival for the heart of Lucie Manette. He also sees himself as consistently depressed, a stand-in in life—virtually dead: "like one who died young. All my life might have been" (*TTC*, 180). Dickens's narrator pities this lost creature, a man "incapable of his own help and his own happiness, sensible of the blight on him, and resigning himself to let it eat him away" (*TTC*, 122). Carton has paralyzed his own will, and *tedium vitae* now has him fully in its grip.

But in this book filled with resurrection men and resurrection imagery, there is hope even for the deadened Carton. At first Lucie, whose name suggests as much, offers that light; then the prospect of personal sacrifice for Lucie lights Carton's way. All this is reinforced by Carton's recollection of the burial service for his father: "he that believeth in me, though he were dead, yet shall he live." Carton makes a turn-around, if not a dramatic conversion. He begins to value life, to leave off drink, and to walk with a more "settled step" (*TTC*, 367). He is, of course, on his way to the guillotine, and his behavior is characteristic both of the determined suicide, whose last days or hours are often marked by energy, and of a determined Victorian, whose life should be guided by willpower. When he confronts Darnay in the cell and begins to effect an exchange of clothes and places, Darnay finds his plan "madness," but the narrator discerns in Carton a "wonderful quickness . . . a strength both of will and action, that appeared quite supernatural" (*TTC*, 380). Carton discovers life through death.

Carton's self-sacrifice has certainly intrigued twentieth-century literary commentators. Recently, John Kucich called it a victory over Darnay as rival. In Lucie's eyes Darnay will never be able to displace Carton's willing and complete sacrifice of self for others. Because of this "tension of the rivalry," Kucich believes that Carton's sacrifice is redeemed from seeming a "savage, suicidal waste."[27] Even more recently, Garrett Stewart has gone further and has found in Carton's "fictional death by proxy" a "displacement of fatality for the reader as well as Darnay,"[28] and so it is. Yet most nineteenth-century readers would have been more concerned with the simpler, Christian message of the self-sacrifice. Carton dies that the Darnays might have life, and have it more abundantly. He, rather than Lucie, becomes a beacon of hope for a family, a France, and an England to come. Like Christ's, his final vision is prophecy.

The vision is also a triumph over Victorian disease—both as fear (of revolution, cruelty, tyranny) and as *tedium vitae*. Carton's self-sacrifice involves self-healing, a Victorian preoccupation that pervades the book. For example, after Doctor Manette is "recalled to life," the Doctor lapses in and out of a "malady" that demonstrates how deeply he has been marked by his confinement. Miss Pross intuits that "not knowing how he lost himself, nor how he recovered himself, he may never feel certain of not losing himself again" (*TTC*, 128), and she proves correct. Later Mr. Lorry speaks to Manette about Manette, trying to get him to diagnose his own malady by thinking of it as a disease affecting some other, fictitious person. Only then does Manette sense the insecurity at the root of his relapses into the silence and shoemaking of his prison days, and only then does he hope to forestall further such relapses. Up to this point, it has been impossible for him to realize that his has been a case in need of self-help—of physician, heal thyself. On the other hand, Carton's diseases—depression, overindulgence, and *tedium vitae*—appear to be more incurable than Manette's relapses. Even Lucie fears that "he is not to be reclaimed; there is scarcely a hope that anything in his character or fortunes is reparable now" (*TTC*, 238). Still Carton does heal himself by losing himself, and Dickens fully sanctions—almost sanctifies—his behavior.

Despite Victorian love of martyred characters like Carton, excesses in martyrdom, as in the case of Matthew Lovat, shocked even the Victorians. Lovat's extraordinary case surfaced again and again in Victorian studies of suicide.[29] Lovat was an Italian shoemaker, a young man subject to attacks of gloominess but initially sane. Much taken by religious exercises, on the day of the feast of his namesake, St. Matthew, Lovat attempted to crucify himself. He constructed a cross from the wood of his bed and proceeded to nail himself to it. Stopped as he was about to pound a nail into his left foot, he ostensibly left off his attempt. Secretly, however, he garnered ropes and more nails, and fashioned himself a crown of thorns. Three years later, in 1805, he tried again. This time he built an amazing contraption for his intended crucifixion. He made a net to hold his cross, and affixed brackets to the cross for his feet. He then stripped naked, placed the cross horizontally on his floor, sat on it, nailed down his right hand and two feet, and slit his side with a knife. Finally, he slid the entire contraption out of the window, him-

The attempted crucifixion of Matthew Lovat, frontispiece, Forbes Winslow's *Anatomy of Suicide* (1840).

self included, and hung suspended from the window-frame in plain view of the people in his street. Rescued, he was reported to have exclaimed, "The pride of man must be mortified; it must expire on the cross!"[30] For early Victorian commentators like Winslow, Lovat's religious melancholia was grisly, fanatical, and incurable. After Lovat's body was healed, remarked Winslow, "his mind retained until his death the same melancholy caste, although he never had another opportunity of putting his sanguinary project into execution."[31] Lovat's attempt seemed like a sick echo of Christianity, but certainly no self-sacrifice for the sake of others.

As the nineteenth century progressed, the Victorians found not only fewer deaths worthy to be called martyrdom but fewer commitments worth willfully dying for. Love and war, for example, seemed more complicated and uncertain, less worthy of self-sacrifice than they once had. Tennyson depicted this uncertainty in *Maud* (1855), when he drew the portrait of a man crazed by dishonor, love, and the need for self-sacrifice. The poem is framed by the two kinds of suicide represented in *Jane Eyre* and in this chapter—selfish self-termination and willing self-sacrifice. The narrator's father appears to have died from a deliberate leap taken as the result of a financial failure:

> Did he fling himself down? who knows? for a vast speculation had fail'd,
> And ever he mutter'd and madden'd, and ever wann'd with despair,
> And out he walk'd when the wind like a broken worldling wail'd,
> And the flying gold of the ruin'd woodlands drove thro' the air.[32]

In the wake of this golden shower of despair, the father has left a broken-hearted widow and a bitter son who says he believes that "sooner or later I too may passively take the print / Of the golden age—why not?" (*PT*, I. 29–30). For the son, the world is pervaded with inescapable mammonism, cheating and death. Yet for him redemption also seems possible, through war and a more honorable kind of suicide—military self-sacrifice.

Maud too believes in patriotism and bravery, and sings of "Honour that cannot die" (*PT*, I. 177). Smitten with her words as with the young woman herself, the narrator longs for a man to arise in him "that the man I am may cease to be" (*PT*, I. 397). In one sense he is saying what all prospective lovers wish to say: "May I be worthy of my love." But in another sense he is simply confirming a suicidal bent and his need for the courage to die. This man does not separate love from death because he holds Maud's family responsible for his father's ruin. Nevertheless, for awhile he deludes himself into believing that love will provide him with the needed loss of self. Only after he kills Maud's brother in a duel does his original motive again surface: to redeem dishonorable suicide—and now murder—through deliberate self-sacrifice.

In the interval between the duel and the poem's conclusion, the narrator endures utter abasement in Tennyson's brilliant madhouse scene:

> Dead, long dead,
> Long dead!
> And my heart is a handful of dust
> And the wheels go over my head,
> And my bones are shaken with pain,
> For into a shallow grave they are thrust,
> Only a yard beneath the street,
> And the hoofs of the horses beat, beat,
> The hoofs of the horses beat,
> Beat into my scalp and my brain,
> With never an end to the stream of passing feet,
> Driving, hurrying, marrying, burying,
> Clamor and rumble, and ringing and clatter;
> And here beneath it is all as bad,
> For I thought the dead had peace, but it is not so. (*PT*, 2. 239–53)

What this narrator imagines is the ignominious burial of a suicide at a cross-roads and thus another disgraceful death in his family, but what he had wanted was quite the opposite—a worthwhile displacement of self unlike his father's surrender to adversity. Tennyson provides him with this and with relief from mad-cells only in the last part of the poem. The winds of the Crimean war wake him "to the higher aims / Of a land that has lost for a little her lust of gold" (*PT*, 3. 38–39) and offer the final opportunity for "making of splendid names" (*PT*, 3. 47). In the poem's famous conclusion, the narrator goes forth to embrace his "doom assign'd" (*PT*, 3. 59).

Although such an ending ostensibly offers an opportunity for heroism, the last part of *Maud* is problematical. In the first place, Tennyson's narrator is unbalanced, throughout the poem incapable of altruism because of his neurotic self-obsession. He swings from hiding and self-abnegation to violent outbursts of passion. Both in his love for Maud and in his hatred of her brother, he ignores Maud's feelings and seems incapable of selflessness of any sort. Secondly, war was itself problematical in 1855. The blunder at Balaclava in October of 1854, with the loss of the Light Brigade, was still fresh in the public's mind. Gladstone faulted Tennyson for offering a bungled and increasingly unpopular Crimean war as a last resort for youthful disillusion and despair. Yet Tennyson was of two minds about Crimea. His "Charge of the Light Brigade" was published along with *Maud* and held both praise for the heroic six hundred and the clear message that "some one had blundered" (*PT*, 1035). Tennyson had hardly overlooked the blindness, in-fighting, and inexperience of the command at Balaclava, but he, like the lookers-on that day, was taken with the picture of a perfectly outfitted, perfectly disciplined young cavalry brigade meeting death in utter order, closing ranks whenever a horse or rider dropped. In publishing his two poems together, Tennyson left undefined the "doom assigned" the narrator of *Maud*. Like the Light Brigade, that young man might die heroically; on the other hand, his death might be ironic waste rather than patriotic self-sacrifice.

Despite the laureate's ambivalent stance on Crimea, his "Charge" itself drew fire from those trying to reduce the suicide rate. Late in the century, Strahan believed that the poem "breathes exactly the same barbaric spirit and contempt for death as did the wild chants of the Sea Kings."[33] Earlier, reform movements trying to end privilege in the buying of commands had stimulated public interest in paintings like Elizabeth Thompson's (later Lady Butler) *Balaclava* (1876) and *The Roll Call* (1874). *Balaclava* depicts privates and noncommissioned officers on the battlefield.[34] *The Roll Call* shows broken and wounded Grenadier Guards at muster, standing in line with one soldier fainting dead in the snow. In both paintings, the callousness and folly of the command are implicit, the focus on common soldiery explicit. Strahan and Thompson did not, however, speak for the many who treasured poems and stories in which such military contempt for death was extolled. There were scores of much-loved ballads that lauded "acts of suicide, in obedience either to orders or to the standing orders of duty and love of country."[35] If many of these poems featured Crimea, it was because the English favored tales about success won over and against heavy odds, and Alma and Inkerman as well as Balaclava offered examples of such bravery. In these ballads about war, the incompetence of the command was usually ignored unless it served as a contrast to the bravery of the common man. Those who were cannon fodder needed desperately to believe in heroic self-sacrifice:

> "For victory!—no, all hope is gone; for life—
> let that go too;
> But for the Colours still work on—the chance
> is left with you."[36]

These are the words of a colonel, soon to be left behind in safety, in Sir Francis Doyle's popular "The Saving of the Colours (22 January, 1879)." The colonel speaks to two commoners, Coghill and Melvill, who will obey, help save the colors, and die.

Such willing deaths under fire certainly gained readers for novelists in Victorian England, as Ouida knew. Her *Under Two Flags* (1867) describes not one but two heroic self-sacrifices, both of lower-class lives lost for one relatively undeserving aristocrat, the Honourable Bertie Cecil, second son of a Viscount and officer of the guards. Handsome Bertie, the "Beauty of the Brigades," is a chaser of women and a racer of horses who eventually winds up in the French army in North Africa. Valiant as well as handsome, Bertie has already inspired the devotion of an anonymous soldier who in battle impales himself on a sword meant for Bertie. The aristocrat saw "the black, wistful eyes of the Enfant de Paris look upward to him once, with love, and fealty, and unspeakable sweetness gleaming through their darkened sight."[37] The possessor of another pair of black eyes, Cigarette, will again save Bertie from certain death nearer the story's end. A young street girl who follows Bertie's regiment, Cigarette is madly and unrequitedly in love with Bertie. She hates the "idle rich" who live from the sweat of workers but is imbued with great personal loyalty to her imagined lover. When she hears of Bertie's impending execution, she wins a reprieve for him through influence with the Marshal and rides hard for eight hours, arriving just in time to stop the bullet meant for Bertie with her own body. Like the Enfant de Paris, Cigarette has proven her self-worth by being fit to serve and loyal to the death; she has fully redeemed her former immorality and has saved herself from becoming an aging camp-follower in the bargain. Among her last words are: "I am only a little trooper who has saved my comrade" (*UTF*, 597). Her white gravestone is carved with a sentimental inscription "on which the Arab sun streamed as with a martyr's glory, "CIGARETTE ENFANT DE L'ARMEE, SOLDAT DE LA FRANCE" (*UTF*, 601). The colors of course fly over her grave.

Like Dickens's, Ouida's brand of melodrama sold books. In less than ten years, from the inception of her literary career in 1859 to the publication of *Under Two Flags* in 1867, Ouida wrote five three-decker novels and a book of short stories. From their proceeds she was able to support herself, her mother, and her grandmother in grand style. By the 1870s, Ouida was earning five thousand pounds a year and was widely read by both women and men. Originally *Under Two Flags* was published in a military periodical, and during its release Ouida became the toast of military parties. As one might conjecture, the melodrama of Ouida's heroic suicides is not unrelated to the melodrama of the deaths of other unfortunates. In the Enfant de Paris's and in Cigarette's sacrifices there is the same focus on passivity and powerlessness that we saw in domestic melodrama. Anonymous common men and fallen women gain stature by showing up the moral indifference of the powerful. Here too we can detect the enactment of the childish fantasy that our parents or our perceived "betters" will only truly appreciate us after we die. Ouida's fictional representation of this fantasy appealed to females who sought the moral superiority of women over men in the substitution of an heroic woman for the more conventional male military hero.

If both in fiction and in fact the lower orders died so that others might live, their military superiors nonetheless basked in their glory. Lord Cardigan, who rode at the head of his Light Brigade through the Valley of Death in October of 1854, landed to a hero's welcome at Dover the following January. Self-sacrificial bravery transferred to the military elite, but it also helped exacerbate a serious problem involving officers: self-destruction off the field. In the two decades following Crimea, statisticians turned with fascination to the question of high rates of suicide among the military, especially among the elite corps and officers. Between 1862 and 1871, civilian rates of death by suicide for males aged twenty to forty-five were less than one third those of the prevailing rate in the army.[38] Counted among the reasons for the frequency of suicide in the armed forces were free access to firearms, a cheapened sense of life's value because of training in killing, ennui, and a sense of lost opportunities for personal self-sacrifice. As one medical man, a Dr. Mouat, put it, having fewer means of killing others or of killing time, soldiers "took to killing themselves instead."[39] Mouat took care to point out that in the army suicides were far more frequent after than before or during a campaign, and related observations were made about naval officers, especially captains. Sir James Anderson, another expert on military suicide, noticed that most naval suicides "occurred at the end of voyages; they happened very seldom where even the ordinary amount of the duties of a captain on a long voyage required attention from him."[40]

Retirement from active service had a similar effect. With their last voyage over and done with, men like Robert FitzRoy, the famous captain of H.M.S. *Beagle*, suffered deeply from a sense of futility and hopelessness. By the 1860s FitzRoy, then an admiral, could not get comfortable at home. He felt extremely tired, both physically and emotionally. All his life the *Beagle's* captain had been a perfectionist, but a perfectionist with a purpose: accurate surveying of the South American coastline, or painstaking preservation of other lives and property, or proper exercise of a deeply felt *noblesse oblige*, or scrupulous presentation of orthodox religious beliefs, or careful working out of a system of storm warnings. Into his retirement FitzRoy carried an intolerance for sloppiness, insubordination, or folly of any kind along with a continuing need to prove his *noblesse*, but alas he had no command. Finally he arrived at a state of irreconcilable contradiction and utter depression.

Darwin had seen FitzRoy like this years before, in 1834 on the *Beagle* when the English naturalist described him as "thin and unwell accompanied by a morbid depression of spirits, and a loss of all decision and resolution."[41] At such times FitzRoy was known to brood over the suicides of two important predecessors—the previous captain of the *Beagle* and his own uncle, Viscount Castlereagh. He was also known at such times to plunge himself even more deeply into work, an intended cure that sometimes led him to the verge of collapse. During FitzRoy's younger years, periods of depression usually preceded recovery followed by new energy and new responsibility. But the end of FitzRoy's life was different. The two projects that took so much of his energy late in life—opposing Darwin's evolutionary theories and working out a system of weather forecasting that he hoped would save lives at sea—were both going badly. By the 1860s, Darwin's theories were gaining credence and FitzRoy's new *Weather Book* was being attacked by the scientific community as prophetic and empirical rather than accurate and factual. FitzRoy fought back with characteristic intensity until he fell into one of his depressions, the last of his life. On 30 April 1865, very like his famous uncle some forty years earlier, Robert FitzRoy went into his dressing room, took up his razor, and cut his throat. Driven by a sense of honor, worried over his wife's concern about him, and seemingly defeated, FitzRoy appears to have opted for what he must have felt was "the honourable thing."

Like FitzRoy's navy, the mercantile marine had a high frequency of suicides, which Sir James Anderson (1874) again attributed to post-voyage let-down, *tedium vitae*, and to the enforced separation of the captain (as "gentleman") from most others in a confined space. Deaths like these would also be numbered among the intriguing subjects of Joseph Conrad's fiction. *Lord Jim* (1899) revolves largely around the question of when merchant mariners die willingly, when they save themselves, and when they die sacrificially. One of the great enigmas of the book is Captain Brierly of the "crack ship of the Blue Star line."[42] At age thirty-two, Brierly has one of the top commands in the East and is a hero. He "had saved lives at sea, had rescued ships in distress, had a gold chronometer . . . and a pair of binoculars with a suitable inscription from some foreign Government, in commemoration of these services" (*LJ*, 49). He was also one of two captains officially called upon to assess the *Patna* situation in which Jim is implicated. The inquiry must look into the motives for Jim's abandoning his badly damaged ship and joining his captain and fellow officers in a lifeboat. Clearly, Brierly is disturbed by Jim's behavior both during the *Patna* incident and at the inquiry. Throughout the questioning, Jim is overeager to take blame and face the issues with zealous courage, attitudes that narrator Marlow distinctly admires. Brierly, on the other hand, sympathizes with Jim but dislikes the blame-taking and thinks that Jim is a patsy for his renegade captain and should "creep twenty feet underground and stay there" (*LJ*, 55) rather than expose himself to further humiliation.

Ironically, Brierly is the one who commits suicide, jumping overboard only a week after the inquiry and only a few days out of port. He simply asks one of his men to confine his dog for awhile, sets and oils his log, carefully hangs his gold chronometer under the rail, hoists himself overboard, and sinks—his pockets weighted with iron belaying pins. His death comes as a total shock and mystery to his mate, Jones. Seemingly a complacent man and certainly another perfectionist and a successful man, Brierly appears to Jones to be ideally suited to live, not to die. But Marlow hints that what Brierly has learned from watching Jim is that at some point anyone can fail in courage or in perfection—it is only a matter of time. A surrogate self for Jim, in one sense Brierly simply quits while he is ahead. Possibly he falls victim to fulfilled ambition, a condition that Anderson felt lethal to youthful captains. He seems to have no higher rungs to climb on the ladder of seamanship, nowhere to go but down—into the sea itself.

Jim, on the other hand, jumps into the sea to live and must spend the rest of his days proving his life worth having. Unlike Brierly, who is a gentleman captain, Jim fights to earn his title "Tuan" ("Lord") and to preserve it. Early in the novel he thinks of himself as so many of Tennyson's contemporaries had thought of the men of the Light Brigade: he would never break rank. Marlow confirms Jim's self-image with his own insights: "He was outwardly so typical of that good, stupid kind we like to feel marching right and left of us in life . . . the kind of fellow you would, on the strength of his looks, leave in charge of the deck" (*LJ*, 39). If so, you would be in trouble, for both Jim's self-image and Marlow's assumptions prove mistaken—or so the *Patna* incident seems to indicate. Conrad causes both Jim and his storyteller to revise early impressions of Jim, but not wholly.

For the deeper mystery inherent in Conrad's look at suicide in this book lies in Jim's life after *Patna* and in his death. The second great leap of Jim's life is to Patusan where he goes to try to live anew in a faraway land. "Romantic," according to those who know him, and determined as well, Jim has not only assumed leadership of a group of natives but has gained their total assent and confidence. His reciprocal good faith he hopes will make him "in his own eyes the equal of the impeccable men who never fall out of the ranks" (*LJ*, 296). Inevitably, the test comes. When a white interloper enters Jim's world and murders one of Jim's most trusted native companions, Jim in turn permits himself to be executed by the murder-victim's father, another willing self-sacrifice.

How one reads this action determines how one reads Conrad's novel. Early in *Lord Jim*, Jim, a minister's son, wishes to be "an example of devotion to duty, and as unflinching as a hero in a book" (*LJ*, 3). Is this final action then heroic and sufficient to redeem the lack of heroics during the *Patna* incident? Jim's eyes send a powerful and brave look toward the natives facing him at his death, but Marlow presents points of view that counter the glory of that look. "It may very well be," says Marlow, "that in the short moment of his last proud and unflinching glance, he had beheld the face of that opportunity which, like an Eastern bride, had come veiled to his side" (*LJ*, 312). On the other hand, one of Marlow's correspondents has contended that

> "giving your life up to them" (them meaning all of mankind with skins brown, yellow, or black in colour) "was like selling your soul to a brute." You contended that "that kind of *thing*" [my italics] was only endurable and enduring when based on a firm conviction in the truth of ideas racially our own, in whose name are established the order, the morality of an ethical progress. "We want its strength at our backs," you had said, "We want a belief in its necessity and its justice, to make a worthy and conscious sacrifice of our lives. Without it the sacrifice is only forgetfulness, the way of offering is no better than the way to perdition." In other words, you maintained that we must fight in the ranks or our lives don't count. (*LJ*, 254)

And Marlow himself views Jim as leaving "a living woman to celebrate his pitiless wedding with a shadowy ideal of conduct," possibly of "exalted egotism" (*LJ*, 312). At the turn of the nineteenth century, it was not easy for Conrad to suggest, nor for his readers to assume, an unironic self-sacrifice of this sort. Jim's possibly heroic death is shrouded in a haze of doubt.

V

Other Times, Other Cultures, Other Selves

Victorians mastered the fine art of displacement, and the taboos associated with suicide helped them along. The threat of suicide might be shifted away from the self by sensationalizing suicides or by retrospectively writing about one's own youthful conquest of suicidal melancholy, as did Mill and Nightingale, but subversive subjects like sex and self-murder could best be discussed indirectly, by distancing. A deeply entrenched sense of history and a growing familiarity with other cultures helped the Victorians distance the fearful. If their culture condemned suicide and prevented full discussion of its contemporary insidiousness, it nevertheless encouraged a close look at self-destruction in other times and in other cultures. People and places remote in time or space offered a set of surrogate selves to examine, praise, or condemn. Displacement provided Victorians with self-protection.

The suicides of history, especially ancient history, had long interested educated British. Cato in particular had captured their imagination. Both John Donne's *Biathanatos* (1608) and Joseph Addison's *Cato* (1713) envisioned Cato's suicide attempt followed by his successful suicide—clawing out his own entrails to avoid Caesar's despotism—as a courageous and noble death. In the seventeenth and eighteenth centuries, love of Rome and Stoicism coupled with love of natural rights to some extent countered Christian strictures against suicide.[1] Even the Roman Catholic Alexander Pope asked if it could be criminal to "act a *Roman's* part."[2] A more convinced advocate of suicide was Joseph Addison's cousin, Eustace Budgell, who invoked both Addison and the ghost of Cato in one of the most notorious suicides of the eighteenth century. Grub Street author, parliamentarian, and gentleman of the bar, Budgell had become involved in intrigue and litigation following the collapse of the South Sea Bubble and eventually committed suicide by plunging overboard into the Thames from a rented boat, his pockets weighted with stones. Theophilus Cibber's account in *The Lives of the Poets* suggests that Budgell had unsuccessfully tried to persuade his young natural daughter to die with him. In any case he left behind one of the most famous suicide notes in English history: "What Cato did and Addison approved, / Cannot be wrong."[3]

In the eighteenth century, Budgell's death functioned as a point of contention in a continuing battle over the heroism of Cato's suicide. Those of a stoical bent cited Cato's bravery; those of conservative religious convictions condemned Cato outright. "Theophilus," for example, a correspondent to the *London Journal* (August 1724), wrote that were Cato or Brutus to meet a contemporary English *felo-de-se*, they would surely declare him a madman or fool. The same writer went on to suggest that this was because Cato and Brutus had not the benefit of Christian morality regarding suicide. Later, in the nineteenth century, sentiments like those of "Theophilus" were intensively echoed and re-echoed. Clergymen, themselves well schooled in the classics, counselled caution in emulating the ancients. Stoics like Cato might be models of how to think, how to write, and even of how to be, but certainly not of how to die. In an 1812 Congregational sermon, *The Dreadful Sin of Suicide*, George Clayton warned against the "unrestricted and unguarded study of Greek and Roman classics which have long been considered as the essential basis of a learned and elegant education. We imbibe, even in our boyhood, the most false and dangerous notions of *honour*; we are taught to form erroneous conceptions of glory, and are dazzled."[4] Turning more specifically to Cato and Budgell, Clayton resumed:

> But how does Cato *die*? And what was the effect of the exhibition on the mind of the unhappy Mr. Budgel [*sic*], who, on retiring (as it is supposed) from the theatre, plunged into the Thames and was found with this defence on his person:—"What Cato *did*, and Addison approv'd, / Must needs be right."[5]

The powerful fear of imitative suicide in the nineteenth century extended even to the example of the ancients, whose self-imposed deaths came to seem like a form of exhibitionism to Christian apologists like Clayton.

Similar attitudes became pervasive in later decades of the century. In 1824 Solomon Piggott warned that the "elements of a learned and elegant education contain in them the seeds of poison; they convey the most dangerous notions of honour, and false glory, and imaginary greatness; and some of the Pagan philosophers and heroes whom we are taught most to admire even praise and extol the crime of suicide."[6] Piggott found poison aplenty in Cato's suicide and in Addison's rendition of it but felt he had an antidote for such poison in the Bible. Job, not Cato, was to be the proper guide for Piggott's readers. Piggott's study, aptly entitled *Suicide and Its Antidotes*, was the nineteenth century's last full-scale religious text discussing suicide. In 1840 came Forbes Winslow's pioneering medical history of suicide, yet it too opened with a chapter on ancient suicides and another warning against "an undue reverence for the authority of antiquity."[7] Winslow posited three causes for the famous suicides of antiquity: avoidance of suffering, vindication of honor, and demonstration of exemplary behavior. To his mind, only the first class was "excusable,"[8] so that Cato also came under harsh judgment from moralistic Winslow. Far from being courageous and magnanimous in death, Winslow's Cato was prideful, timid, "enfeebled," "depressed," distracted, and disappointed. In fact he sounds more like a victim of Victorian *tedium vitae* than a defeated Roman warrior. Moreover, to the alienist Winslow, Cato appeared not only despondent but insane:

> It was not the placid, judicious Cato of former years, but the depressed Cato, *impos mentis*, committing a rash action, contrary to all his former great reasoning, and virtuous persevering conduct. It was, in fact, Cato's act of insanity; it was not dying to serve his country, but to effectually rob Caesar of his eminent services; it therefore appears more the effect of private pique and despondency than a demonstration of public virtue or courage.[9]

Here Winslow does what many Victorians chose to do with the ancients: he transforms Cato into a Victorian in antique dress. Winslow's Cato has become what Frank Turner calls a "distant contemporary,"[10] an ancient resurrected as a modern. Winslow recalls him in order to make him a surrogate Victorian and then show the timelessness of Winslow's own views of suicide. Cato becomes one of Winslow's cases, retrospectively diagnosed, sealed, and delivered to the author's Victorian readers.

Through to the end of the century, medical texts on suicide—like William Wynn Westcott's *Suicide* (1885) and S.A.K. Strahan's *Suicide and Insanity* (1893)—opened with backward glances at ancient suicide. Strahan found it both "interesting and instructive" to look "hastily at voluntary death as it occurred among the ancients." It would enable him "to contrast the suicide of past ages with that of today, to see in what they differ, and aid us in endeavouring to discover the causes of such differences as may be found to exist."[11] Yet a far more popular forum for evaluating historical suicides than medical texts was the poetry of the age. Although Elizabeth Barrett Browning warned her fellow poets that "To flinch from modern varnish, coat or flounce, / Cry out for togas and the picturesque, / Is fatal,—foolish too,"[12] many of the most famous of her male, classically trained contemporaries paid her little heed. If novelists were turning a penny by sensationalizing suicide, poets seized the day by appealing to a more serious audience. Both university men like Matthew Arnold and Tennyson and working-class men like Thomas Cooper cried out for togas when looking for ways to present the compelling subject of suicide.

In the late 1840s Arnold looked to ancient suicides as a source of comfort for his readers and a means of self-definition for himself. In "Courage" (written 1849 or 1850) he turns to Cato to help settle his own unease over the philosophical question of the will. Like Carlyle, Arnold believed that the Victorians "must tame our rebel will,"[13] but like Byron, he also prized the force of rebellious souls. For him Cato was an exemplar of utter courage:

> Yes, be the second Cato praised!
> Not that he took the course to die—
> But that, when 'gainst himself he raised
> His arm, he raised it dauntlessly. (*PMA*, 13–16)

Characteristically, Arnold compared Victorian lack of willful determination with ancient resoluteness:

> Our bane, disguise it as we may,
> Is weakness, is a faltering course.
> Oh that past times could give our day,
> Joined to its clearness, of their force! (*PMA*, 25–28)

After penning these words, Arnold certainly continued in his admiration of ancient virtues. But in the early 1850s he would suppress his earlier fascination with ancient suicides. "Courage" appeared in his 1852 volume of poems but was not included in the 1853 collection and was never again reprinted by Arnold. Likewise "Empedocles on Etna," the title poem of the 1852 edition, was removed from the 1853 *Poems, Second Series*.

In the famous preface to the 1853 volume, Arnold formally states what he believes were his aims in writing "Empedocles." He had quite deliberately sought a distant contemporary in the ancient philosopher:

> I intended to delineate the feelings of one of the last of the Greek religious philosophers . . . living on into a time when the habits of Greek thought and feeling had begun fast to change, character to dwindle, the influence of the Sophists to prevail. Into the feelings of a man so situated there entered much that we are accustomed to consider as exclusively modern. . . . What those who are familiar only with the great monuments of early Greek genius suppose to be its exclusive characteristics, have disappeared; the calm, the cheerfulness, the disinterested objectivity have disappeared: the dialogue of the mind with itself has commenced; modern problems have presented themselves.[14]

Certainly Arnold himself shared the alienation of Empedocles. "Wandering between two worlds, one dead, / The other powerless to be born" (*PMA*, p. 288), or, as David Sonstroem so ably paraphrased it, "one death and the other powerless to be life,"[15] Arnold created an Empedocles who duplicated his own distress. Arnold's friend J. C. Shairp wrote to Clough in the summer of 1849 that Matt "was working at an 'Empedocles'—which seemed to be not much about the man who leaps in the crater—but his name and outward circumstances are used for the drapery of his own thoughts."[16] If Arnold saw the Victorians' similarity to his hero, Arnold's friends saw Matt's own likeness to Empedocles.

Still, Arnold would deny that likeness just as he would suppress his poetry of suicide. To Henry Dunn he discredited the notion that he used "Empedocles and Obermann as mouthpieces through which to vent [his] own opinions."[17] By the early 1850s he no longer desired to describe and diagnose "modern problems" so much as he wanted to cure the modern malaise and heal himself in the bargain. He wrote Clough that "modern poetry can only subsist by . . . becoming a complete *magister vitae* as the poetry of the ancients did: by including as it did religion with poetry."[18] Yet "Empedocles" presented what Arnold considered an unsatisfying "creed." Were it a satisfying one, said Arnold to Dunn, Empedocles "ought to have lived after delivering himself of it, not died."[19] More than Cato, Empedocles had led Arnold to an impasse. Arnold's Cato had chosen death in preference to the end of freedom; for him to become Caesar's pawn was clearly a fate worse than suicide. But Arnold's Empedocles was in bondage not to a human conqueror but to his own unrest. His suicide put a desperate end to what Arnold felt were desperately unresolvable dilemmas. In 1853 his creator pronounced Empedocles as in a condition "in which the suffering finds no vent in action; in which a continuous state of mental distress is prolonged, unrelieved by incident, hope, or resistance; in which there is everything to be endured, nothing to be done. In such situations there is inevitably something morbid, in the description of them something monotonous."[20]

Arnold's concern over and rejection of "Empedocles on Etna" lay partly in his fearful consciousness—realized and signified in the poem—of the ultimate use of willpower: to end life. In Act I, Empedocles delivers a kind of Victorian sermon about the will to Pausanias. We must curb our wayward wills, do our duty, and stoically live out our existence, he tells his friend. Carlyle could have written this counsel. But in Act II, in his "dialogue of the mind with itself," Empedocles uses willpower in order to define himself through death. As Dwight Culler has observed, Arnold had read the *Bhagavad Gita* as well as the fragments of Empedocles's philosophy and "realized that the disposition of one's mind at the hour of death is very important in determining the soul's state after death."[21] This disposition becomes all the more crucial when one realizes that for a post-romantic hero like Arnold's Empedocles—much as for the Empedocles of the fifth century B.C.—there would have been a primary responsibility to one's mental integrity. If youthful vitality, friends, and society all weary him, one thought—that of immortality—does not. Although Empedocles is clearly not after the "feigned" "bliss / Of doubtful future state" (*PMA*, 1. 402–03) that Pausanias seems to desire, he still wishes "not to die wholly" (*PMA*, 2. 406). For him immortality is neither eternal bliss nor endless reincarnation but rather a state of equilibrium achieved through a death that alone "can cut his oscillations short, and so / Bring him to poise" (*PMA*, 2. 232–34). "There is," says Empedocles, "no other way" (*PMA*, 2. 234).

To attain that poise, Empedocles must will to die at a moment of inner balance. Yet according to Empedocles's lesson to Pausanias, such poise cannot come about purely as a result of one's own free will. A man is wrong, says Empedocles, to "make his *will* / The measure of his rights" (*PMA*, 1. 154–55). Instead he must take into consideration other elements at play in the universe and achieve poise within a context considerably broader than that of the self. Arnold's prose summary of this part of Empedocles's advice to Pausanias explains the idea in greater detail:

> We have a will;
> we find we cannot freely give it scope;
> we are irritate, and account for it on different theories into which
> we carry our irritation.
> But look at the matter calmly.
> We arrive, a new force, in a *schon* existent world of forces.
> Our force can only have play so far as these other forms will let it.[22]

In the poem itself, Empedocles goes on to remind Pausanias of some of " 'these other forms'," which are also part of the universe. These must be reckoned with, regardless of one's will or even of one's state of purity:

> Yet even when man forsakes
> All sin—is just, is pure,
> Abandons all which makes
> His welfare insecure—
> Other existences there are, that clash with ours.
> Like us, the lightning-fires
> Love to have scope and play;

The stream, like us, desires
An unimpeded way;
Like us, the Libyan wind delights to roam at large. (*PMA*, I. 242–51)

These stanzas serve as a prophecy of what is to come when Empedocles is about to seal his own fate. He addresses the elements as his "friends" but does not at first accept their autonomy. Instead he proceeds to invest them with his own consciousness, his own "pent will." Only when he becomes aware of his use of the pathetic fallacy and endows the elements with their own state of being, does he become free to recognize the true power of Etna's volcano. Acknowledging that the volcano has a will just as he does, Empedocles realizes that he can attain poise only if their two wills become harmonious, and his soul now "glows" to meet the elements. Death is accomplished at a moment that promises him accord with what Arnold called the "*schon* existent world of forces" and allows the state of poise that brings immortality.

By putting his death under his own power, Empedocles has finally conquered those haunting self-doubts that tortured him throughout most of Act II, and the tension of Arnold's dramatic poem is fully resolved. Mind is now under the control of will, and doubt and paralysis are under the control of action. Thus Empedocles's suicide becomes like the suicide Antonin Artaud dreamed of and described so well:

By suicide, I reintroduce my design in nature, I shall for the first time give things the shape of my will. I free myself from the conditioned reflexes of my organs, which are so badly adjusted to my inner self, and life is for me no longer an absurd accident. . . . Now I choose my thought and the direction of my faculties, my tendencies, my reality. . . . I put myself in suspension, without innate propensities, neutral, in the state of equilibrium.[23]

In a sense, Arnold was too good an historian. His Empedocles became such a close contemporary that Arnold rejected his poem as being too modern. Through Empedocles Arnold solved the problem of Victorian *Angst*; he offered willed death as a final confirmation of personhood in times when society threatens to dissolve personal identity. But he was repelled by his poem's fitting resolution; it did not meet his extra-literary needs. He had once told Clough that the spectacle of the 1848 revolution in France would be a "fine one" to an "historical swift-kindling man, who is not over-haunted by the pale thought, that after all man's shiftings of posture, 'restat vivere'."[24] For Arnold himself it remained to will life, not to plunge into revolutionary self-destruction. "Empedocles on Etna" functioned as a kind of eloquent suicide note that negated the need for suicide itself; it was a substitution of sign for experience. Through displacement to Empedocles, Arnold found that "the dialogue of the mind with itself" led to the brink of suicide. He then withdrew himself and his work from the crater's edge and turned toward the more personally acceptable role of Victorian sage.

In his own use of ancient suicide Tennyson was quite different from Arnold. The poet laureate did need to dissociate himself from his modern poems about potential suicides. "Supposed Confessions" was withdrawn from the volumes after 1830 and republished only in 1884; and in reference to his presumed likeness to the narrator of *Maud*, Tennyson quipped, "Adulterer I may be, murderer I may be, suicide I am not yet."[25] But when it came to the ancient Lucretius, Tennyson sought the philosopher's differences from himself more than his similarities and avoided the problem of identification. Arnold's Empedocles is a sympathetic character. Like Arnold and so many Victorians, he looks anxiously for religious reintegration with the universe. Tennyson's Lucretius is an embodiment of materialistic philosophy and served as a warning to the Victorians to turn toward a more spiritual existence.

In 1866, two years before the publication of "Lucretius," Tennyson told Bradley that he approved of a Parisian who ordered and ate a good dinner and then committed suicide, covering his face with a chloroformed handkerchief. "That's what I should do," said Tennyson "if I thought there was no future life."[26] Earlier, in "The Two Voices" (1833), Tennyson's ambivalent persona was saved from suicide and a tempter's voice only by a redemptive Sabbath voice that bid him live. The poet implied fear of external condemnation but hope of grace and transcendence for the death-wisher. Tennyson's Lucretius, on the other hand, is trapped in ancient Rome and precluded from any hope of an afterlife. If they exist, his gods are indifferent to him. The original Lucretius was an Epicurean who denied the soul's immortality. Tennyson—like St. Jerome whose *Chronicle* was probably his source—was determined to discredit Lucretian philosophy.

What sympathy one feels for Tennyson's Lucretius stems from his victimization by a love philtre. Discouraged by Lucretius's sexual coldness, his wife has administered the drug that has sent the philosopher over the brink. Lucretius now dreams only of his violent atomistic universe and of maddening, voluptuous women. In his waking moments, he discourses on suicide. If the gods exist, why not join them in their calm withdrawal? If they do not, why not die, enter the atomistic universe, and end the lustful dreams? As it is, Lucretius is blasted "with animal heat and dire insanity."[27] Tennyson has brought his monologist to a state of dissipation, madness, and despair that most Victorians would have immediately associated with suicide. Through the use of the philtre, he has also paralyzed Lucretius's will:

> But now it seems some unseen monster lays
> His vast filthy hands upon my will,
> Wrenching it backward into his. (*PT*, 219–21)

Made beast by this demon, Lucretius resolves to commit suicide in an effort to reassert his humanity:

> Why should I, beastlike as I find myself,
> Not manlike end myself?—our privilege—
> What beast has heart to do it? And what man,
> What Roman would be dragg'd in triumph thus?
> Not I. (*PT*, 231–35)

Like Arnold's restless Empedocles, Lucretius wishes union with "Great Nature"—but unlike him he is wearier and expects only reincarnation or atomization, not reintegration. Richard Jebb, the famous Victorian classicist, caught the essence of their difference in a review of "Lucretius" for *Macmillan's*: "Empedocles died because he could not find peace; Lucretius, because he had found and lost it."[28] From the point of view of Tennyson's Lucretius, both Lucretius himself and his work are ended; his "soul flies out and dies in the air" (*PT*, 273). Thus Tennyson here presents suicidal willpower as manly but not redemptive. But again, as line 234 so carefully states, Lucretius was a "Roman," not a Victorian. For the Victorians Tennyson implied other choices, and most of his contemporaries inferred as much and liked what they inferred. Jebb lauded Tennyson's historical accuracy, while others applauded Tennyson's message. Only the reviewer for the *Christian Observer* missed the moral and berated "the first poet of this Christian land" for rendering "the benighted sentiments of a heathen philosopher heading for self destruction."[29]

Many such heathen philosophers were rendered by Thomas Cooper in his grandiloquent if often puzzling *Purgatory of Suicides* (1845), a work he called a "mind-history." Imprisoned for two years for Chartist activities, Cooper wrote the *Purgatory* during his confinement. It is a ponderous poem in ten books, framed in Spenserians and presenting men and women of many eras, all of whom have taken their lives and await a paradise on earth while serving out purgatorial years in a large cavern. The parallels to Cooper's own imprisonment are obvious. His suicides too are distant contemporaries, like Cooper awaiting a better day, and through them Cooper purged some of his own bitterness and despair. Each book opens with an exordium offering Cooper's own feelings and finishes with a look at the suicides. The point of it all is radical in every sense of the word: Cooper questions whether life is worth living in a world so rife with oppression and cruelty. Possibly the suicides have shown wisdom in electing death. Yet Cooper recoils from the thought of utter annihilation and places his hope in the world of tomorrow.

An amazing autodidact, Cooper chose liberally from among ancient suicides. Carbo attracted him because Cooper was convinced that the orator destroyed himself out of intolerance for his countrymen's vices. Lucretius served him as counsellor to a love-tormented Sappho; Lucretius informs her that despite her individual misery, "the Universe is perfect."[30] Empedocles, on the other hand, is for Cooper a far less noble character. The pride and aspiration toward immortality that had captured Arnold's imagination repelled Chartist Cooper who envisions Empedocles on a mountain, sitting "with raised right hand to mock the pomp of Jove / Hurling his lightnings" (*PS*, 2.24). Clearly, working-class Cooper despised such pretension. His Empedocles needs reproofs by two others of Cooper's ancients to help bring him to his senses. Cleombrotus first calls his bluff, pointing out the pride and folly inherent in pretending to be a god, while Indian Calamus finds him a total fraud:

> but I joy
> That Vulcan's fabled forge cast out, in scorn,
> The sandal's brazen soles, for base alloy,
> And thus the flimsy veil in twain has torn
> That hid thy apish godhead. (*PS*, 2.64)

Neither Cooper's tough free-thinking nor his sentimental overlay of Christianity can brook the hubris implicit in Empedocles's famous leap into Etna. The mountain did well to belch up humble footware as evidence of the philosopher's vulnerability. Thus Empedocles became no surrogate self for Cooper. Exercise of pretended godhead and great efforts of willpower were not of much use to an incarcerated Chartist in the late 1840s. Still, his long look at suicide enabled Cooper to urge his fellows of the working class not to accept willed death as an alternative to deliverance but rather to fight through to deliverance itself. Meanwhile in his *Purgatory* they could read with pleasure about the spectacle of the latter-day ruling-class vainglorious who destroyed themselves as had Castlereagh.

As the century progressed, Victorian poets turned less to ancient suicides than to modern for their poems about self-destruction. Suicide laws became more lenient and classical education less prevalent, and it seemed more permissible to represent contemporary self-destructives. To many Victorians it also became more obvious that the ancients were not really contemporaries after all. A writer for *Chambers's* magazine in 1884 observed that this differs essentially from the suicidal era of the ancients, being psychical rather than physical. Whereas theirs was born of sheer exhaustion and satiety, with want of belief in a future state of existence, that of the present day is the melancholy of a restless and unceasingly analysing soul, eternally brooding over the insoluble problems 'Whence?' and 'Whither?' which disordered state not unfrequently leads to incapacity for action, and finally to inability to live.[31]

Strahan too had to admit that "what were the chief causes of suicide among the ancients have ceased to be incentives to self-destruction among European peoples today."[32] George Meredith had already realized this thirty years earlier and had created a contemporary version of the restless, brooding, analyzing soul in the narrator of *Modern Love* (1862)—a man confused and anxious over the suicide of his wife. Past personal history was difficult enough to fathom, let alone ancient history. For Meredith's part, Empedocles could be consigned to bathos:

> He leaped. With none to hinder,
> Of Aetna's fiery scoriae
> In the next vomit-shower, made he
> A more peculiar cinder.
> And this great Doctor, can it be,
> He left no saner recipe
> For men at issue with despair?
> Admiring, even his poet owns,
> While noting his fine lyric tones,
> The last of him was heels in air![33]

As Meredith's career attests, not all poets disagreed with Elizabeth Barrett's exhortation to leave off depicting togas and start representing "the age, / their age" (*AL*, 163). Nevertheless, more often than not Victorian poetry of suicide involved displacement—if not to another time, then to another culture. When, for example, Barrett's husband wrote of suicide, he preferred French to English subjects. Among them were three men in a Paris morgue in "Apparent Failure" (1864) and a religious fanatic in contemporary Normandy in *Red Cotton Night-Cap Country* (1873). *Red Cotton Night-Cap Country or Turf and Towers* certainly offers an odd sort of displacement, a serious, pseudo-factual look at "heels in air." It is the story of a Paris jeweller named Leonce Miranda and is based both on hearsay and on public records of an actual case. Browning's Miranda is a troubled man. Raised in the village of St. Rambert, he blindly accepts the local religious lore and wholeheartedly believes in the miracles of La Ravissante, a statue of the Virgin housed in a nearby church of the same name. His religious aspirations are symbolized by the "towers" of the Church, represented in Browning's subtitle. But Miranda has another aspect. Also drawn by the "turf," the earthy side of life, he forms a liaison with the blossomlike Clara de Millefleurs, and then renovates an old Clairvaux Priory for their love nest. Soon afterwards, Miranda's mother activates terrible conflict within her son. Playing upon his guilt, she suggests that his life with Clara endangers his spiritual life. In despair over seeing no possible resolution to this conflict, Miranda attempts but fails to commit suicide in the Seine. Shortly thereafter Miranda's mother dies, and an even more guilt-ridden Miranda vows to relinquish "turf" forever. Violently he burns off his hands in an effort to destroy Clara's letters, and eventually he mounts to the Belvedere atop Clairvaux and attempts to fly to the distant steeple of La Ravissante to prove his faith: "A sublime spring from the balustrade . . . / A flash in middle-air, and stone-dead lay / Monsieur Leonce Miranda on the turf."[34]

Sensational in the extreme, this is the outline of *Red Cotton Night-Cap Country*, a poem that Browning claimed was so factual that he was forced to alter the names of his characters to avoid a libel suit. Yet from the outset Browning did distort fact. When his friend Milsand told him the story of Mellerio (the original name of Miranda), without consulting the records, Browning immediately "concluded that there was no intention of committing suicide" and said to himself that he would "treat the subject *just so*."[35] Furthermore, when he did look at the documents of the case, he changed and omitted facts at will. Mellerio's immersion in the Seine was originally reported only to have been a bath; in his last two years Mellerio was seen by all concerned as degenerating in mind and body; and in the court case that followed Mellerio's death, the plaintiffs argued in favor of a verdict of suicidal lunacy.[36] Browning, however, converted Mellerio's story into a kind of Pyrrhic victory. His final leap becomes an act of faith and courage, prefaced by a long, sympathetic soliloquy in which Miranda reveals his belief that the Virgin Mary's angels will bear him to La Ravissante.

Browning had reasons for his fanciful distortions of record. Like Empedocles, Miranda is a surrogate Englishman. Through him Browning transports suicide across the Channel and harries the French for their hypocrisy in trying to reconcile turf and tower by looking first one way, then the other. At the same time he focuses on English concerns, for if the English Victorians were less likely than the French to hold double standards, they were quite as likely to suffer conflicting desires. As Jerome Buckley describes Victorian society, it "was forever subject to tensions which militated against complete spontaneity and singleness of purpose."[37] Such tensions are reflected in Victorian poetic characters like Empedocles and Miranda and are resolved only by their deaths. For his part Browning was not so troubled over this kind of resolution as Arnold had been. His Miranda is neither so bright nor so admirable as Arnold's Empedocles. Instead Miranda is a fascinating, if sympathetic, example of how not to be. He foolishly brings a brand of medieval faith into the nineteenth century and dies a fruitless and anachronistic death. He fails to realize what Browning himself persistently attempted to convey in his poems: that body and soul are counterparts and must dwell comfortably together. Tensions were the essence of life for Browning; not to waiver was to die. In *Red Cotton Night-Cap Country*, Browning neither condemns materialism, as did Tennyson, nor exalts Miranda's choice:

> Miranda hardly did his best with life:
> He might have opened eye, exerted brain,
> Attained conception as to right and law
> In certain points respecting intercourse
> Of man with woman—love, one likes to say;
>
> Also, the sense of him should have sufficed
> For building up some better theory
> Of how God operates in heaven and earth,
> Than would establish Him participant
> In doings yonder at The Ravissante.
> The heart was wise according to its lights
> And limits; but the head refused more sun,
> And shrank into its mew, and craved less space. (*CPW*, 771)

Browning's contemporaries were less satisfied with *Red Cotton Night-Cap Country* than was Browning. Although they relished sensationalism in newspapers and novels and would love *The Ring and the Book* (1868–69), they felt uneasy over sensational poetry *sans* togas or other exotic garb. The reviewer for *The Spectator* did not think that Browning "succeeded in giving any true poetic excuse for telling a story so full of disagreeable elements"[38] like suicide, and most reviewers agreed. Only Chesterton felt it "worth noting that Browning was one of those wise men who can perceive the terrible and impressive poetry of the police-news which is commonly treated as vulgarity, which is dreadful and may be undesirable, but is certainly not vulgar."[39]

Anything but vulgar, Walter Pater—like Browning—looked across the English Channel for examples of self-destructiveness. In his *Imaginary Portraits* (1887) he colored his history with fiction and invented a semi-factual medium for hunting distant contemporaries. In his "Sebastian van Storck," he set that medium to work on the problem of suicide. Like Tennyson's "Lucretius," the portrait is an admonition against materialism, but it is an even stronger warning against nihilism. Young Sebastian lives in seventeenth-century Holland at the peak of Dutch power and prosperity. As a member of a prominent, well-to-do family, he appears to have a life of ease and affluence ahead of him. Instead, he opts for a self-destroying philosophy of negation that he patterns partially on Spinoza and through which he has "come to think of all definite forms of being, the warm pressure of life, the cry of nature itself, as no more than a troublesome irritation on the surface of the one absolute mind."[40] In Sebastian there is no Miranda-like war between sensuality and spiritualism. A convinced intellectual, he is determined to silence his senses in order to join "the calm surface of the absolute, untroubled mind" (*IP*, 132). For him the ever-present sea becomes a metaphor for that desired surface—"barren and absolutely lovely" (*IP*, 133).

From the outset there is little contest in Sebastian's mind between Dutch materialism and this nihilistic monism, although seventeenth-century Holland, according to Walter Pater, was not a wholly unattractive place. It had "a minute and busy wellbeing" (*IP*, 117) rather like its famed *genre* paintings, which were "of the earth earthy—genuine red earth of old Adam" (*IP*, 118). Sebastian soundly rejects this welter of wellbeing and art, refusing to become a part either of his prominent family or of the family portrait for which his mother begs him to sit. He will not help immortalize either materialism or materiality in paint. "Why add," he muses, "by a forced and artificial production, to the monotonous tide of competing, fleeting experience" (*IP*, 119). He also turns his back on the one eligible young woman who sheds a bit of warmth on his cold isolation. Instead he continues to long for pallid absolutes:

> He seemed, if one may say so, in love with death; preferring winter to summer; finding only a tranquillising influence in the thought of the earth beneath our feet cooling down for ever from its old cosmic heat; watching pleasurably how their colours fled out of things, and the long sand-bank in the sea, which had been the rampart of a town, was washed down in its turn (*IP*, 126).

Pater clearly did not side with Sebastian's choice. A lover of color, variety, and flux, Pater accepted finiteness. In *Plato and Platonism* he called "the literal negation of self" a "kind of moral suicide,"[41] and in "Sebastian van Storck" he appears to lead Sebastian toward just such a death. When his hero thinks of the dead, primeval Dutch, he has "the odd fancy that he himself would like to have been dead and gone as long ago, with a kind of envy of those whose deceasing was so long since over" (*IP*, 123). Eventually, Sebastian goes to the sea to make this death wish a reality. What Pater calls his "dark fanaticism" has created a correspondingly "black melancholy" in him (*IP*, 135), and he desires to "make 'equation' between himself and what was not himself" (*IP*, 137). Ironically, nature, flux, and fate take over the initiative in Sebastian's death. No calm oceanic surface greets him, but "an undulation of the sea the like of which had not occurred in that province for half a century" (*IP*, 137). Sebastian is found dead after having saved the life of a small child whom he has placed in a high tower out of the reach of the ravaging sea. His intended suicide has altered to an heroic self-sacrifice.

"Sebastian van Storck" was a kind of parable for Victorians, another study in wrong thinking. Clearly Sebastian's philosophy is suspect. Because death is inevitable, Pater intimates, one does not need to die before one's time. Pater discountenances Sebastian's retreat from family, from love, from responsibility, and from society. His hero, he tells us, is diseased, the victim both of the black melancholy and of tuberculosis. He is a sick man of Europe, a contemplator of romantic suicide—an affliction that Pater seems to have considered out of place in any era or culture but typical of many times and many places. Certainly Sebastian affords no tonic for life-weary Victorians, but then neither does the rest of Pater's seventeenth-century Holland. If Sebastian is too withdrawn from the society around him, that society is itself less than ideal, beset as it is by parental pressures and overeager husband hunters. And in any case, bourgeois Dutch civilization is also soon to come to an end. According to Pater, tuberculosis will strike Europe as it has stricken Sebastian and will attack "people grown somewhat over-delicate in their nature by the effects of modern luxury" (*IP*, 137). These words, the last of Pater's portrait, are surely cautionary. As Knoepflmacher says, all of Pater's "fictional recreations of the past are conditioned by the needs of the present."[42] It is as though Pater were urging, "Wake up Victorians! end romantic suicide, look out for nihilism, beware of materialism, and live!"

But live how? Pater suggests no easy answers. Compassion reaches his Sebastian only by chance and only *in extremis*. Nevertheless it does lay hold of him in the end, much as it does Marius in Pater's *Marius the Epicurean* (1885). Like Pater, Marius believes in the life of the senses but finds himself in need of moral prerogatives. In searching for them, he rejects first philosophical materialism and then idealism and comes to the emptiness of relativism. Ultimately he dies in place of one of his Christian friends, a self-sacrifice not unlike that of Sebastian. Thus readers of *Marius* are offered a rather unconvincing and sentimental "*Nachshein* of Christianity," what Knoepflmacher calls "the Christian death of a pagan by an almost accidental act of will."[43] Such enfeebled Christianity glimmers only weakly and only at the ends of the stories of two men whose "age and our own," as Pater would say of Marius, "have much in common—many difficulties and hopes."[44] Pater attempted to choose those difficulties and hopes with a scholar's skill and to embellish seventeenth-century Holland and Antonine Rome with somber shades from an artist's palate. Yet in doing so he ultimately reinforced a belief that the sensitive intellectual's fate seemed suicidal no matter what culture or what time one might examine. For people like Pater displacement came hard. Their own selective sense of history and their own sense of despair kept telling them "*plus ça change, plus c'est la meme chose.*"

Biased selectivity in choosing historical examples had begun to trouble historians, if not litterateurs, earlier in the century. It had become more apparent that "who controls the present controls the past."[45] Lessons from the past were never really selected randomly but with a taste for timeliness. People like Julius Hare lost all respect for historians who "not having the right insight into the necessary distinctions of ages and nations . . . measure others by their own standard and therefore misjudge them."[46] Later in the century, A. P. Stanley voiced kindred concern because he felt that "in historical matters, the power of seeing differences cannot be too highly prized. The tendency of ordinary men is to invest every age with the attributes of their own time."[47]

Stanley's dissatisfaction arose during a period when history was no longer the only window for viewing alternate kinds of human experience. By the third and fourth quarters of the nineteenth century, social anthropology had begun to come into its own, revealing customs and beliefs of peoples far removed from Western civilization and its roots in ancient Greece and Rome. In 1861, in his classic study of *Ancient Law*, Sir Henry Maine surmised that "the tone of thought common among [the British] would be materially affected if we had vividly before us the relation of the progressive races to the totality of life."[48] By the 1880s that tone of thought had altered sufficiently to make cultural relativism a main focus of the new field of anthropology and a new dimension in writings about suicide. And by 1898, when Strahan opened chapter one of his *Suicide and Insanity*, he could begin with the subheading "Suicide in Early Times and among Primitive Peoples." The latter topic now fascinated his contemporaries, who generally still defined the primitive broadly to mean both atavistic and non-Western. They gave themselves free rein to survey the exotic suicidal customs of the world. Sir James Frazer turned to Africans and Eskimos, while Edward Westermarck looked at dozens of other cultures,[49] but nearly all anthropologically inclined students of suicide sooner or later studied the Indian practice of *suttee*, the self-immolation of wives on their husbands' funeral pyres.

The British were obsessed with *suttee*, an obsession attested to by the thousands of pages of parliamentary papers devoted to its consideration. Beginning in 1815, in India the British Raj instituted a system to police *suttee* in an attempt to insure against unwilling sacrifices and deaths of young girls who had not yet reached puberty. At home, public opinion against the practice grew as returning missionaries sought opposition against *suttee*. By 1829 Lord Bentinck, Governor General of India, had wholly banned *suttee*, although it continued throughout the century in spite of the ban. The surprising thing about this particular British obsession was that *suttee*, though appalling to Westerners then as now, was neither so prevalent nor so widespread as British attention to it would suggest. From 1817 to 1827 there were some four thousand *suttees* in a population of over 160 million, and most of those were localized to Bengal—Calcutta in particular. In an essay on colonial death ritual, C. A. Bayley speculates that nineteenth-century concern over *suttee* was intensive because, beginning in about 1820, feelings against Hinduism ran high, and *suttee* was the most blatantly barbaric custom that could be used in an anti-Hindu campaign.[50] But the concern was certainly also a displacement. Increased attention to *suttee* paralleled not just anti-Hinduism but an ensuing interest in and fear of self-destruction that came with altered suicide law after 1823, and later in the century, with a fear of "redundant women,"[51] a term used to refer to a surplus of unmarried females. Commentators on suicide showed interest in *suttee* beginning with Piggott, who in 1824 compared the self-immolation of Hindu widows with what he considered to be the nobler self-sacrifices of Europeans. Hindu wives he saw simply as barbaric life-wasters. "How different is this," he believed, "from that voluntary sacrifice of life to achieve durable benefits for our country, for the world, for our own souls, and for God; where heroic virtue excites the true patriot to daring deeds of valour and the imminent risk of personal safety, or where the love of God and our Saviour animates the Christian to the greatest of privations, and to embrace the burning stake!"[52] It seems never to have occurred to Piggott that he had found a parallel more than a contrast, that he had uncovered a Brahmin belief as deeply held as any Christian one. Increasingly, interest in *suttee* was also a manifestation of the feminization of suicide. Many Victorians wanted to believe that "redundant women" had really no place to go but toward death. *Suttee* offered a flagrant case in point and was sufficiently distanced from England to become a topic for open discussion. The British were shocked at the Indians' apparent solution to redundancy but were fascinated by it all the same.

Investigators of *suttee* later in the century did not share Piggott's brand of cultural blindness. As Maine realized, it was becoming necessary for imperialist Britain to try to understand colonial customs—even this most puzzling form of self-destruction. Maine himself tried to explain *suttee* in terms of law. In Roman law, legal obligation and religious duty had been separated; in Hindu law, on the other hand, the religious element acquired "complete predominance." Family sacrifices became "the keystone of all the law of Persons and much of the Law of Things."[53] Therefore contemporary Britons had to view *suttee* in terms of an entirely foreign legal framework in order to judge it at all. Strahan, too, in his treatise on suicide and the insane, marvelled over but accepted what seemed to be Brahmin "contempt" for life,[54] as did his late-century contemporaries in anthropology. What Strahan termed "contempt," Frazer called Eastern "indifference to human life which seems so strange to the Western mind."[55]

Meanwhile Edward Westermarck, the influential Finn who taught at the London School of Economics, directed himself toward non-Western peoples as exemplars of high culture. Chinese and Japanese civilizations seemed especially relevant to his discussion of suicide. Westermarck saw Oriental suicides as honorable in the extreme and observed that "in spite of imperial prohibitions, sutteeism of widowed wives and brides has continued to flourish in China down to this day, and meets with the same public applause as ever."[56] Westermarck's extensive global survey of suicide, which included primitive peoples, led him to two important conclusions. The first was that because attendant circumstances and notions about future life vary so enormously from suicide to suicide and culture to culture, moral valuation also must vary to "an extreme degree."[57] Westermarck's second conclusion was that the more lenient judgment passed upon suicide "by the public conscience of the present time"[58] was unlikely to be regressive.

Thus by the end of the century historical displacement seemed naive, and the safety net once afforded by cultural displacement had come to resemble a maze. If other peoples in other places were to be of use in distancing one's own fears of suicide, they had first to be understood on their own terms, possibly even on their own turf. Such difficulties did not, however, prohibit many late Victorian anthropologists from pronouncing rigid moral judgments against suicide. The final version of a chapter in Frazer's *Golden Bough* concludes with these shrill and scathing words:

According to one account, the Sicilian philosopher Empedocles, who set up for being a god in his lifetime, leaped into the crater of Etna in order to establish his claim to godhead. There is nothing incredible in the tradition. The crack-brained philosopher, with his itch for notoriety, may well have done what Indian fakirs and brazen-faced mountebank Peregrinus did in antiquity, and what Russian peasants and Chinese Buddhists have done in modern times. There is no extremity to which fanaticism or vanity, or a mixture of the two, will not impel its victims.[59]

Victorian taboos against suicide faded slowly, even in the new light of cultural relativism, a light that sometimes failed Victorian luminaries.

VI

Monsters of Self-Destruction

This is a chapter about fictions and fantasies, about projections of freakish creatures who will to die. Such projections show the dark side of the Victorian psyche, coupling deep-seated fear of violent and willful death with irrational terror of hidden bogeys that may lurk within the mind. With its horrid and ultimately vengeful monster, *Frankenstein* (1818) is the romantic prototype of this sort of literature. Frankenstein's monster gradually evolves an immoral interior to match his hideous frame and eventually builds his own blazing funeral pyre to consume his own desolate life. This kind of fantasy took hold in the Victorian era, when propriety and self-denial masked a powerful sense of alienation and estrangement.[1] People who did not believe that they bore monsters within eagerly sought stories of monsters without. They preferred to feel subject to dark, external forces rather than search for them as inner demons as we post-Freudians do today. Like Victor Frankenstein just after his creation of the Monster, they hid from their demons, not realizing that they might be their "own vampires," their "own spirit let loose from the grave."[2] Improbable worlds thus became popular worlds as Victorian readers relished tales like Shelley's and those of the brothers Grimm. Displaced fears of suicide were relocated in the realm of fantasy where ghoulish other selves became perpetrators of suicide. Meanwhile there was little conscious recognition that monsters were images or dreams of one's own self. Most Victorians could not countenance Schiller's dictum, "All creatures born by our fantasy, in the last analysis, are nothing but ourselves."[3]

The mid-century abounded in such fantastical fictions. About the time that Matthew Arnold was agonizing over Empedocles on the brink of Etna, the publishing house of E. Lloyd, Esq., Salisbury Square, London, was offering its avid readers Varney the Vampire, boldly vanishing into the mouth of Vesuvius. *Varney the Vampire, or The Feast of Blood* (1847) came to be one of the most popular mid-century "penny dreadfuls." For a single penny, Victorian readers could relish the first four parts of this feast, since parts two, three and four came free with the purchase of part one. Sir Francis Varney proved a hard man to kill, a man whose life spanned generations, and whose lengthy story needed considerable space for its telling and eventually gained thousands of pounds for its publishers. A titled gentleman who had once died by hanging and had then been revived by a young medical student, Varney was in fact no man at all, but a freak, an anomaly. Instantly revivable when bathed in moonlight, he could not die by any natural means but was condemned to immortality. His creators tell us that "he would gladly have been more human and lived and died as those lived and died whom he saw around him. But being compelled to fulfill the order of his being, he never had the courage absolutely to take measures for his own destruction, a destruction that should be final in consequence of depriving himself of all opportunity of resuscitation."[4] Like Empedocles, then, Varney became a surrogate Victorian, another self. Capable of endless resuscitation as Empedocles is of endless reincarnation, Varney fulfills the Victorian yearning for immortality. Guilty of selfishness and blood-letting, he deserves the Victorian punishment of death. Whatever the order of his being, however, Varney seems not to have had the right to take his own life.

Unlike Empedocles, Varney is a distorted, fantastical self, free from most human constraints. Through him working-class Victorians could experience the forbidden, just as Arnold's more refined readers could through Empedocles. When Varney's *tedium vitae* becomes unendurable, the vampire determines to destroy himself. His visionary powers reveal to him that death by drowning could put an end to his existence. Carefully, he stages his demise, throwing himself overboard from a ship with little hope of rescue. Found and presumed dead, he is carried off to a "boneyard," but, alas, moonbeams enter the vault where he has been placed, and Varney once again comes to life. Varney next puts himself in the care of a priest, hoping to be reformed. But the vampire really has no faith in religion and so devises a last, desperate attempt to die. Accompanied by a witness, Varney makes his way to the crater of Mount Vesuvius and disappears. "Tired and disgusted with a life of horror, he flung himself in to prevent the possibility of a reanimation of his remains."[5]

Varney's tale ends with this event, but Varney's readers would have been left unsettled, all the same. For what *Varney the Vampire* is saying is really what "Empedocles on Etna" says: when the burden of life becomes too heavy, it is acceptable to lay it down. If immortality means a continuation of mental or metaphysical suffering, suicide can be preferable. This subversive message is again made safe for Victorians because it occurs in tales whose characters seem far removed from nineteenth-century England. Empedocles, as Arnold carefully pointed out, "was a Sicilian Greek born between two and three thousand years"[6] before the mid-Victorian day in Britain. Varney, his authors also take care to announce, is inhuman: "There are some good points about the—man, we are going to say—and yet we can hardly feel justified in bestowing upon him that title,—considering the strange gift of renewable existence which was his."[7] The monstrous or uncanny, like the past, is not subject to acceptable Victorian codes of behavior. Death-wishing that can be displaced far enough from home can be fully depicted, discussed, and examined.

In the case of Varney, there was both something to remove him from the haunts of his working-class reader and something to bring him close. As a vampire and a gentleman, he seemed remote from everyday life. But in his *tedium vitae*, in his mixture of good and bad, and in his final despair over religion, he was akin to many. Lloyd's writers carefully stressed these points. If Varney were really immortal, they go so far as to suggest, his monstrous self could still be present:

> If it were as, indeed, it seemed to be the case, that bodily decay in him was not the result of death, and that the rays "of the cold chaste moon" were sufficient to revivify him, who shall say when that process is to end! and who shall say that, walking the streets of giant London at this day, there may not be some such existences? Horrible thought that, perhaps seduced by the polished exterior of one who seems a citizen of the world in the most extended signification of the words, we should bring into our domestic circle a vampyre![8]

More than working-class mistrust of aristocracy underlies this passage. London's streets might conceal ghoulishness and suicide as well as treachery.

Some forty years after the publication of *Varney*, a blatantly true-life monstrosity was indeed walking the streets of London in the person of John Merrick, the Elephant Man. Merrick, subject of the modern play and film *The Elephant Man*, is nearly as well known to us as to the Victorians. Exhibited in side-shows because of his hideous growths and shape, he was eventually rescued by Dr. Frederick Treves, who described his patient as "deformed in body, face, head and limbs. His skin, thick and pendulous hung in folds and resembled the hide of an elephant—hence his show name."[9] Merrick was housed in the London Hospital where he remained until his mysterious death from suffocation. What he became was a kind of pet monster for upper-class Victorians, a man who took the fear away from strangeness and otherness by proving himself wholly domestic. Once saved from the savagery of exploitation, Merrick revealed a gentleness far greater than that of his persecutors. Eventually he entertained royalty, read widely, learned of the lively arts, and visited the beautiful countryside. They called him "such a gentle, kindly man, poor thing!"[10] Ugly on the outside but sterling within, Merrick seemed the perfect fairy-tale Beast.

Actually, he was a naive and ill man whose final years were not filled simply with ease and friendly callers. His disease was worsening, its crippling effect becoming more painful. For hours he would sit staring into space, despondently and rhythmically tapping at his pillow or the arm of his chair with his distorted right hand. Officially, however, Merrick gave his contemporary well-wishers what they wanted—gratitude and a sentimental feeling that theirs was a good world:

"Tis true my form is something odd,
But blaming me is blaming God;
Could I create myself anew
I would not fail in pleasing you.

"If I could reach from pole to pole
Or grasp the ocean with a span,
I would be measured by the soul;
The mind's the standard of the man."[11]

The second of these two verses appeared at the end of a pitiful document handed out at the freak-shows in which Merrick had been exhibited. Both verses capped a statement of thanks to his benefactors that was appended to an account of him published in the *British Medical Journal*. There Merrick confirms his inner goodness and, like Varney, accepts his God-given lot.

One wonders, however, if he did so to the end, for Merrick's death was unexpected enough to warrant an inquest. On the last day of his life he seemed quite as usual, so very usual that Treves found the circumstances of his death "peculiar." Merrick had chatted with his nurses and had accepted his lunch and yet two hours later was found dead, his food still untouched. He was presumed asphyxiated, the weight of his huge head having choked off his air supply when he lay down on his back to sleep. This was odd, because Merrick knew well how to live with his enormous head. He never slept recumbent but had always tucked himself into a fetal position and dozed sitting up, with the weight of the head supported by his knees. The "Report of the Coroner's Inquest" published in the *Times* for 16 April 1890, also contains a peculiarity: "The Coronor said that the man had been sent round the shows as a curiosity, and when death took place it was decided as a matter of prudence to hold this inquest." Surely there could not have been much precedent for an inquest based on these premises. The death of the Elephant Man seems shrouded in a mystery as impenetrable as the full-length cloak and strangely curtained hat that covered Merrick from head to toe when he went out on the streets. Since there was no sign of a struggle, could Merrick have taken his own life?

Treves never says so directly, but he certainly implies as much in his 1926 pamphlet, "The Elephant Man." Written nearly three decades after Merrick's death, the pamphlet retrospectively strives to account for its circumstances. Treves claims of Merrick:

> He often said to me that he wished he could lie down to sleep "like other people." I think on this last night he must, with some determination, have made the experiment. The pillow was soft, and the head, when placed on it, must have fallen backwards and caused a dislocation of the neck. Thus it came about that his death was due to the desire that had dominated his life—the pathetic but hopeless desire to be "like other people."[12]

Treves posits that the Elephant Man grew tired of being a Victorian other self. More practically, Merrick was also very insecure about his lodgings. Because of two successful, large-scale appeals by the London Hospital, he had been allowed to stay on in his hospital rooms until he died. Since he was not expected to live long, his stay was not projected as an impossible financial drain. But Merrick never got over the idea that he might be moved at any time, an obsession that Treves also focuses on in his narrative. This insecurity, coupled with his occasional despondency and his fear of people's gaze, might indeed have accounted for a desire to sleep forever. Merrick felt so deeply marked by the eyes of others that he told Treves he wanted his next move to be to an asylum for the blind. Perhaps he had been reading *Frankenstein* and recalled that the Monster's only gentle treatment came from an old blind man.

Thus there was darkness still in this man's new life. Gentle, spiteless, and uncynical he might have been, free from sadness and anxiety he was not. Earnestly, Treves acknowledges that darkness in the conclusion to his pamphlet:

> He had been plunged into the Slough of Despond, but with manly steps he gained the farther shore. He had been made "a spectacle to all men" in the heartless streets of Vanity Fair. He had been ill-treated and reviled and bespattered with the mud of Disdain. He had escaped the clutches of the Giant Despair, and at last had reached the "Place of Deliverance," where "his burden loosed from off his back, so that he saw it no more."[13]

Here his doctor rewrites Merrick's life not as that of a monster but as that of a pilgrim, echoing one of the Victorians' favorite stories. Merrick was converted by Victorian doctors, blue bloods, and show people from Elephant Man to Everyman. Small wonder his death was sentimentalized. Despite the inquest and Treves's concern over "peculiarity," there could be little official talk of suicide in Merrick's case. Invested with Victorian projections of goodness and divested of all taint of the demonic or bestial, John Merrick had become a symbol of perseverance in the face of affliction. In the end, he came to embody the other self as angel, not devil.

Treves fictionalized Merrick much as Dickens had Little Nell in *The Old Curiosity Shop* (1841). In discussing Freud's Wolf Man, Peter Brooks points out the connection between case history and fiction. Case histories are stories didactically presented to the public; they are exemplary biography.[14] Certainly the lives of both Merrick and Little Nell served as lessons to the Victorians. Both figures emerge as long-sufferers who earn death as relief from pilgrim-like wandering, travail, and victimization. Both have heroic rescuers who remove them from society and find them sanctuaries in which to die. And the praises of both are couched in similar language. Dickens's schoolmaster in *The Old Curiosity Shop* listens to Nell Trent with astonishment:

> "This child!" he thought. "Has this child heroically persevered under all doubts and dangers, struggled with poverty and suffering, upheld and sustained by strong affection and the consciousness of rectitude alone! And yet the world is full of such heroism."[15]

Dickens and Treves chronicled their stories as they did because they felt that their readers wanted to believe in such heroism and in easeful death as a reward for it. But then so did the two authors. Dickens always tried to reassure himself that his young sister-in-law, Mary Hogarth, had died peacefully and was in some way requited for her good, short life. Similarly, Treves needed over thirty years to convince himself that his charge had not laid down his ungainly head in order to spare London Hospital the trouble of his upkeep, but in fact had simply needed to "sleep" like others.

There is nonetheless a darker side to Little Nell's story as there is to Merrick's and to Dickens's own. For if Dickens's memory canonized Mary Hogarth, it also captured horrific and macabre images of dead men in the Paris morgue. In "Travelling Abroad," from *The Uncommercial Traveller* (1861), the novelist would write that he was haunted by a mental picture of a drowned man whom he had seen laid out in that house of death. Darkened and disfigured by water, the remembered and recreated drowned man pursued Dickens to the public baths and then onward for the better part of a week. Earlier, in Dickens's fiction, Daniel Quilp, Little Nell's cruel, lecherous persecutor in *The Old Curiosity Shop*, knew just such a disfiguring death. In more ways than one it would befit him, for Quilp, like Varney, was a monster of self-destruction.

From his first entry into Dickens's novel, Quilp is depicted as deformed both inside and out:

> The child was closely followed by an elderly man of remarkably hard features and forbidding aspect, and so low in stature as to be quite a dwarf, though his head and face were large enough for the body of a giant. His black eyes were restless, sly, and cunning; his mouth and chin, bristly with the stubble of a course hard beard; and his complexion was one of that kind which never looks clean or wholesome. But what added most to the grotesque expression of his face, was a ghastly smile, which, appearing to be the mere result of habit and to have no connexion with any mirthful or complacent feeling, constantly revealed the few discoloured fangs that were yet scattered in his mouth, and gave him the aspect of a panting dog. (*OCS*, 65)

Later, Kit calls him "the ugliest dwarf that could be seen anywheres for a penny" (*OCS*, 95), while others dub him "monster." Like Merrick, Quilp is of freak-show proportions, although unlike him he becomes everybody's dreaded, darker other self, especially Nell's. Dickens makes this clear by creating several more innocuous "monsters": the crippled Master Humphrey, the deformed factory worker, and the group of circus freaks. None of these figures has an interior to match his physical deformity, a realization that Nell quickly makes. Her sympathy with them and her horror over Quilp are meant to be a moral index for Dickens's readers. Quilp will eventually haunt Nell's nightmares and become confounded in her dreamlife with Mrs. Jarley's waxwork figures of murderers and wild boys. By day a sexual threat, Quilp becomes by night a threat to life itself.

Thus Quilp comes to serve as Nell's moral opposite. Evil is excluded from Nell, good from the monstrous Quilp. In keeping with their deserts, they are meted out their deaths. It is important to realize that in *The Old Curiosity Shop* no one escapes death.[16] Although Dickens's devotees clamored to save Nell's life, Dickens had to kill his young heroine. Death in this book is inevitable, but it can either be a release—a beautiful and easy transition like Nell's—or a torment like Quilp's miserable, self-induced drowning. "Everything in our lives," Dickens tells us, "whether of good or evil, affects us most by contrast" (*OCS*, 493). Nell has been faced with inhumanity both in the city, where "ruin and self-murder" crouched "in every street" (*OCS*, 172), and on the road; eventually, however, she finds an Edenic, prelapsarian place and slips into a death that seems more like birth. Quilp, on the other hand, locks himself away from all possible aid, loses his footing, and drowns miserably in the Thames:

> Another mortal struggle, and he was up again, beating the water with his hands, and looking out with wild and glaring eyes that showed him some black object he was drifting close upon. The hull of a ship! He could touch its smooth and slippery surface with his hand. One loud cry now—but the resistless water bore him down before he could give it utterance, and, driving him under it, carried away a corpse. (*OCS*, 620)

Quilp is one of Dickens's "accidental" suicides. Attempting to escape his fate like cruel Bill Sikes in *Oliver Twist*, Quilp actually seals it. In each of their cases, self-destruction works like the hand of justice. Their worlds are bestial, primitive, and sexual—frought with dangerous forces seemingly beyond individual control. Nevertheless their excessive desperation to live is what causes their demise. In the world of *The Old Curiosity Shop*, to accept death quietly is to conquer it, while to attempt to escape it is to succumb to it. Dickens reinforces this lesson by making the deaths of his two characters nearly simultaneous. In Nell's case, he tells us,

> it is hard to take to heart the lesson that such deaths will teach, but let no man reject it, for it is one that all must learn, and is a mighty, universal Truth. When Death strikes down the innocent and young, for every fragile form from which he lets the panting spirit free, a hundred virtues rise, in shapes of mercy, charity, and love, to walk the world, and bless it. Of every tear that sorrowing mortals shed on such green graves, some good is born, some gentler nature comes. In the Destroyer's steps there spring up bright creations that defy his power, and his dark path becomes a way of light to Heaven. (*OCS*, 659)

In Quilp's case, however, we learn of the harsh consequences of excessive and senselessly cruel vitality. Quilp has become the primitive, death-fearful second self that many Victorians strove to hide or kill. Fittingly, the inquest on his body determines that Quilp was *felo-de-se*, and he is left to be buried at a cross-roads with a stake through the heart. Although rumor contends that this grisly ceremony was dispensed with, it is clear that Dickens wanted his villain associated with the demonic in the minds of his readers.

Dickens paired sentimental and suicidal deaths in several of his earlier novels. In *Dombey and Son* (1848), young Paul Dombey embraces death and is easily borne away on an ocean of immortality, while Carker meets a bloody end by suicide on the railway tracks. In *Nicholas Nickleby* (1838–39), Smike is unafraid to die and "almost" does not wish to recover from his final illness, while his father, Ralph Nickleby, shakes his fist at the world in frenzied hatred as he prepares to hang himself. Carker and Ralph Nickleby are not accidental suicides. Tired of their misdeeds, these two will to die. More men than monsters, they finish life aware of their capacity for cruelty. They therefore do not become emblems of bestiality but rather of calculated and misguided behavior—in death as in life.

Thus the demonic imagery of otherness that surrounds Quilp inside and out haunts Ralph Nickleby mainly from the outside. On his last night, Nickleby conjures up images of suicide. As he passes a graveyard, he recalls being a juryman for a *felo-de-se*, remembers the look of the corpse, and then sees a macabre, hump-backed figure performing what looks like a dance of death. For a while he becomes softened, but a vision of crippled Smike on his deathbed rekindles his hatred of Nicholas Nickleby. When he looks about—and inside—for a devil to help him out of his frenzy, only the image of the suicide appears. And Ralph Nickleby, who could have converted himself into a better man as Scrooge does, instead transforms himself into a dead man. As Nickleby prepares to hang himself, he is addressed by voices on the other side of the door. When he answers, the outsiders do not at all recognize his voice, " 'That's not Mr. Nickleby's voice surely,' was the rejoinder. It was not like it, but it was Ralph Nickleby who spoke,"[17] says Dickens's narrator. The voice belongs to a living man who has already pledged himself to death—to Ralph Nickleby as other. Nickleby has sealed his fate by internalizing the suicide that so haunted his memory.

Haunted suicides, who like Nickleby are plagued by phantoms of the self, appear with some regularity in Dickens, but they abound in the fiction of the Irish writer Joseph Sheridan Le Fanu. Dickens himself was fascinated by the work of Le Fanu and printed Le Fanu's "Green Tea" in his periodical, *All the Year Round* (1869). Dickens's correspondence regarding that publication is itself of interest. Convinced that Le Fanu was an expert on "spectral illusions" because of the writer's passages on Swedenborgianism, Dickens requested that Le Fanu send on to Madame de la Rue all possible information about such illusions. One of Dickens's friends, Madame de la Rue had suffered from spectres for thirty to forty years, and Dickens had already tried mesmerism as a cure. Le Fanu's own haunted figures are, however, not women but male aristocrats like Varney. Tormented by grotesque hallucinations and personifications of evil in the form of various others—ghosts, spectral monkeys, or other preternatural beings—ultimately they are driven to their deaths. Here once again their phantoms seem to be aspects of the self displaced and imagined as things or people outside the self. Some seem palpable, witnessed by people other than those they haunt, while others only manifest themselves to the haunted. All are equally destructive.

In Le Fanu's "The Fortunes of Sir Robert Ardagh" (written 1838–

40), for example, Ardagh is plagued by a foreign valet named Jacque, known to Ardagh's servants as "Jack the devil":

This man's personal appearance was, to say the least of it, extremely odd; he was low in stature; and this defect was enhanced by a distortion of the spine, so considerable as almost to amount to a hunch; his features, too, had all that sharpness and sickliness of hue which generally accompany deformity; he wore his hair, which was black as soot, in heavy neglected ringlets about his shoulders, and always without powder—a peculiarity in those days. There was something unpleasant, too, in the circumstance that he never raised his eyes to meet those of another; this fact was often cited as a proof of his being something not quite right, and said to result not from the timidity which is supposed in most cases to induce this habit, but from a consciousness that his eye possessed a power which, if exhibited, would betray a supernatural origin.[18]

Like Dickens's deformed Quilp, black Jacque delights in the distress of others. When Ardagh's son and heir is stillborn, the valet chuckles with merriment. Nevertheless, Ardagh is deeply attached to Jacque and treats him as a second self; "His commands are mine" (*PP*, 28), Ardagh tells another servant. Eventually, Jacque leaves the household, much to the relief of all but Sir Robert himself. From the day of his departure, Ardagh sinks into apathy, becoming more and more indifferent and abstracted. Bit by bit, he declines into death, or so goes the second version of Sir Robert's story, "authenticated by human testimony" (*PP*, 22).

"The Fortunes" is actually a twice-told tale. In the first version, Le Fanu recounts "tradition" (*PP*, 21) and credits Sir Robert with a much more violent end. This version views Ardagh himself as a "*dark* man . . . morose, reserved and ill-tempered" (*PP*, 15). As time wears on, Ardagh withdraws and is heard to argue with himself, becoming agitated and pacing about wildly. During these occurrences, he manifests what Le Fanu calls "paroxysms of apparent lunacy" (*PP*, 17). Finally, a foreign stranger comes to the house and Ardagh desperately protests his admittance. Sir Robert is heard wrestling with someone or something on the ledge of a precipice outside his door and is found dead at the foot of that precipice, "with hardly a vestige of a limb or feature left distinguishable" (*PP*, 21). In death he has lost the physically distinguishing marks of humanity.

The double telling of this tale and the mystery surrounding the circumstances of death cast doubt as to just what has happened to Ardagh. So does the careful distancing of the tale in the past. It is hard to get hold of facts here, but this seems to be Le Fanu's point. Apparent suicides are all mysteries, especially as to cause; in Le Fanu's words from

Willing to Die, suicide is both "the maddest and most mysterious of crimes." With all cases of *felonia-de-se* murderer and murdered are one, and both are always inaccessible. Thus with every suicide something unsettling occurs. Inquests hold no final answers, only conjectures. Explanations are wanted but can never be authoritative. Even suicide notes can be fictions, written by persons who may have been beside themselves. Le Fanu draws upon all this doubtfulness. In positing mysterious others who echo looks or behavior—doubles who may stand for the suicide both as victim and as self-murderer—he metaphorically separates murderers from murdered and feeds Victorian fears and uncertainties about death by suicide. Was Ardagh insane? Was he really a suicide? Was he a terrible sinner? Was he pursued and tormented by a dark stranger, or by himself? Did he conceal a dreadful secret of some sort? What indeed drives a man to his death? Le Fanu's readers are left with these awful questions but with no certain truths. Whether it is traditional or "authenticated," no narration will fully illuminate Le Fanu's dark world of suicide.

Le Fanu would re-emphasize this in his next tales of self-murder. In "A Chapter in the History of a Tyrone Family" (1839), his young heroine and primary narrator is wholly unable to decode the mystery of her husband's death. Found with his throat slit—a more obvious self-murderer than Ardagh—Lord Glenfallen has taken his secrets with him to the grave. Possibly Glenfallen was a bigamist, as Charlotte Brontë's Rochester would be, but unlike *Jane Eyre* this story affords no surprise brother-in-law from Jamaica to recount the past and set the record straight. If guilt over helping to frame and incarcerate the woman who may have been the first Lady Glenfallen has driven Glenfallen to madness and suicide, no one will ever know. Even his current young wife is at a loss to say. "All, then, was over; I was never to learn the history of whose termination I had been so deeply and so tragically involved," she sadly confesses.

In line with his penchant to rework the mysteries that absorbed him, Le Fanu retells this young woman's story thirty years later as *The Wyvern Mystery* (1860). Similarly, he would recast "Some Account of the Latter Days of the Honorable Richard Marston of Dunoran" (1848) as three separate works of fiction: "Some Account," "The Evil Guest," (1851) and *A Lost Name* (1868). And he would later rewrite "The Watcher" (1847) as "The Familiar" (1872). Critics of Le Fanu have contended that he revamped these stories because plotting came hard for him.[19] Surely he was also deepening a connection between the mystery of suicide and the inscrutability of the haunted minds of its victims. As he himself had said of the relentless pursuit in "The Watcher," "however the truth may be, as to the origin and motives of this mysterious persecution, there can be no doubt that, with respect to the agencies by which it was accomplished, absolute and impenetrable mystery is like to prevail until the day of doom."[20]

"The Watcher" is in several ways typical of Le Fanu's stories of suicide. Its protagonist, Captain Barton, prides himself on his rationalism, declaring that he is "an utter disbeliever in what are usually termed preternatural agencies" (*GS*, 13) but knows all the same that he is pursued by the hollow sound of footsteps. A friend also notices that he is trailed by an odd-looking foreigner with a menacing, "almost maniacal" mein (*GS*, 20). Barton fears yet shrugs off his pursuer, attributing his fear to overwork. But as time wears on, Barton wears down, though his watcher does not. Now subject to "blue devils"—defined in Le Fanu's day as despondency or hypochondriac melancholy—Barton finds that his mind has turned in upon itself. The pursuer becomes an "apparition" (*GS*, 29) to him. Deeply disturbed, Barton consults both a clergyman and a high-ranking army officer about his plight. While the cleric tells him that he is his "own tormenter" (*GS*, 35), the general good-naturedly offers to "collar the ghost" (*GS*, 40) and free his friend.

The man of the cloth unfortunately proves to have been right: Barton's only freedom will come with death, his ultimate release from self-torment. Like Ardagh and many suicides he loses hope and *joie de vivre*, becoming uncannily tranquil. He looks for a last encounter with his demon, is heard to scream out piercingly in agony, and is found dead. In a kind of a postscript or coda to his tale, we discover that eight years previously Barton had formed a guilty attachment to a girl whom he ill-treated and who subsequently died of a broken heart. Barton's blue devils, then, are avengers of that earlier death, and no rationalizing, no uninformed members of the establishment in the guise of doctors, preachers, or military men have the power to stop them. Barton ultimately falls victim to his own past.

Such is the fate of all of the murderers among Le Fanu's suicides. In *Checkmate* (1871), one-time murderer Yelland Mace goes so far as to have his face rebuilt to suit what he hopes will be a new life and new name, Walter Longcluse. But the spectre of Mace haunts Longcluse, who becomes weary of himself. In the fictional world of Le Fanu, whatever a man's visage or name, his past cannot be eluded or denied; it is encoded within him. Thus changes in aspect or prospect, as when he moves to England, are insufficient to save Mace/Longcluse, who eventually poisons himself in despair. Anxious somehow to be transformed but incapable of inner conversion, Mace/Longcluse resorts to the most desperate of all remedies.

About this checkmated man, there is something pitiful and vulnerable. About Silas Ruthvyn in *Uncle Silas* (1864), there is little to pity. Silas is the dark alter ego of Austin Ruthvyn, a double to his own brother. When that brother dies and his daughter, Maud, is sent to live with Silas, Le Fanu unfolds a shocking mystery of character. Along with young Maud Ruthvyn, Le Fanu's narrator, we wonder: who is Silas, what is he? Slowly we find that he is anything but holy, fair, and wise, although at first he appears to be all three. Silas is himself the ghost of a man. Sealed off in a world of laudanum and Swedenborgian visions, he seems like a spectre to his niece:

> Uncle Silas was always before me; the voice so silvery for an old man—so *preternaturally* soft; the manners so sweet, so gentle; the aspect, smiling, suffering, *spectral*. It was no longer a shadow; I had now seen him in the flesh. But after all, was he more than a shadow to me? When I closed my eyes I saw him before me still, in *necromantic* black, ashy with a pallour on which I looked with fear and pain, a face so dazzlingly pale, and those hollow, fiery, awful eyes! It sometimes seemed as if the curtain opened, and I had seen a *ghost*.[21]

Silas is self-haunted, but he also is ruthless, as his name might imply. Having murdered once, he is willing to murder again—this time his young niece. Saved by her wits, Maud lives to retell her story and to try to unravel the riddle of her own haunter, Silas, "Child of the Sphinx" (*US*, 116).

Yet even in the end, Silas eludes both Maud and her readers. He appears to die from an overdose of laudanum which his inquest determines to have been "accidentally administered by himself" (*US*, 423). But Silas is an expert in dosages and unlikely to have taken too much or too little. Had even Uncle Silas had enough of evil, enough of life? Here once again, suicide is unprovable. In discussing mystery novels, Patrick Brantlinger has observed that they are paradoxical because they "conclude in ways that liquidate mystery: they are not finally mysterious at all."[22] This could never be said of a novel like *Uncle Silas*, where we believe Silas's murder victim to have been a suicide until close to the novel's end; where the people of the novel have certified that same man self-murdered for years; and where the riddle of Silas Ruthvyn's own death remains.

In Le Fanu's suicides so far discussed, what is missing are the inner reflections of the victims. There are no suicide notes, no shared confidences. But in the Doctor Hesselius stories from *In a Glass Darkly* (1872), something quite different occurs. Hesselius's assistant, in "Mr. Justice Harbottle," has seen an important paper in the Judge's own handwriting and has access to one of Harbottle's own "dreams," which brings the reader much closer to the world of the haunted. The dream is fraught with both the ghostly presences of Harbottle's severely judged and hanged victims and a huge "dilated effigy" of the judge himself—Chief Justice Two-fold, "an image of Mr. Justice Harbottle, at least double his size, and with all his fierce colouring, and his ferocity of eye and visage enhanced awfully."[23] Harbottle's dream world has thus split his tormenters into two groups, a set of externalized others and an alter ego, larger than life; and Le Fanu's art has led us directly through the dark door of Harbottle's nightmare. This second, surrealistic judge condemns Harbottle to die for his crimes in a month's time and leaves him with four weeks of "blue devils" and desperate rationalizations before he is found hanging from the banister at the top of his own staircase and pronounced *felo-de-se* by his coroner's jury.

In the ghost stories of *In A Glass Darkly*, Le Fanu becomes far more cautious in attributing causes for suicide. There is no coda discussing Harbottle's guilt, no overhearing of melodramatic death throes. There is only mention of "medical evidence to show that in his atrabilious state it was quite in the cards that he might have made away with himself" (*IGD*, 298). Despite Harbottle's injustices and despite this medical jargon, here the motives and mystery of suicide have deepened, and this is even more true in the case of the Reverend Mr. Jennings in "Green Tea." Jennings is the only one of Le Fanu's suicides who is a good man with no apparent guilt or reason to kill himself. He is not indifferent to others, nor ruthless, lecherous, or full of arrogant rationalism. He seems to need no self-punishment. All the same he is the most relentlessly haunted of all the suicides, and his is also the most carefully documented of the stories of self-destruction. Hesselius is not only a recorder here but the tale's inner narrator and an actor in the drama as well; and Jennings himself is also a painstaking and minute observer and revealer of his tormenter, his environs, and his own inner states.

Jennings's story is an odd one. A man of the cloth, he has few bad habits, though for a time he had been addicted to drinking strong green tea. Four years earlier he had begun working hard on a study of religious metaphysics of the ancients, all the while indulging heavily in the tea, but at the same time had never found existence so pleasant. Suddenly, however, when sitting in an omnibus, he is astonished to catch sight of a small, black monkey with reddish glowing eyes. At first he believes it to be real, but when he pokes at it with his umbrella, the nub seems to pass right through the animal. Horror grows as Jennings's relationship with this apparition moves through what Hesselius documents in three stages. First Jennings considers the monkey as a manifestation of disease. Next he believes it hellish. Finally he hears it "singing through"[24] his head, urging him to crime and self-destruction. By the time he consults Hesselius, Jennings verges on total despair. Hesselius nevertheless assures him of a cure, remarking that he has had a great success rate with similar cases. Jennings is simply to summon Hesselius the very instant that the apparition reappears. Inevitably the monkey does return, but when it does, Hesselius is sequestered, ironically, working on the Jennings case. And by the time Hesselius gets to Jennings, the minister has slit his own throat in desperation.

In its bare outline, this story is mysterious enough, but when one tries to fathom just why poor Jennings is the victim here, it becomes even more so. How to account for the appearance to such a decent man of a leering, malignant, black monkey with a red aura? Le Fanu gives a number of explanations, none very satisfactory. First and foremost, there is the Swedenborgian insight into the case. In an effort to understand his plight, Jennings has been reading Swedenborg's *Arcana Celestia*. According to Swedenborg, evil spirits from hell can inhabit the world of humankind for a time. When they do so, they are no longer in infernal torment but reside in the thoughts and affection of the person with whom they associate. In this situation they appear as "correspondences" to what they are in the eyes of their infernal associates, and take "the shape of the beast (*fera*) which represents [the] particular lust and life, in aspect dire and atrocious" (*IGD*, 31) of their human associates.

If the monkey is a representative of Jennings's lust and life—a Swedenborgian or pre-Freudian manifestation of his darker side, a kind of Dorian Gray portrait—there is little evidence in "Green Tea" that Jennings has merited such an incubus. His only vices seem to have been green tea and ancient metaphysics, and he has wholly given up the tea. The vision of the monkey is not drug-induced. It could, however, be guilt-induced, and Le Fanu's Swedenborg also says that the man in consort with spirits must be a man in good faith, "continually protected by the Lord" (*IGD*, 29). In retrospect Jennings admits that the pursuit of ancient metaphysics is "not good for the mind—Christian mind" (*IGD*, 46–7). Possibly he felt guilt over his delight in paganism; certainly the monkey begins its torments in church, squatting on his open book so that Jennings cannot read to his congregation, and in the second phase constantly interrupting his prayers. But Jennings persists with prayers and clerical responsibilities; we never see him give over attempts at communication with a Christian God. If apostasy is Jennings's crime, Le Fanu is not eager to make this evident, although Victorian readers of "Green Tea" would surely have been prepared for a link between religious doubts and suicide. Daily and weekly papers and the *Annual Register* were full of suicides attributed to "religious melancholy." Jennings, however, exhibits something more than the usual melancholic symptoms of doubt and depression. He lives in utter horror of his peculiar, red-ringed monkey.

Medical explanations for Jennings's condition and death are even less satisfying. There are three doctors involved in his case, and all three fail him. Before consulting Hesselius, Jennings has seen a Dr. Harley, whom he classifies as "a paralytic mind, an interest half dead . . . a *mere* materialist" (*IGD*, 36). Clearly the eminent Harley has little belief in the monkey. Hesselius, however, has Jennings's confidence because his medicine is of another order. Himself influenced by Swedenborg, Hesselius believes that there are sometimes human insights that move one from the material to the spiritual world. Through a rending of the veil, for a time "the mortal and immortal prematurely make acquaintance" (*IGD*, 89). In consulting Hesselius, whose writings he has read, Jennings comes self-diagnosed. He likes the Swedenborgian insight into his problem but nevertheless deliberately seeks out a medical practitioner rather than turning to Swedenborg's own solution of God's protection. Unfortunately, Hesselius proves less than in control of his healer's art. He is a careless empiricist, a derelict in duty, and a very materialistic spiritualist. He begins with a "theory" about Jennings even before he hears out the man's case; then he fails to be accessible at the very moment when his patient needs him. In the end his great disappointment comes not when he loses Jennings the man, but when he loses Jennings the case. Full of hubris and denial, he feels cheated because he has not had a chance to make Jennings his fifty-eighth success story in the business of sealing a patient's inner eye. All that was needed, he believes, was a treatment of the fluid in our bodies, which we hold in common with spirits. Since green tea opened Jennings's inner eye, something as simple as eau de cologne might have closed it. Ironically, these absurdly material assumptions become the most profound ones that the great Doctor Hesselius can offer. They are carefully prefaced and edited by yet another, younger doctor who is translating Hesselius's most striking case histories with reverential interest.

In his and Le Fanu's final paragrah, Hesselius totally divorces himself from Jennings. According to Hesselius, Jennings was not really one of his failures because he was never really one of his patients. Hesselius had not begun a cure, and just as well. For what Jennings finally succumbed to, decides Hesselius, was not after all the open inner eye but "hereditary suicidal mania," a grand Victorian catch-all, killer of FitzRoy of the H.M.S. *Beagle* and numerous less eminent Victorians—

a kind of Victorian original sin. So while Hesselius and his editor wind up looking irresponsible and foolish, Le Fanu's readers continue puzzled over the eerie monkey and haunted clergyman. Which returns them again to the nagging questions: Why would a man, happily going about his business, quite suddenly be plagued by a spectral monkey? Is the beast a symbol of lust? of the mysterious jungle? of the more mysterious East? Or is it a primitive ancestor of humankind? And, more importantly, why would such a monkey drive a man to take his life? Like Hesselius's answers to it, the last question begins to seem more than a little absurd.

Certainly Le Fanu must have meant it to be. As Jack Sullivan says of "Green Tea," "the strange power of the tale lies in the irony that something intrinsically ridiculous can drive a man to destroy himself."[25] Here Le Fanu reveals the tenuousness of all human life, its susceptibility to sudden, unsuspected—and seemingly pointless—alterations, and the Victorians' and our own limitations in coping with such alterations. We linger over "Green Tea" because the story of Jennings is Le Fanu's most deeply troubling story and the spectre of the monkey is his most deeply disturbing spectre. As we hear his anxious recountings to Hesselius, we feel for this tormented man. Jennings is not a decadent aristocrat, not a xenophobe, or a murderer, or a representative of a heartless professional class like Harbottle or even Hesselius. Jennings seems an Everyman, even a superior man, whose intellect and decency are unable to save him from his bogey. Blue devils, green tea, hereditary insanity, religious melancholy—Le Fanu offers no satisfying explanation for Jennings's complaint. His disease reflects Victorian unease and feeds our own discomfort as we ponder what it really is that causes a person not to want to live. In an era drenched in *Aberglaube* (Arnold's "extra" beliefs "beyond what is certain and verifiable"[26]) and bathed in a certain "*Nachshein* of Christianity"[27] that withholds men like Teufelsdröckh and Carlyle from suicide, a lurid monkey may in fact have seemed a fitting symbol for an inexplicable will to die. And a ghost story—mysterious and equally inexplicable—must have seemed the perfect medium for conveying the ultimate mystery of suicide.

Le Fanu's mysteries are also Victorian fantasies, fulfilling Todorov's definition of the fantastic as "that hesitation experienced by a person who knows only the laws of nature confronting an apparently supernatural event."[28] They posit, but they hesitate to confirm, spiritual other selves. Like Dickens's pairings of sentimental and suicidal characters and deaths, they flirt with surrogation or doubling—in Jennings's case with a fictional version of autoscopic doubling. In autoscopy, an individual hallucinates a second self, whether through anxiety, fatigue, drugs, or psychosis.[29] Such surrogation can be distinguished from dissociation, a more dramatic type of doubling represented in Robert Louis Stevenson's *The Strange Case of Dr. Jekyll and Mr. Hyde* (1886). Jekyll and Hyde are like a dual personality, a single entity dissociated into two. They have become what Otto Rank calls opposing selves. According to Rank, the double in primitive societies is conceived of as a shadow, representing both the living person and the dead. This shadow survives the self, insuring immortality and thus functioning as a kind of guardian angel. In modern civilizations, however, the shadow becomes an omen of death to the self-conscious person. Doubles become opposites and demons rather than guardian angels.[30] This is particularly true in inhibited or self-restrained modern societies like that of Victorian Britain.

In *Dr. Jekyll and Mr. Hyde*, Hyde thus becomes Jekyll's demonic, monstrous self. Certainly Stevenson presents him as such from the outset. Hissing as he speaks, Hyde has "a kind of black sneering coolness . . . like Satan."[31] He also strikes those who witness him as being deformed—"pale and dwarfish" (*SC*, 40) and simian-like. He is both monster and shadow *par excellence*—another self not only for Jekyll but for all the presumably upright Victorian bachelors of the story who perceive his deformities and for whom he becomes both devil and death knell. *The Strange Case* unfolds with the search by these men to uncover the secret of Hyde. As the narrator/lawyer, Utterson, says, "If he be Mr. Hyde . . . I shall be Mr. Seek" (*SC*, 38), and so will they all. Utterson begins his quest with a cursory search for his own demons. Fearing for Jekyll because the good doctor has so strangely altered his will in favor of Hyde, Utterson examines his own conscience, "and the lawyer, scared by the thought, brooded a while in his own past, groping in all the corners of memory, lest by chance some Jack-in-the-Box of an old iniquity should leap to light there" (*SC*, 42). Like so many eminent Victorians, Utterson lives a mildly double life and feels mildly apprehensive about it. An ugly dwarf like Hyde may jump out from his own boxed self, but for him such an unlikely creature is still envisioned as a toy. Although, from the beginning Hyde fills him with a distaste for life (*SC*, 41), not until the final, fatal night, after he storms the cabinet, can Utterson conceive of the enormity of Jekyll's second self. Only then does he realize that "he was looking on the body of a self-destroyer" (*SC*, 70); Jekyll and Hyde are one in death as they must have been in life.

Poole, Jekyll's servant, and Lanyan, his medical colleague, are even more incredulous. When Poole sees Jekyll/Hyde in his final form, he thinks he sees his master with a "mask" on his face: "that thing was not my master and there's the truth" (*SC*, 66). Again, Poole's "thing" is monkey-like and dwarfish, and it weeps "like a woman or a lost soul" (*SC*, 69). When Poole and Utterson hear Jekyll on the opposite side of the door that last night, they react like Ralph Nickleby's would-be rescuers. The voice they hear sounds like something "other," not like the peson they know. Lanyan, alas, never survives to that final night. An earlier party to the knowledge that Jekyll and Hyde are one, he has already lost his life to that secret. A man who believes in rationalism and moral rectitude, Lanyan simply cannot adapt to the truths uncovered in the revelation of Hyde: improbability and "utter moral turpitude" (*SC*, 80). He sinks slowly into death, his body following the lead of his "sickened" soul. His too is a kind of suicide, a death permitted, if not willed. Lanyan simply cannot accommodate himself to the horror of Jekyll unveiled.

And neither can Jekyll himself, who is a suicide, as his name indicates ("*Je*" for the French "I"; "kyll" for "kill"). His double is killing him even in the early stages of their association, when he believes that he can with impunity rid himself of Hyde at any time. Initially, Jekyll does not care whether or not Hyde survives: "I cannot say that I care what becomes of Hyde; I am quite done with him" (*SC*, 52). But as his opposing selves prove inextricably bound, Jekyll becomes "careless" of life itself (*SC*, 97). He knows he risks death in taking his drug, but he does so quite deliberately. If not uppermost in his mind, suicide lurks there all the same. Jekyll often uses telling language, words like "I had come to a fatal cross roads" (*SC*, 85). Yet his Hyde-self totally fears death. As Jekyll becomes "occupied by one thought: the horror of my other self" (*SC*, 95), he simultaneously delights in realizing he has the power of death over Hyde. On the other hand, Jekyll is fascinated by Hyde's "wonderful" love of life and remarks, "when I know how he fears my power to cut him off by suicide, I find it in my heart to pity him" (*SC*, 96). These vacillations continue until the cabinet door is forced—and with it Jekyll/Hyde's nearly involuntary suicide.

Through Jekyll/Hyde's equivocal attitudes toward self-murder, Stevenson leaves the mystery of his tale in place, much as Le Fanu did. Because all of Stevenson's characters are wanting in self-knowledge, they ultimately fail to understand the links between duality, demons, and death. Stevenson's readers are therefore forced to try to solve the mystery of the strange case. More than Le Fanu, however, Stevenson leads us in this attempt. For even *in extremis*, his Jekyll fears exposure more than death. This is why he finally kills himself when the door is forced. Hyde must be hidden if it takes death to hide him, and Jekyll must ultimately be his own murderer to avoid full disclosure of the duality. Here Stevenson is not only revealing human nature's deeply intertwined double nature; he is also castigating Victorian hypocrisy. The kind of double life that characters in this book lead is not only false but suicidal. As Stevenson says in his essay "Lay Morals": "We should not live alternately with our opposing tendencies in continual see-saw of passion and disgust, but seek some path on which the tendencies shall no longer oppose, but serve each other to common end."[32] To behave otherwise, his tale implies, is to court the death of authenticity, the loss of one's self. If altruism and bestiality are both embedded in human nature, one must not only know this rationally as did Jekyll, but must live comfortably with this knowledge.

Many of Stevenson's contemporaries did not live so, nor did they like the link with suicide that Stevenson's story forged. John Addington Symonds wrote Stevenson that one "ought to bring more of distinct belief in the resources of human nature, more faith, more sympathy with our frailty than you have done. . . .The scientific cast of the allegory will act as an incentive to moral self-murder with those who perceive the allegory's profundity."[33] But Stevenson was nonetheless acting as a moralist. His "shilling shocker," conceived in a dream and written in a white heat, captured both his own deepest divisions and insights into the callous folly of late-Victorian hypocrisy. Stevenson had himself considered suicide at least three times and yet persisted through ill health to natural death.[34] Far from counselling "moral self-murder," his dark story of monstrous alter egos was counselling integration. Far from starting another Werther-craze, *Dr. Jekyll and Mr. Hyde* pioneered as a modern admonition of blind, self-destructive behavior. Stevenson's fictional lawyers and scientists show dangerous second sides because they have not persisted in self-knowledge. His fictional workers, like the butler, Poole, see masks in place of the "horrors" that their presumed betters have become because they have opted for distorted vision over clear-sightedness.

In all of these traits they resemble the knights of King Arthur's disintegrating realm in Tennyson's *Idylls of the King* (1857–88). Caught between Arthur's ideals and the realities of human longing and lust most of these characters represent deeply divided people. For Tennyson as for Stevenson, natural man threatened moral and social man. Ideals that aim too high here again lead to hypocrisy and unleash concealed bestiality. Most of the *Idylls* deal with this subject in one way or another, but "Balin and Balan," written in 1885—when Stevenson was also at work on *Jekyll and Hyde*—delves deepest into the devils and doubles that result from misplaced ideals. Its Balin, "the Savage," becomes a near-tragic monster of self-destruction, carrying along with him his own twin brother, Balan.

Like Jekyll, Balin wants to meet the high expectations of his culture. He models himself on Lancelot, chief knight of the Round Table, who seems to move "far beyond him."[35] At the outset of Tennyson's idyll, Balin desires to redeem himself in his own and Arthur's eyes because in anger he had once smitten a churl of Arthur's court. Forgiven by Arthur for his earlier offense, he remains at court to learn courtesy and self-restraint, while his twin rides out to destroy a "demon of the woods," a fiend who "strikes from behind" (*PT*, 128). As he leaves, Balan tells Balin to externalize his own demon, to subdue his violent moods by holding them as "outer fiends" (*PT*, 138), capable of defeat. But Balin doubts himself:

> "Too high this mount of Camelot for me:
> These high-set courtesies are not for me.
> Shall I not rather prove the worse for these?
> Fierier and stormier from restraining, break
> Into some madness even before the Queen?" (*PT*, 221–25)

Balin's self-diagnosis is perceptive. Like Hyde—who "came out roaring" (*SC*, 90) after strong restraining—he will "rather prove the worse" for "high-set courtesies."

What triggers Balin's monstrous bestiality is his discovery of the liaison between Lancelot and Guinevere. Wild to ease his disillusionment, Balin rides out to remove the "demon of the woods." Recalling his brother's advice, he looks for an external monster to kill rather than tearing himself apart with rage. "Savage among savage woods" (*PT*, 479), Balin nevertheless feeds that rage in encounters with Arthur's enemies, who reinforce his anger over the hypocrisy of Lancelot and Guinevere. When a teasing and vicious Vivien completes this disillusionment, Balin screams out a "weird yell / Unearthlier than all shriek of bird or beast" (*PT*, 535–36). With awful irony, Balan hears the shriek and mistakes it for that of the wood-devil he had come to quell. Blindly, the brothers clash and eventually destroy one another.

As Tennyson surely knew, twins like Balin and Balan make perfect doubles. In this case, one is courteous man and one natural man, but like Jekyll/Hyde, they are mortally bound to each other. Thus "Balin and Balan" becomes Tennyson's parable about monstrous other selves who must die. As Rank points out,[36] twins function like the shadow, with the guardian angel—in this case Balan—becoming transformed into an omen of death. Balan knows that his twin/double must kill inner demons, but in counselling him to destroy them as though they were outer fiends, he signs the death warrant for both brothers. Balin himself becomes a demon in his search for the wood-devil and is thus aptly but tragically murdered by a knightly twin who knows how to quell monsters but not how to manage unpredictable brothers.

Of course the brothers together represent divided Victorians. Tennyson, more than Stevenson, was fearful of humankind's bestial instincts. He saw them as far more dangerous than humankind's repressive side. His Tristram, heedless of everything but his own physical desires and natural instincts, is brutally cloven through the head by a betrayed King Mark. Likewise Balan dies at the hand of a beast who is his own angry, subterranean and uncontrollable half. Balin and Tristram signal the end of Arthur's reign, much as Tennyson thought unbridled naturalism and materialism might signal the end of Victoria's. This is why, unlike Stevenson, Tennyson sought to quell monsters through a continued presentation of the ideal. Arthur might pass, might lose both his Round Table and his life to the dark forces within his knights as they "reeled back" to the beast, but without him there would never have been a ray of light in the first place. Tennyson saw that Victorian hypocrisy stemmed from a discrepancy between what human nature could aspire to and what it could accomplish, but he did not hold idealism accountable for a bestiality that bore its own seeds of self-destruction.

By 1891, when he published his *Picture of Dorian Gray*, Oscar Wilde could project a world in which integration is impossible and where all of life's paths lead to self-destruction. As in *Dr. Jekyll and Mr. Hyde*, hypocritical bourgeois culture is beastly dangerous, but so is every alternative to it. If Stevenson's society exhibits fragmented selves, Wilde's reveals a fractured place where everyone is doomed to untimely death. Appropriately, this world of *Dorian Gray* is described as monstrous throughout. Cynical and manipulative Lord Henry sees law and the temptations its repressiveness fosters as "monstrous,"[37] while Dorian perceives his own delight in the altering portrait of him as "monstrous" (*PDG*, 143) and later considers people smitten with "vice and blood and weariness" as "monstrous," too (*PDG*, 161). And artist Basil Hallward, painter of the infamous picture of Dorian Gray, feels the secret of his soul lies in that beautiful portrait but sees in the end that it indeed "has the eyes of a devil" (*PDG*, 174).

Far from being a refuge from brutal reality, then, the sphere of art in this book is also deadly dangerous. Hallward is cruelly murdered by Dorian after he uncovers the secret of the portrait that Dorian has so carefully hidden away (as Jekyll does Hyde). The living Dorian, still looking so like the beautiful, untainted picture that Hallward loves, has gone rotten at the core. In worshipping and depicting Dorian's beauty, Hallward has helped create the monster of his own destruction. He is another suicide, killed by his own misjudgment. And so is actress Sibyl Vane. Living in a theatrical world of make-believe and melodrama, Sibyl cannot accept the reality of Dorian's rejection. When she decides to give up acting for his love, she is shocked at Dorian's callous, "without art you are nothing" (*PDG*, 100), followed by his desertion. Steeped in theatrics, Sibyl commits suicide like Ophelia, not like the Juliet she so hoped she might play to Dorian's Romeo. Yet Sibyl is not a heroine of melodrama, for heroines of melodrama triumph in the end. Sibyl, a victim of art, dies from swallowing prussic acid, her only tribute being the brief record of her inquest and verdict of "death by misadventure" (*PDG*, 139) which is recorded in *St. James's*.

Beautiful but deadly Dorian will drive many such admirers to suicide before he destroys his portrait and himself. A young boy of the guards; Adrian Singleton; Allen Campbell—Dorian's victims are many. To all of them Dorian must have seemed something other than what he was. Yet for a long time double life is a "pleasure" to Dorian, who asks, "is insincerity such a terrible thing? I think not. It is merely a method by which we can multiply our personalities" (*PDG*, 158). Only near his end does he desist from toying with others' lives and then prides himself when he leaves a village girl before destroying her too. Lord Henry teases him with the query, "how do you know that Hetty isn't floating at the present moment in some star-lit mill-pond, with lovely water-lilies round her like Ophelia?" (*PDG*, 233). Dorian, who at last discovers in himself the vestiges of a conscience, resents having any conscience at all, and so projects that conscience into the picture. When he tears at the painting with the very knife that had stabbed Basil Hallward, he is determined to "kill this monstrous soul-life" (*PDG*, 247). Instead he takes on the "withered, wrinkled, and loathsome" (*PDG*, 240) visage of the portrait, emblem of his corrupted soul, and himself dies. Dorian *is* the now hideous portrait; it is his other self.

The ending of this novel was problematical for late Victorian readers. Wilde's odd preface, which reads like an aesthetic's version of Blake's "Proverbs of Hell," warns that "there is no such thing as a moral or an immoral book" (*PDG*, 5) and that "those who read the symbol do so at their peril" (*PDG*, 6). Nevertheless many did read the symbol and wondered whether the book were moral or immoral. Did it say that conscience cannot be denied and that all people who do deny it become self-destroying monsters? And if so, was suicide then justifiable as a kind of self-extermination of evil? Or did it say, as a reviewer for the *Daily Chronicle* surmised, that sensation is all?

Mr. Wilde says his book has a "moral." The "moral," so far as we can collect it, is that man's chief end is to develop his nature to the fullest by "always searching for new sensations," that when the soul gets sick the way to cure it is to deny the senses nothing, for "nothing," says one of Mr. Wilde's characters, Lord Henry Wotton, "can cure the soul but the sense, just as nothing can cure the senses but the soul." Man is half angel and half ape, and Mr. Wilde's book has no real use if it be not to inculcate the "moral" that when you feel yourself becoming too angelic you cannot do better than rush out and make a beast of yourself.[38]

A concerned Wilde reacted to this statement in a letter to the *Chronicle*, published on 2 July. "The real moral of the story," he states, "is that all excess, as well as renunciation, brings its punishment." One of *Punch*'s reviewers, the Baron de Book-Worm, disagreed:

If Oscar intended an allegory, the finish is dreadfully wrong. Does he mean that, by sacrificing his earthly life, Dorian Gray atones for his infernal sins, and so purifies his soul by suicide? "Heavens! I am no preacher," says the Baron, "and perhaps Oscar didn't mean anything at all, except to give us a sensation, to show how like Bulwer Lytton's old-world style he could make his descriptions and his dialogue, and what an easy thing it is to frighten the respectable Mrs. Grundy with a Bogie."[39]

All the same, the bogey was there for the frightening. For Dorian was a monster quite opposite to the benign Elephant Man; he was beautiful on the outside but ugly within. And "ugliness," Wilde's narrator tells us, "was the one reality. The coarse brawl, the loathsome den, the crude violence of disordered life, the very vileness of thief and outcast, were more vivid, in their intense actuality of impression, than all the gracious shapes of art, the dreamy shadows of song" (*PDG*, 206). Like Tennyson's fictional Camelot, Wilde's portrait of *fin de siècle* England is of a land reeling back to the beasts, but with no hope for a second coming of a King Arthur to save it. The fantasy of Dorian Gray's portrait is not a Faustian story of a hero giving up life for knowledge, but a black fairy tale in which a spoiled boy gets his one wish—endless youthfulness and sensuality—and becomes a suicide because he cannot handle its implications. Wilde may have deserved the harsh criticism of his contemporaries, but like other Victorian creators of fictions and fantasies about monstrous selves who will to die, he discerned something deeply disturbing about his own culture. His Hallward, Dickens's Nell, Le Fanu's Jennings, Stevenson's Dr. Jekyll, and Tennyson's Balan all had "a little shadow that went along with them." That shadow was a dark, distorted other self, "a hideous hunchback," to use Matthew Arnold's paraphrase of Dr. Pusey, "seated on [their] shoulders and which was the main business of [their] lives to hate and oppose."[40] Often that subversive hunchback was beckoning them on toward death.

VII

Suicidal Women: Fact or Fiction?

Women were fictionalized and mythologized much as were monsters in Victorian England. They too were made into "others"—weaker vessels or demons, angels in the house or fallen angels[1]—and suicide was displaced to them much as it was to demonic alter egos. For the most part, fictions about women and suicide became more prevalent and seemed more credible than did facts. The facts themselves were clear: throughout the nineteenth century women consistently had a suicide rate lower than that of men.[2] Consistent too were the means of suicide. In most cases, women chose poison or drowning over bloodier deaths by gun or knife, a pattern that continues today. These facts were well-established even before mid-century and were well-confirmed after 1858, when William Farr improved record-keeping for cause of death. Lower incidence among women proved, however, easier to determine than to accept. Despite all evidence to the contrary, most Victorians believed what they wished to believe about the frequency of female suicide.

In the main they did so because they wanted and expected suicide, like madness, to be a "female malady."[3] Since women were statistically over-represented among the mentally ill—primarily because in Victorian England they were more often confined to "homes" for the insane and were more easily countable than were men—they were generally thought to be more vulnerable to madness. The reasoning for linking women and suicide went something like this: more women are confined for insanity than men and suicide is a result of insanity; therefore more women should commit suicide than men.[4] Or else it went like this: woman is a lesser man, a weaker being, both physically and mentally. Resisting suicide takes willpower and courage; therefore women should fall victim to suicidal impulses far more readily than should men. Unless the weaker sex were to be credited with unwanted strength, the fact that women killed themselves less frequently than men required considerable explaining. Such was the price of retaining the displacement of self-destruction to women in a patriarchal society that was dedicated to championing male mental and physical superiority and to rationalizing sexual differences.

Throughout the century, men's explanations for the discrepancy between statistics and expectations centered on what was presumed to be the female disposition. In 1857, writing for the *Westminster Review*, George Henry Lewes attributed the cause for the lower suicide rate among women to women's "greater timidity" and to "their greater power of passive endurance, both of bodily and mental pain."[5] Lewes was echoed in 1880 by a writer for *Blackwood's* who asserted that women were "habitually better behaved and quieter; they have more obedience, more resignation, and a stronger directing sentiment of duty. . . . They possess precisely dispositions of temperament and teaching which best withhold from voluntary death."[6] Female analysts of suicide rates were less likely to make naive pronouncements about female character, but they too felt called upon to explain away the statistics. After observing that "nearly three men commit suicide to one woman," Harriet Martineau concluded that "as there is no such disproportion in the subjects of what we may call natural insanity, we may attribute the majority of male suicides to the habit of men to incur the artificial insanity caused by intemperance."[7] For women's timidity, she simply substituted men's weakness toward another Victorian *bête noir*, the demon bottle.

At century's end, men like S.A.K. Strahan and Havelock Ellis made less generous conjectures about the female temperament and suicide than had Lewes. Strahan believed that women were weaker contenders in the struggle for existence and therefore less prone to its aftereffects—like suicide. For him, their lower suicide rate depended upon woman's "lack of courage and her natural repugnance to personal violence and disfigurement."[8] Female ignobility, not nobility, marked his suppositions. Ellis's similar judgments hinged less on the rate than on the means of suicide. Referring to what he called the "passive" methods of suicide (drowning, for example), Ellis found women temperamentally irresolute in opting for means that required both less preparation and less gore. More violent forms of suicide offended "against women's sense of propriety and their intense horror of making a mess" and reflected their fear of public scrutiny after they were dead. "If it were possible to find an easy method of suicide by which the body could be entirely disposed of," said Ellis, "there would probably be a considerable increase of suicides among women."[9]

Inherent in these observations is an absurd prejudice in favor of bloodier suicides as being braver and therefore more manly. Ellis makes means of suicide so much a point of honor that he begins to glorify self-destruction and loses sight of his real argument about suicide as a "morbid psychic phenomenon." Inherent here too is a more insidious prejudice against women and women's bodies, a male supposition that women must wish to dwindle away to nothing. This is a confirmation of the Victorian ideal of the female self that dissolves into others, much as does Dickens's Esther Summerson in *Bleak House*. Frances Power Cobbe metaphorically described this ideal as exhibited in marriage. It is as though a male tarantula devours a female spider and incorporates the female wholesale into his own being.[10] When the female atomizes into the male, there is simply no longer any "other" to contend with. Cobbe's description can also serve to characterize a state of death-in-life, where there is still a remaining female body, but only a living corpse. In this state, the female's logical end becomes suicide. She is like a child or a mistress who exists but must not be seen, and eventually relinquishes her existence as a confirmation of the way in which she is perceived.[11] The Indian institution of *suttee*, so fascinating to Victorians, well exemplifies this perception of women. The Englishman Ellis certainly posits something similar in his fanciful alternative to accepting the reality of suicide statistics: rates of self-destruction would be much higher for females if women's bodies could disappear along with their sense of self.

The conjectures of Ellis, the famed pioneer sexologist, help confirm the fact that men displace self-loss in sex to women and therefore displace death to them as well. But Ellis did not really deny the statistics; he only wanted them to be otherwise. It took J. W. Horsley, a prison chaplain in the last quarter of the century, to argue resolutely that suicide was predominantly a female crime. Drawing upon his own experience at Clerkenwell Prison dealing with women rescued from suicide attempts and brought to him for "reform," Horsley became convinced that women had a greater propensity to suicide. They were simply less successful in its execution. He contradicted himself, however, when he suggested how easily such intrinsic female suicide might be prevented: "Hysterical girls make demonstrations on the Embankment, and a pail of water over their finery would often be more efficacious a deterrent or cure than the notoriety they gain (or perhaps seek) by apprehension."[12] Horsley's lack of compassion could hardly have been instrumental in "reforming" Clerkenwell's inmates. He himself asserted that hardly five days at the prison went by without sight of a repeated suicide attempt by a woman. With his own callous attitudes, Horsley seemed determined to help substantiate his belief that suicide was beyond a doubt "a specifically female crime."[13]

Ellis and Horsley show the lengths to which intelligent Victorian men could go to continue displacing self-destruction to women. Taken along with theories of passive endurance, their assumptions lead to the heart of a puzzling contradiction. Was women's comparative immunity to the suicidal impulse the result of will-lessness or of willpower? Were women really too weak to commit suicide, or were they morally stronger than men and therefore more courageous in resisting it? If they were simply weak, they better fit Victorian expectations of them. As John Stuart Mill pointed out, women were inculcated to believe "that their ideal of character is the very opposite of that of men, not self-will, and government by self-control, but submission and yielding to the control of others."[14] Such people, sentiment ran, would hardly be bent toward self-destruction, for they lacked the fortitude to kill themselves, much as Ellis and Horsley posited. On the other hand, should they run counter to both statistics and expectation, their inherent weakness was at fault. In either of these cases, they proved baser, lesser beings. But what if they were in fact stronger than men in withstanding suicide? This alternative was by far the more troubling one for Victorians—so troubling that more fallacious reasoning was concocted to explain it away. Argument was diverted from the courage not to die and from the female sense of duty to those "self-willed" women who opted for death. Late in the century, Ellis tried unsuccessfully to prove that the growing number of women whose working lives most resembled men's were more prone to suicide, but he had to admit that women's tendency to suicide versus men's was continually decreasing. Others had been even less generous to women. The famous case of Mary Brough, who slit the throats of her six children and then unsuccessfully tried to kill herself in the same way, raised enormous hostility—more because of Brough's "long-indulged self-will" than because of the child murders. Brough was reported to have been an unfaithful wife who became deranged as a result of her immoral life; her insanity was consequently "self-created."[15] To most Victorians, self-will, Carlyle's first line of defense against suicide, was unnatural in woman—an indication that something was radically wrong. Charles Kingsley, for example, disliked Tennyson's Princess Ida because of her "self-willed and proud longing to unsex herself." She had substituted "her own self-will" for "the womanhood which God [had] given her." As a result she was "all but a vengeful fury, with all of the peculiar faults of a woman and none of the peculiar excellences of man."[16]

Women with willpower struck a different chord with women writers. When Anna Jameson wrote about Cleopatra in her book on Shakespeare's heroines, her imagination thrilled to the "idea of this frail, timid, wayward woman dying with heroism from the mere force of passion and will."[17] Women also looked askance at the timidity that allowed other women simply to dwindle away to death. In *Shirley*,

Charlotte Brontë's Mary Cave dies by starvation for love and significance rather as the anorectic Nightingale nearly did. Her death may be a suppressed rebellion, but it is clearly cautionary. In this sort of rebellion, the woman dies in order to become noticed or missed. In *Shirley*, young Caroline Helstone, the love-starved niece, must learn to read Mary Cave's lesson and live. Brontë's own sympathy lay more with Frances Henri in *The Professor*, who scorned voluntary death in the hope that she would "have the courage to live out every throe of anguish fate assigned me."[18] Later in the century, Victoria Crosse (Vivian Corey) took on Grant Allen's *The Woman Who Did* (1895) in her *The Woman Who Didn't* (1895). Allen had described a broken, fallen heroine who initiates suicide by taking prussic acid and then arranges herself on a bed with white roses at her breast. Crosse's heroine, Euridyce, lives on and employs willpower to endure a loveless marriage and defy premature death.

Despite the insights of such women writers, the image of woman as the strong-willed, "vengeful fury" better approaches the dominant Victorian view of female willfulness and suicide because it begins to make myth of willful womanhood.[19] A decade and a half after Kingsley wrote about Ida, a male writer for the *Westminster Review* (1865) sketched in the image of the fury. She was the new woman abroad, one who possessed "not only the velvet, but the claws of the tiger." She was "no longer the Angel, but the Devil in the House." With her in mind, this writer reframed an old proverb to read, "man proposes, woman disposes."[20] This sentiment was virtually paraphrased by the painter Edward Burne-Jones, who said of woman: "Once she gets the upper hand and flaunts, she's the devil—there's no other word for it, she's the devil . . . as soon as you've taken pity on her she's no longer to be pitied. You're the one to be pitied then."[21] And so she-wolves grew in place of pet dogs. Monstrous women represented female energy bristling with will, whereas male monsters like Hyde depicted masculine energy dispossessed of will. Even when they disposed of themselves, such women were insidiously dangerous because they then threatened the very being of males who were their counterparts in willpower. Ever "vengeful," these monstrous women suggested that willpower was a way into, not out of, self-destruction. They began to displace displacement and needed to be mythologized endlessly in efforts to distance them. Fear of Mary Brough's sexuality and of her anger caused her rebirth in the press and in the popular mind as an utterly appalling miscreation. Fear of Bertha Rochester's female loss of control caused the fictional Rochester in *Jane Eyre* to lock her up like an animal, to dehumanize her into the ultimate monster she became until she set fire to her cage-like home, destroying both herself and, for a time, the will of Rochester in the bargain. A broken man, the once potent Rochester could only be restored by the intuition and ministration of Jane.

Making monsters of women was not only the pastime of the press or of novelists during the nineteenth century. Criminologists like Cesare Lombroso, an Italian who was widely admired in England, included women in their theories of evolutionary regression or atavism. For Lombroso, criminals became a manifestation of such atavism; they were less evolved beings, closer to other primates than were most people. And because women were already lesser beings than men, female criminals were the most atavistic of all. In *The Female Offender* (1893), Lombroso discussed woman's hysteria, hand and facial anomalies, lunacy, tattoos, and of course suicides. To his mind, female offenders were appallingly dangerous because in them piety and maternalism were missing. In their place were "strong passions and intensely erotic tendencies, much muscular strength and a superior intelligence for the conception and execution of evil." To Lombroso "it was clear that the innocuous semi-criminal present in the normal woman," had in these women been "transformed into a born criminal more terrible than any man." His "criminal woman is consequently a monster."[22] Lombroso also believed that women were less impelled to suicide than were men because they felt pain less. When thwarted in love, however, their monstrously passionate natures leapt to the fore, so that far more than men, women in love turned into self-destructives.

Lombroso reached an English soil well prepared for his coming. Nevertheless liberals like Mill and feminists like Cobbe had earlier raised voices of protest against such dehumanizing of women. In *On the Subjection of Women* (1869), Mill questioned the right of men "to worship their own will as such a grand thing that it is actually the law for another rational being."[23] Absolute domestic tyrants were for him "absolute monsters"; lesser tyrants, more the rule in Victorian England, were "savages," "little higher than brutes."[24] Mill thus found more primitiveness in men than in women. So did Cobbe, who also thought that to treat woman, who "has affections, a moral nature, a religious sentiment, an immortal soul . . . as a mere animal link in the chain of life" was itself "monstrous."[25] These two earlier writers helped stand the myth of atavistic womanhood on its head. Later, Oscar Wilde would further invert and deflate it. In *The Importance of Being Earnest* (1895), Jack says of Lady Bracknell, "she is a monster, without being a myth, which is rather unfair."[26]

But it was not necessary to treat women as fiends in order to distance them from men. Other myths about their nature would serve equally well, especially when it came to suicide. When suicidal women were not feared as willful Medusas, they were usually disdained or pitied as the yearning lovelorn. They displayed that second-class will so often projected upon them. If men had been their main reason to exist, one important supposition went, losing them meant indifference to life. Of all the constructs about women and self-destruction, this one had the deepest hold on the Victorian imagination for the longest time. A catalogue listing all works of art on this subject would have to run on for pages. Domestic melodrama snatched dozens of jilted women from the jaws of suicide, while broadsheet after broadsheet sensationalized their plight. Ophelias and Crazy Janes, madwomen frenzied for want of their lovers,[27] haunted the pages of Christmas books and annuals. In *Forget-Me-Not: A Christmas and New Year's Present for 1827*, the orphaned Ida is abandoned by her higher-born beloved, Osmond, in favor of a wealthier bride. Poor Ida gazes on Osmond's nuptial pride and turns her "lone footsteps to the shore." "A plunge was heard—a dying groan— / A bubble in the moonbeam shone; / A light form rose, then sunk again, / And Ida slept beneath the main."[28] The strength of Ida's stereotype would be confirmed by Victorian coroner's juries like Margaret Moyes's, that would ask: "Was this dead woman crossed in love?"

Ida and her jilted sisters—both real and imagined—were often sympathetic figures, victims of men who were superior to them in status, power, or physical strength, and the source of sympathy for them very often lay in male perceptions of female honor. Many believed with De Quincey that "there is no man who in his heart would not reverence a woman that chose to die rather than to be dishonoured."[29] But deserted women who committed suicide did so not only out of bereavement. Many were seduced as well as abandoned. They killed themselves rather than face the shame of "falling," for fallen women immediately gained new willpower in Victorian eyes. Sinful creatures now considered responsible for their own destinies, they became blameable for their wrong choices.[30] If they lived on, as most did both in Victorian literature and in actuality, they might either become prostitutes or else atone for their sin through good works, through death-in-life, or through some untimely demise. Ruined Hetty Sorrel in George Eliot's popular *Adam Bede* (1859), for instance, became an infanticide. After killing her illegitimate offspring, she was punished for her fall by a sentence of hanging—later commuted to transportation but followed by an early death. More common than infanticide for the women who fell was a further fall into prostitution. In *Household Words* (1853) Dickens tells of "case number fifty-four" at the Home for Homeless Women who "had stayed out late one night, in company with a 'commissioner' whom she had known abroad, was afraid or ashamed to go home, and so went wrong."[31] The Home itself was an attempt to counter such prostitution. Established in the late 1840s by a group of women, it set out to find work for young women who had "already lost their character and lapsed into guilt" or to lend an opportunity to "fly" from the "crime" of prostitution.[32] In literature more than in life, losing character did mean losing life. William Acton's classic study of prostitution pointed out that prostitutes did not have a high rate of suicide.[33] In popular poetry like William Bell Scott's "Rosabell," however, when the woman "goes wrong," she before long develops the scornful laugh of the street-walker. People like Scott's narrator can then only moan: "Descent is easy: stage to stage / Facile, they say, and swift, alas."[34] The usual end of such an archetypal fall was self-destruction. Scott's poem concludes with a fatal prophecy for such women: "And every lamp on every street / Shall light their wet feet down to death."

Fallen women were considered deadly to more than just themselves. Scott's Rosabell was led astray not only by her male lover but by the already hardened Joan. Unfallen Victorian women, like those who established the Home for Homeless Women, had to be careful to avoid the taint of the fallen. In discussing the importance of Ladies Committees to female penitentiaries, John Armstrong saw both pros and cons for their existence. Ladies could show requisite pity for their sisters, but it might not be "advisable for pure minded women to put themselves in the way of such a knowledge of evil as must be learned in dealing with the fallen members of their sex."[35] Moreover, the taint from an actual fall could cling to middle-class or even upper-class women for the rest of their lives, another stigma widely illustrated in Victorian literature. In Arthur Wing Pinero's *The Second Mrs. Tanqueray* (1893), Paula, the cynical second wife of Aubrey Tanqueray, is much beloved by her husband but resented by his daughter, Ellean. By an odd quirk of fate, the daughter falls in love with a former lover of the second Mrs. Tanqueray. To save Ellean from that lover, Paula tells Aubrey of her own affair but then refuses to save herself. She had once revealed to Aubrey that she would have killed herself had they ever parted, but now commits suicide rather than live with his and Ellean's knowledge of her past. Similarly in Dickens's *Bleak House* (1852–53), after her illegitimate liaison is discovered, Lady Dedlock wanders on to self-induced death by exposure, a fitting metaphor for the revelation of her fall.

Paula Tanqueray and Honoria Dedlock die willingly but only after attempts to live down a deeply internalized sense of descent. Other women in Victorian literature choose death-in-life after a self-perceived fall. They live disheartened, suicidal lives that confirm what they feel friends or society must think of them. Marian Erle in *Aurora Leigh* (1856) becomes a living dead person twice in Barrett Browning's poem. First she flees home to avoid falling victim to a neighboring squire, running until she drops, and then she feels "dead and safe."[36] Years later she is more severely victimized. Drugged and raped, not "seduced" says she, but "simply murdered" (*AL*, 223), she becomes pregnant but indifferent to her own life. "I'm dead," she admits. "And if to save the child from death as well / The mother in me has survived the rest / Why that's God's miracle you must not tax,— / I'm not less dead for that" (*AL*, 224). Marian is only restored by the ministrations of another woman, Aurora Leigh. Less revivable is Dahlia Fleming in George Meredith's *Rhoda Fleming* (1865), one of the most profound Victorian studies of living death after sexual fall. Dahlia and Rhoda are the two flower-like daughters of a dead, garden-loving mother. Beautiful, natural, and naive, Dahlia goes to the city, is seduced by Edward Blancove, the worldling son of a banker, and when he deserts her, she evades her family. She is about to marry a ruffian when she is discovered by Rhoda's suitor. Morally strong but blindly unaware of the dangers of supposedly correct behavior, Rhoda is willing to see Dahlia married off after her fall because it will make her respectable again. Only very slowly does Rhoda realize that acts like marrying off are what constitute immorality. Meanwhile, Dahlia dies to life as had Marian Earle. Unable really to accept anything but Edward, she maddens, unsuccessfully attempts suicide, and then succumbs to *tedium vitae*. Eventually Edward decides he will indeed have her, but by then she has deadened to him as well.

Central to Meredith's portrayal of Dahlia is others' misapprehension of her deathlike indifference. It begins while Edward is still present, on the night when he will leave her. Dahlia, again like Marian Erle, directly states that she is dead, but Edward counters her statement with baby talk. Meredith brilliantly reads both sides of the gulf between his characters. Edward thinks of Dahlia as a child, a will-less, lesser being, and so feeds her child's talk. But Dahlia is love-starved, not weak, and resents this gibberish "as not the food she for a moment requires."[37] It sickens her and in turn disgusts Edward, who is about to go out to his club for dinner. Intuiting Dahlia's feelings, Edward glances at the real plate of food that Dahlia is about to have and muses to himself that the "potatoes looked as if they had committed suicide in their own stream" (*WGM*, 100). First realizing, then denying, the growing compassion he suddenly feels for Dahlia, he rationalizes that no person of character could knowingly sit down to a meal like Dahlia's, and he abruptly leaves. Much like Edward, Rhoda too lives on the opposite side of the abyss from Dahlia, who after Edward's abandonment becomes like one

John Everett Millais, *Ophelia* (1851–52).

of the damned. This new Dahlia, who does "not wish to live but cannot die" (*WGM*, 381), puzzles Rhoda, who "had imagined agony, tears, despair, but not the spectral change, the burnt out look" (*WGM*, 380). The sisterly gulf is finally bridged, but like Hetty Sorrel, Dahlia lives for only a few years and then only as a kind of nurse to Rhoda's children. Her heart in "ashes" except regarding her nieces and nephews, Dahlia dies uttering the words, "Help poor girls" (*WGM*, 499). These final words of the book, an 1886 revision of the 1865 text, leave Meredith's reader recalling Dahlia's will to die more than Rhoda's new fecundity and corrected moral vision. In 1865, the story had ended with Edward's wondering whether Dahlia's ultimate independence from him meant that she was a greater or lesser being than before—with his trying, as it were, to fit her into a new mythology. Dahlia's last words refocussed the novel as a plea to alleviate women's pain.

Earlier in *Rhoda Fleming*, Meredith had Dahlia imagine "that perchance if she refrained from striving against the current, and if she suffered her body to be borne along, God would be more merciful" (*WGM*, 382). What Dahlia envisioned here is another female-associated type of death, dissolution into a body of water. Suicide by drowning, a common route for those women who did take their own lives, was the way most visual artists and many writers of the Victorian era imagined female suicide. It was as though women drowned in their own tears, or returned to the water of the womb, or, as Freud believed, were delivered of a child [38] when they made their final retreat into water. Fallen women thus drowned in grief or in conjunction with childbearing, both of which were associated with their state and with female fluids in general. In Victorian literature, many fallen women openly acknowledged this affinity with water. Fronting the river, Martha Endell in *David Copperfield* exclaims, "I know it's like me! . . . I know I belong to it. I know that it's the natural company of such as I am!"[39] Martha's creator, Charles Dickens, certainly seems to agree. Nancy in his *Oliver Twist* also feels destined to drown. "How many times," she ponders, "do you read of such as I who spring into the tide. . . . It may be years hence, or it may be only months, but I shall come to that at last."[40] And in "Wapping Workhouse" from *The Uncommercial Traveller*, Dickens's narrator, looking down into dirty water from a swing bridge, hears of women "always a headerin' down here,"[41] down to the water.

If Dickens presented a phalanx of fallen women moving toward the Thames, Thomas Hood preferred to focus on only one. In his enormously popular and influential "Bridge of Sighs" (1844), Hood, who had been moved by Mary Furley's suicide attempt and trial for infanticide, determined to write about "Waterloo and its suicides."[42] Hood's poem opens by presenting "One more Unfortunate, / Weary of breath, / Rashly importunate, / Gone to her death." Basically, the poem is an impassioned plea for charity toward this homeless, "lost" woman, and predictably, men like Horsley found it too soft. For Horsley "it tinged suicide with a halo of romance, and afforded a justification of cowardice and crime to the unreasoning and hysterical."[43] Nevertheless its strong sentiment deeply stirred most Victorian consciences. Hood's unfortunate is described with great tenderness. As she is brought up dead from the water, the poet sings her a merciful kind of dirge:

> Touch her not scornfully;
> Think of her mournfully,
> Gently and humanly;
> Not of the stains of her
> All that remains of her
> Now is pure womanly. (*SP*, 15–20)

Once she is plucked from the river, Hood sees her as washed clean of her sins, in effect baptized by the Thames. Yet kindly as Hood is toward his "unfortunate," one can hardly miss an underlying message that the only good prostitute is a dead prostitute:

> Make no deep scrutiny
> Into her mutiny
> Rash and undutiful:
> Past all dishonour
> Death has left on her
> Only the beautiful. (*SP*, 21–26)

This poor woman has been willful, but has been punished and bathed into attractiveness by the river—left clean, limp, will-less, but dead.

Like the famous Victorian painting of *Ophelia* (1851–52) by John Everett Millais, Hood's poem on his unfortunate's death has a quietude and beauty that belies its subject. And like many Victorians, both Hood and Millais had Shakespeare's flower bedecked corpse in mind when they thought of the suicides of jilted, fallen, or mad women. Recall Wilde's Lord Henry teasing Dorian Gray by suggesting that his Hetty might be floating in a mill-pond with water-lilies all around her. Such Ophelias became a phenomenon in Victorian England. Elaine Showalter has uncovered the fact that asylum superintendents with cameras actually dressed up inmates in Ophelia-like costumes in order to get "authentic" photos of the phenomenon. Then art, trying to imitate life, which was really imitating art, sent stage actresses to the asylums to study the crazy Ophelias there. Showalter believes that "the figure of Ophelia eventually set the style for female insanity."[44] Certainly Hood was fascinated by the image when he selected "Drown'd! drown'd" from *Hamlet* as the epigraph for "The Bridge of Sighs." Hood's epigraph in turn was chosen by Abraham Solomon as the title for a painting that he exhibited at the Royal Academy in 1860. Solomon's representation, now extant only in a lithographic reproduction, features yet another woman pulled out of the water from beneath Waterloo Bridge. A waterman with grappling hook stands nearby, and a woman folds the dead girl in her arms. Other lookers-on in this visual narrative remain more indifferent, and Solomon seems to be relaying the same overt message as Hood: "Londoners, learn to show more compassion!" Interestingly, a reviewer for *The Athenaeum* (12 May 1860) directly compared Solomon with Hood and found Solomon lacking because his drowned female was not beautiful like Hood's:

> What respect does not Hood pay to the beauty of the fallen! how singularly felicitous are the epithets throughout! how he dwells upon the natural inci-

Gustav Doré, *The Bridge of Sighs*.

George Frederic Watts, *Found Drowned* (ca. 1848–50).

dents of the suicide, forming a background, as it were, full of living nature, to his picture in words! We may be sure that had the brush been the exponent of Hood's wise-heartedness, he would never have neglected to show, with all possible fidelity, the awful stillness of the dawn looking down upon the climax of guilt, confident as he must have been that by painting Nature alone could he do her justice.

The contrast between loveliness in death and guilt in life, between will-lessness and willingness, was what the Victorians wanted to see in art about suicidal women. It amounted to a kind of necrophilia.

In the visual arts, the Thames and its bridges came to represent the end of the line for such desperate women. For two decades after the publication of Hood's poem, artists like Solomon rendered women as dead or about to die on the banks or bridges of London's central river. Gustav Doré's *The Bridge of Sighs*, with its darkened arc of a bridge, forlorn female figure, and hulking church dome, epitomizes these works. From 1848 to 1850, George Frederic Watts worked on *Found Drowned*, a portrait of a woman washed up by the tides under Waterloo Bridge, her body laid out in the form of a cross. Then came Phiz's illustration for *David Copperfield* (1849–50) entitled "The River." It

Hablôt K. Browne, *The River*, illustration for Charles Dickens's *David Copperfield* (1849–50).

shows Martha Endell staring out into her kindred river, one toe already in the water, with a ruined vessel jutting out behind her and St. Paul's dome in the background. And the third and last painting of Augustus Egg's series *Past and Present* (1858) would depict the adulterous wife wrapped in a shawl, with the thin, small legs of her illegitimate child protruding out from under it. She stares at the moon from underneath the Adelphi Arches near Waterloo Bridge. If the tide is out for the moment, it will not be for long; the woman's beloved moon will see to that. Meanwhile she awaits death by resting under a poster bearing the word "VICTIMS."

In each of these pictures, arches or arcs frame the women. Even Phiz's etching, which is free of bridges, has an arched sky at its upper edge. The same is true of Paul Delaroche's *The Christian Martyr*, an 1855 French painting of a drowned woman floating with a life-ring drifting beside her, placed on the canvas like a halo above her head. Above her, too, the heavens are opening. This popular painting passed into British hands in 1866 and was hailed as the French *Ophelia*.[45] *Ophelia*, of course, was also framed with an arched upper edge, suggesting that arcs were a convention for rendering drowned, female suicides in the visual arts.

Augustus Leopold Egg, *Past and Present, no. 3, Despair* (1858).

They might have been chosen as reminiscent of religious altar paintings, by association purifying weaker vessels, much as did Hood's poem. Certainly Delaroche's work demands such an interpretation. Or they might have functioned as subtle reminders of eggs or of the womb, enclosing women in symbols of their beginnings, their power, or their fall. They also serve to distance the viewer from the suicides, replicating proscenium-arched stage sets and reinforcing the drama of suicide. Whatever their other functions, they certainly helped draw attention to women, water, and death.

A second image that saw a series of visual representations during the Victorian period was that of women plunging through the air from a height. The woodcuts of deaths from the Monument—with Margaret Moyes dropping like a lead weight or with her counterpart in the 1841

Paul de La Roche, *The Christian Martyr* (1855).

suicide flying with arms outstretched, skirts billowing, and collar uplifted like wings—became prototypes for a number of graphics, mostly associated with popular literature. Reynolds's *Mysteries of London* (1844–46) was illustrated with a young woman fleeing from the embraces of a royal "personage" and leaping into space. Her arms fan out in a ballet-like gesture of entreaty, and her skirts fly like a parachute. In 1848, George Cruikshank etched a now famous flying woman for his series *The Drunkard's Children* and entitled it "The Poor Girl Homeless, Friendless, Deserted, Destitute, and Gin-Mad, Commits Self-Murder." His scene combines pathos with brilliance and bridge arcs with flying. Cruikshank's young woman's body bends upward at the middle, virtually reversing the arch of the bridge in its unwillingness to die. As she falls, the Drunkard's Daughter covers her eyes, and her hat trails her skirt and hair, which almost touch one another as she arches her back. Two onlookers, a horrified man and impassive woman, peer over the edge of the bridge. This powerful rendering yielded a host of imitations, particularly as illustrations for melodramas.[46] Act I, Scene 6 of *After Dark* (1868) was provided with a woodcut reminiscent of Cruikshank, Egg, and Doré, all three. In it young Eliza drops from Blackfriars Bridge and flies like a witch across the moon, but with hands held up to the sides of her head in despair. The perspective from under the arching bridge is like Egg's in *Past and Present*, *no. 3*, but here a St. Paul's prominent on the horizon and a gibbet-like bridge-support looming up on the right both cry out in condemnation of the girl's rash action. Closer to Cruikshank was an 1886 cover illustration for Charles Selby's melodrama, *London by Night* (1844), a production that actually tried to incorporate a scene dramatizing Cruikshank's Drunkard's Daughter. The illustration repeats Cruikshank's scene but with only one onlooker and a nearly vertical woman. Here once again the arms are outstretched in flight, but this young person is trailed by a cape and looks rather like an angelic superwoman.

All these images of airborne women bear a message different from the Victorian Ophelias. These women are not deadened or will-less. Their soaring is—for a moment—an act of autonomy or self-assertion. Symbolically, flying signifies raising oneself, both in terms of status and in terms of morality. In her plunge, Reynolds's heroine is trying to escape compromise. The others, shown flying rather than falling, are choosing the course of their own descent. They are kindred to Lady Cecilia Harborough in Reynolds's *Mysteries*, who, thinking of the Monument, had theorized that "from the river I might be rescued; but no human power can snatch me from death during a fall from that dizzy height."[47] If these figures confirm "fallen" woman's status, they also convey determination. And probably because of their imminent deaths, Victorians made momentary heroines rather than monsters of these women. They were not associated with witches, those legendary fliers who are always considered willful and dangerous. Witch flights represent magical powers, and judges in witchcraft trials presupposed the reality of their flying.[48] But in Victorian flights like Eliza's from Blackfriars, men look on in horror rather than anger, hailing rather than impaling the young Eliza. In the case of these doomed Victorian fliers, sentiment won out over fear.

Repeated representations of women and water and women and flight confirmed the statistical knowledge of female means of suicide. Ellis points out that women chose falls from heights twice as often as did men.[49] Yet the profusion of images also helped perpetuate the inaccurate myth of frequency of female suicide,[50] another myth that women writers strove to counter. In literature by women of all classes, female characters most often lived on past suicidal urges and pointless atonements. Charlotte Brontë certainly took Elizabeth Gaskell to task for killing off her heroine in *Ruth* (1853). After a long and heroic struggle to respectability and self-reliance, Ruth dies of a fever contracted while nursing her one-time seducer back to health. To Gaskell, Brontë vehemently protested what seemed a needless sacrifice. "Why Should she die? . . . And yet you must follow the impulse of your own inspiration. If *that* commands the slaying of the victim, no bystander has a right to put his hand to stay the sacrificial knife, but I hold you a stern priestess in these matters."[51] Brontë's own protagonists live on, sometimes against great odds like those faced by Lucy Snowe in *Villette*. So does Lady Blessington's Clara Mordaunt in *The Governess* (1839). After her father's suicide, Clara survives, but with "a dark cloud" over her past and a "shadow" over her future.[52] And so do George Eliot's fearful, weak Hetty and gentle, Zionist Mirah. These well-known characters had powerful counterparts in lesser-known works of fiction about working women. Nelly, in Sarah Whitehead's two-volume novel, *Nelly Armstrong* (1853), works as a maid in Edinburgh, becomes pregnant, loses her job and then her baby, despairs, but refuses to kill herself because she hopes for a heavenly reunion with the child. Another Nelly, the sister of Lucy Dean in Eliza Meteyard's "Lucy Dean; the Noble Needlewoman" (1850),[53] has an illegitimate child and is deeply distressed but goes off to Australia instead of off of a bridge.

When not busy saving their heroines, women writers also denied myths about female suicides by turning the tables and depicting male suicides—including male self-sacrifices and men made miserable by liaison or love. Charlotte Brontë refused to banish Jane Eyre to exhaus-

The Leap from the Window, illustration for G.W.M. Reynolds's *Mysteries of the Courts of London*, n.s. 2 (1849–56): 25.

tion and death as a missionary in India, but Brontë's St. John Rivers meets such an end. So does Mary Augusta Ward's Robert Elsmere, who consumes his existence in self-sacrifice for others in the novel named after him (1888). Frances Trollope, in *Jessie Phillips: A Tale of the Present Day* (1843), destroys the male as well as the female in an illegitimate partnership. Young Jessie, a beautiful seamstress, is seduced and abandoned by wealthy Frederic Dalton. Dalton leaves her to a fate that includes childbirth, a workhouse, a coma, and a trial for an infanticide committed by Dalton. Worn out, Jessie eventually dies a natural death,

George Cruikshank, *The Drunkard's Children*, "The Poor Girl Homeless, Friendless, Deserted, Destitute, and Gin-Mad Commits Self-Murder" (1848).

LONDON BY NIGHT.

A DRAMA, IN TWO ACTS.

BY CHARLES SELBY.

First Produced at the Strand Theatre, January, 11th, 1844.

Cover illustration for Charles Selby's *London by Night*, Dick's Standard Plays, no. 721 (1886).

but Dalton commits suicide by throwing himself into a raging stream; Trollope uses water to punish her villain, not to bear off her heroine. With a different intent, Elizabeth Gaskell sends one of her male characters to the Thames to drown. This poor man, a sailor in "The Manchester Marriage" (1858), returns to England after a long absence. Presuming him dead, his wife has remarried. Unbeknownst to the wife, a nursemaid has allowed the long-lost man into the house to see his child, born while he was away. He prays next to the child's bed and afterwards flings himself into the Thames in a gesture of grief and self-sacrifice over the wife's new happiness. Although his wife never learns of all this, the second husband does and becomes a more thoughtful man as a result. Here Gaskell leaves the woman entirely free of the taint of suicide, which is used both as a symbol of male grief and as an admonishment urging male growth.

How unmanly such male suicides for love must have seemed to some Victorians becomes clear when one recalls Gilbert and Sullivan's *Mikado* (1885). There masculine suicidal lovelornness is spoofed in "Titwillow," sung by Ko-Ko, the Lord High Executioner of Titipu. Ko-Ko first hears the sound "titwillow" burst from a sad, suicidal "Dicky-bird" whose "willow, titwillow" echoes from his "suicide's grave" under a "billowy wave." Ko-Ko then croons his own "Titwillow" to the elderly Katisha:

> Now I feel just as sure as I'm sure that my name
> Isn't Willow, titwillow, titwillow,
> That 'twas blighted affection that made him exclaim,
> "Oh, willow, titwillow, titwillow!"
> And if you remain callous and obdurate, I
> Shall perish as he did, and you will know why,
> Though I probably shall not exclaim as I die,
> "Oh, willow, titwillow, titwillow!"[54]

If women writers showed less robust humor than Gilbert and Sullivan toward men dying for love, it may have been because they had in mind the fates of women trying to cope after male self-murders. Most men did not die lovelorn, but as we know, more men were pronounced *felo-de-se* than were women. The consequences were often both bitter loneliness and utter destitution for female survivors, even if confiscation did not occur. Early in the century, Harriet Cope's four-part poem, *Suicide* (1815),[55] looked into three instances of women suffering after suicides—Chatterton's bereft mother; a young wife who in her shame and grief over her husband's suicide begins to ignore her child; and a young unmarried woman whose father forbids her marriage, whose

Eliza's attempted suicide, illustration for Dion Boucicault's *After Dark; A Tale of London Life* (1868).

lover then kills himself, and who considers suicide herself but has a vision of God warning her against self-murder. Imagined scenarios like Cope's dealt mainly with bereavement, but economic deprivation equally stunned the actual survivors of suicides. An 1825 family letter, written by a woman in London to a step-son in America from whom she had not heard for twenty-two years, tells a tale worthy of Brontë or Dickens. Ten years earlier, Ann Jewett's husband had become a debtor. He was taken off to Fleet Prison and from there on to Bedlam, where he ended his own life in despair. Left destitute, Ann had lived on minimal parochial aid and on the few shillings she could get by plying her needle. At fifty-nine, however, she wrote to her step-son saying that she was still grateful to have learned sewing years before in convent school, but that her eyes were now failing her as was her subsistence. The letter is not a plea for financial help from a long-lost son nor a statement fraught with self-pity, but rather a moving assessment of the way things were, coupled with a contrasting look at the past. Ann ached for her old father who "brought her up with greatest tenderness," and wondered what he would feel if he should "rise from his grave" to see her at age fifty-nine.[56]

Ann Jewett's letter brings us back to the painful reality behind the statistics of suicide, much as the deaths or suicide attempts of real women can bring us back to the reality behind the myths. Beliefs about women and suicide were ingrained in women as well as men—so ingrained that some women opted to live them out. Mary Wollstonecraft had once, when deserted by a lover, filled her pockets with lead and tried to drown herself. Nina Auerbach sees George Eliot's *Mill on the Floss* as a mythic expression of Eliot's obsession with Wollstonecraft's attempt to live and die the myth of abandonment.[57] And for most of her married life Thackeray's wife Isabella lived hidden away, almost like a madwoman in the attic—much to Charlotte Brontë's embarrassment when she found out about Isabella only after dedicating *Jane Eyre* to her greatly admired Thackeray. Isabella made repeated attempts on her own life, all graphically described in Thackeray's letters to his mother. On an 1840 steamship voyage to Ireland, says Thackeray, "the poor thing flung herself into the water (from the water-closet) & was twenty minutes floating in the sea, before the ship's boat even *saw* her. O my God what a dream it is! I hardly believe it now I write. She was found floating on her back, paddling with her hands, and had never sunk at all."[58] Having failed as the distracted, drowned Ophelia, the next night Isabella again tried to die. Thackeray says he then tied "a riband round her waist, & to my waist, and this always woke me if she moved."[59] The novelist's descriptions move one to compassion for him, poor "Titmarsh," who asked himself "O Titmarsh Titmarsh why did you marry?"[60] But they move one to even greater concern over the miserable Isabella, a confused Victorian woman, but hardly a heroine from *Hamlet*.

Wollstonecraft outlived the myth of suicide-by-drowning only to die later in childbirth; while poor Isabella Thackeray subsisted in various private asylums only to outlive Thackeray by thirty years. The novelist lamented in 1848 that the institutionalized "poor little wife of mine . . . does not care for anything but her dinner and her glass of porter."[61] Isabella indeed became a timid, childlike ghost of a person, an enduring but will-less Bertha Mason. On the other hand, Elizabeth Siddal, who suffered the ignominies of chill and cramp when posing in a bathtub for Millais's *Ophelia* and who came to represent the enduring image of Ophelia-madness after mid-century, succeeded in killing herself. Known to us almost exclusively through others' eyes, Siddal is a difficult person to grasp. A milliner discovered by the Pre-Raphaelite brothers and frequently used as a model by Rossetti, Siddal is the woman whose eyes Christina Rossetti saw looking out from so many a Rossetti canvas. On canvas, Siddal became part of the Rossetti myth, the saintly angelic woman or, after her marriage to Rossetti, the silent mysterious icon. In both cases, she was envisioned by her paramour as "other," a figment of his Victorian woman-worship, rather than a living partner. This artistic mythologizing seems to have entered the very lives of Siddal and Rossetti, but Siddal had difficulty living out a romanticized ideal with a man who was so often unfaithful, moody, and inattentive. Throughout their long engagement, Siddal gained Rossetti's attention through illness and talk of impending death. She wanted to appear mortal, not merely to be immortalized in paint. After the Rossettis' marriage, Siddal's illnesses continued, as did veiled suicide threats. In Brighton with her sister Lyddy, trying to recover her health, Siddal wrote to Rossetti that "I should like to have my water-colours sent down if possible, as I am quite destitute of all means of keeping myself alive. I have kept myself alive hitherto by going out to sea in the smallest boat I can find."[62]

All this suicidal misery was compounded when Siddal gave birth to a stillborn daughter. For months afterwards she would sit by the fire, rocking and staring at the empty cradle. Georgina Burne-Jones believed that Siddal "looked like Gabriel's *Ophelia* when she cried with a kind of soft wildness"[63] by the childless cradle. So often represented as Ophelia, Siddal seems finally to have become obsessed with Ophelia's lot, to have decided to live—and die—a fiction. Like her husband, she both painted and wrote poetry, the latter haunted by images of watery death. In her "A Year and a Day," the poem's persona reviews a dreamlike life and imagines a scene that all but recreates Millais's painting in words:

> Dim phantoms of an unknown ill
>   Float through my tiring brain:
> The unformed visions of my life
>   Pass by in ghostly train;
> Some pause to touch me on the cheek,
>   Some scatter tears like rain.

The river ever running down
    Between its grassy bed,
The voices of a thousand birds
    That clang above my head,
Shall bring to me a sadder dream
    When this sad dream is dead.[64]

All dreams ended for Siddal on 10 February 1862, when, retreating to her room after a dinner out with Swinburne and Rossetti, she emptied a laudanum phial. After a few hours of labored breathing, Elizabeth Siddal Rossetti relinquished dead dreams and entered the ranks of the dead.

VIII

Century's End: "The Coming Universal Wish Not to Live"

"*Men everywhere* are becoming more weary of the burden of life,"[1] wrote an essayist for the *Contemporary Review* in 1881. By the last quarter of the nineteenth century, simply being alive had become a severe trial to many. Hopelessness beset the dispossessed and sensitive alike, and vitality seemed to be eroding away with the century. Men, especially, seemed to find it harder to displace anxiety and death. They felt out of control, powerless against the force of their own inventions—runaway science, runaway technology, runaway urbanism. Lost and homeless in an alien universe, the articulate among them spun eloquent metaphors to define their plight. Looking back to the 1870s and 1880s, Havelock Ellis recalled that he "had the feeling that the universe was represented as a sort of factory filled by an inextricable web of wheels and looms and flying shuttles, in a deafening din. That, it seemed, was the world as the most competent scientific authorities declared it to be made. It was a world I was prepared to accept and yet a world in which, I felt, I could only wander restlessly, an ignorant and homeless child."[2] John Ruskin in 1884 found that "harmony is now broken, and broken the world round: fragments, indeed, of what existed still exist, and hours of what is past still return; but month by month the darkness gains upon the day, and the ashes of the antipodes glare through the night."[3] A disillusioned Arthur Balfour referred to human life as "an accident, [man's] story a brief and transitory episode in the life of one of the meanest of the planets."[4] And Francis Adams's hero in *A Child of the Age* (1884; 1894) seems to have spoken both for his creator and for his age when he exclaimed:

> "Was I *never* to have rest, peace, comfort, self-sufficiency, call it what you please,—that spiritual sailing with spread canvas before a full and unvarying wind? *Why was it, why?* Was it really because the strange shadow of Purposelessness is played the perpetual-rising Banquo at Life's feast for me? . . . I didn't know, I didn't know! I wished I were dead."[5]

Adams made good his own and his hero's wish when he killed himself in 1893. By century's end, with everything else in flux and with death harder to distance, suicide seemed more often courted and was more often condoned.

Throughout the Victorian era, compassion for suicides and for their families had certainly grown. Late in the century, coroner's juries most often brought in verdicts of "temporary insanity" in cases of suicide. In an 1885 pamphlet, *The Right to Die*, T. O. Bonser asked for two things from his contemporaries: "(1) A legalization of suicide in extreme cases. (2) A mitigation of the harsh prejudice with which it is regarded."[6] Many Victorians were on the way to granting both of these requests in Bonser's day. By 1870 public opinion about suicide had already liberalized sufficiently to allow for the abolition of forfeiture, and the bodies of suicides were no longer sent to anatomy classes for dissection. Then in 1879 and 1882 came two further legal revisions. Suicide was no longer classed as homicide, so that the maximum sentence for attempted suicide would be reduced to just two years; and suicides were at last granted the right of burial in daylight hours, although the clergy were to decide on the question of allowing Christian rites. Also by the last quarter of the century, public records and statistics on suicide were far more reliable than they had ever been, so that more suicides were recorded and rates seemed higher. W. Knighton's 1881 article "Suicidal Mania" drew upon Morselli's statistics to show how much more common suicide was becoming, "not in England only, but all over the civilized world."[7] The implications of this seemingly indisputable statement were beginning to gnaw at the Victorians, and throughout the latter part of the century, essays in periodicals began to speculate as to just what this increase meant in terms of Victorian civilization and ethics.

One of the most comprehensive of these essays on suicide appeared in *Blackwood's* in June of 1880.[8] Called simply "Suicide," it aimed to explain the increase in self-destruction by correlating the suicide rate with changes in the quality of life. In it, the interests of the statisticians were reviewed—incidence of suicide, method of self-destruction, and the influence of climate and culture—but the author was far more interested in just what it was about his era that caused the frequency shown in the statistics. He found that the intensity of agitation and disillusionment over life had made suicide appear like an antidote, "an outburst of the universal appetite for calm; because every man who wilfully terminates his life does so, necessarily, with the idea of improving his condition."[9] He also speculated that the growth of cities had led to more suicide, for there was, said the author, a greater sense of solitude in cities than in smaller towns and also "more misery and more despondency, with less encouragement of restraint."[10] Like many another writer who would enter what became a Victorian debate about suicide, this anonymous author also doubted that morals without religion would ever be sufficient deterrents to suicide.

This type of concern had become the crux of the most heated argument over suicide to occur in the last quarter of the century, and nowhere was more heat generated in this controversy than in the pages of *Nineteenth Century*. Edited by Tennyson's friend James Knowles, this periodical sponsored several symposia on questions of belief.[11] Then, in September of 1877, it printed an article that posed the ultimate question: "Is Life Worth Living?" The author W. H. Mallock, a young Oxford graduate, approached his question by directly attacking atheists. To his mind modern atheism was grounded in research, experiment, and proof. Its god was Nature, an immoral god incapable of correcting the malaise of the age or enspiriting humankind with a sense of morality or of life's meaning. This became the heart of his argument: Could such contemporary secularism give contemporary human beings "something worth living for, some goal to work towards when the very notions of a God and a future life have left us, and have evapourated even out of our imaginations"?[12] Mallock's answer was that it could not, since its morality was founded upon a vague sense of human betterment rather than upon time-tested doctrine.

Mallock's views were soon challenged, again in the pages of *Nineteenth Century*. In the December 1879 issue, L. S. Bevington concluded a two-part essay, "Modern Atheism and Mr. Mallock," in which she vehemently defended the secular morality that he had attacked. "So far as human life is worth living," she argued, "so far is it worth protecting. So far as it is not worth living, so far is it needful to ameliorate it. Duty, on secular principles, consists in the summarized conduct conducive to the *permanent protection* and *progressive amelioration of* the human lot."[13] Bevington doubted both Mallock's logic and his heart. She could not be convinced that what she called "the felt value of life" was dependent upon believing that life would last forever, and she would not be convinced that any belief in life's worth could come from reasoned demonstrations of morality such as Mallock's. Bevington believed that secular moralists like George Eliot, whom Mallock denigrated, based their ethics in feeling and compassion, not in dogma or argumentation. Such social thinkers would do what they could to improve the human condition on earth. If religion was in fact losing its hold on the nineteenth century, then "Religion's foster-child, Society, must eventually learn to trust her own two feet of civil and moral law, and run alone."[14] It was of course this sort of positivism that had originally goaded Mallock into writing his own article. So the wheel turned round and round in the late 1870s. The suicide rate appeared to be up, and no one really knew why—except that something fearful was undermining even the will to live.

By 1880, Victorian artists too felt both the pervasiveness of suicidal mania and the weight of hopelessness. No longer could poets like Tennyson as readily subdue their dream-worlds to the call of duty or action. Now one of their tasks was to describe both the empty universe and the psyches of those who were deterministically caught in its grip. Mid-Victorian morality had slipped into a void, with its religious groundwork washed out from under it. In November of 1881, Tennyson published a dark dramatic monologue, "Despair," in which he "hypothesized the feelings of a would-be suicide in the latter half of our nineteenth century."[15] Narrated by the would-be suicide himself, this melodramatic poem depicts total disillusionment with life, hope, God, and the promise of an afterlife. Both the narrator and his wife have attempted self-destruction by walking into the sea. Although the wife has been drowned, the narrator has been rescued by a minister of the Calvinistic sect to which the couple had once stoutly belonged. Before their suicide attempt, the two had become thoroughly desperate over their loss of faith and hope and as thoroughly contemptuous of the Calvinism that they believed had led them to their pass. Tennyson's narrator castigates the minister for having saved him, fiercely and directly asserting his right to die to a world so harsh and comfortless.

This grim tale was based on an account taken from a newspaper and suggested to Tennyson by Mary Gladstone, and it was just the sort of subject to attract Tennyson at this time. Sir Charles Tennyson tells us that late in 1881 the Laureate was deeply depressed—both personally and morally.[16] He had recently suffered profoundly over the loss of James Spedding, a friend from his Cambridge days, and had been affected, too, by the deaths of Dean Stanley and Carlyle. He had consequently been brooding over questions of death and immortality. In 1881 he went so far as to join in the founding of the Society of Psychical Research, hoping for, but not finding, clues to the secret of life after death. Meanwhile he too felt bleak over what he thought were a growing loss of faith and a tendency toward evil in the world; what was needed, he deduced, was the advocacy of feeling and spirit over against both rationalism and darkness. Yet the dramatic monologue that flowed from the Laureate's pen in late 1881 was ambiguous, not reaffirming. In "Despair," Tennyson's narrator is weak and self-pitying, so that the reader is invited to condemn both his viewpoint and his attempt at suicide. Like Tennyson, however, this narrator is deeply affected by the ills of his day so that he also gains the sympathy of the reader.

We do not know whether Tennyson had read and pondered Bevington's 1879 essay before writing "Despair," or James Thomson's powerful *City of Dreadful Night* (1870–74), which appeared in volume-form for the first time in 1880. But Thomson's long poem shows the same concern with suicide and the meaning of life in a godless world as do Mallock's and Bevington's essays and Tennyson's poem. Thomson's narrator poses the question that is posed by the essayists: "When Faith and Love and Hope are dead indeed, / Can Life still live? By what doth it proceed?"[17] His answer is that it does not proceed. Thomson's Necessity suggests that " 'if you would not this poor life fulfill, / Lo, you are free to end it when you will, / Without the fear of waking after death' " (*PW*, 14.767–69). Here, as in Tennyson's poem and in so much late Victorian literature, the universe is a vast stranger, an abyss dotted with widely separated stars. In such a universe, a river like the Thames begins to seem like a refuge, much as does the salty sea in Tennyson's "Despair." This "River of the Suicides" beckons humans to "perish from their suffering surely thus, / For none beholding them attempts to save, / He may seek refuge in the selfsame wave" (*PW*, 19.971–74). Indifference to all but the death-wish devours those who people the City of Dreadful Night. The English despair of the 1870s and 1880s had found one of its most despondent voices in James Thomson, and self-destruction was on its way to becoming a central metaphor for *fin de siècle* England.

Suicide took on the status of trope quite readily. Discussion of self-destruction, so much more open by the end of the century, had become an important form of social criticism as suicide was more directly related to the evils of the day. According to the Reverend J. Gurnhill in 1900, "the causes which lead to suicide are many of them of a social character, that is, they take their rise in the unsatisfactory condition of those social problems, whether industrial, civil, or domestic, on the well-ordering of which the contentment, welfare, and happiness of the people so greatly depend."[18] Suicide, then, first became an indicator of social illness, a measure of what was wrong with late Victorian Britain and her institutions. It next became a symbol of social malaise. Take suicide and the city, for example. Like Thomson, many Victorians forged links between London and self-destructiveness.[19] The 1880 writer for *Blackwood's* contended that the preponderance of urban suicides was not so much attributable to greater suffering in cities as to "the lesser disposition to support that suffering."[20] In 1892, W. R. Lethaby called the capital city a place where men "grow sickly like grass under stone,"[21] a place of withering, dying, and burial—the appropriate site for suicides. When Jack London visited London at the turn of the century, he found life there "cheap and suicide common," with suicide attempts rousing little more interest or compassion in police courts than did drunkenness.[22] He posited a loss of instinct for life as the cause for this indifference. The great western metropolis had become a necropolis; it was suicidal, an emblem of emotional deadness.

Near the heart of this symbolic necropolis lay George Gissing's New Grub Street, fictional last outpost of the literary world. If, early in our era, Carlyle, Mill and Nightingale wrote themselves back toward affirming life, Gissing's earnest characters in *New Grub Street* (1891) write themselves toward death at its end. Old Grub Street, the haunt of Dr. Johnson, knew failures and poverty, but Gissing's new Grub Street, haunt of Harold Biffen and Edwin Reardon, knows total hopelessness as well. Setting his novel in the early 1880s, just after the article on "Suicide" in *Blackwood's*, Gissing wrote of a city so joyless that suicide for some seemed an improvement over life.

Central to Gissing's book is the conflict between writing as trade and writing as art. Survivors like Jasper Milvain write to grub for money; self-destructives like Reardon and Biffen want to write good three-volume novels or innovative neo-realism but are doomed from the start. Gissing makes this clear in his very first chapter through the mouthpiece of Milvain. A pragmatist himself, Milvain expects the idealistic Reardon to become a suicide, for "he is just the kind of fellow to end by poisoning or shooting himself." Milvain's Reardon cannot "keep up literary production as a paying business,"[23] and certainly that much is true. Saddled with an ambitious wife and an exacting conscientiousness, he exhausts himself in an attempt to satisfy both. The wife, Amy, proves more prophetic than Milvain when she points out to her husband that "if one refuses to be of one's time and yet hasn't the means to live independently, what can result but break-down and wretchedness?" (*NGS*, 81). Yet Reardon plugs on, continues to write triple-deckers—an increasingly less popular art form—and to spin daydream fantasies about ancient and modern Greece with his friend, Biffen. A man following the dictates of an earlier Victorian time, Reardon anachronistically drudges away at his painstakingly long novels and at the same time uses willpower to sustain his life. In Gissing's late Victorian London, however, this kind of integrity is no road to salvation. Because Reardon does not play their game, those fellow Grub Streeters who review Reardon's work take it to task. And because he refuses to bend, Reardon becomes brittle in health, haunted by despair and nightmares, and enfeebled in body, much as Amy predicted he would.

Still, Gissing does not permit suicide for poor Reardon and opens his own third volume with interesting reasons why:

REFUGE from despair is often found in the passion of self-pity and that spirit of obstinate resistance which it engenders. In certain natures the extreme of self-pity is intolerable, and leads to self-destruction; but there are less fortunate beings whom the vehemence of their revolt against fate strengthens to endure in suffering. These latter are rather imaginative than passionate; the stages of their woe impress them as the acts of a drama, which they cannot bring themselves to cut short, so various are the possibilities of its dark motive. The intellectual man who kills himself is most often brought to that decision by conviction of his insignificance; self-pity merges in self-scorn, and the humiliated soul is intolerant of existence. He who survives under like conditions does so because misery magnifies him in his own estimate. (*NGS*, 373)

Reardon is one who lives on to natural death by virtue of his tolerable self-pity. He fights for life in the end. Not so his friend, Biffen, a near alter-ego to Reardon. While Edwin Reardon struggles with the vulgar by refusing to pander to crude tastes or to show vulgarity in his work, Harold Biffen "delights" in "vulgar circumstances" because his "life has been martyred by them" (*NGS*, 174) and opts to write a realistic novel about a grocer. At one point, a despairing Reardon is told by Biffen that he must not commit suicide because of his love for beautiful Amy. Although Reardon responds that she is precisely why he could kill himself, Biffen is right: Reardon cannot die mainly because of Amy, and Biffen does willfully die after he realizes he can never have a woman like the widowed Amy. Ultimately Reardon rejects both Amy and his vision of Greece, while Biffen embraces but renounces them to complete Reardon's destiny. Biffen's final moments come in a peaceful, parklike setting that is described with a lyricism usually reserved in this book for descriptions of the Greek fantasy.

Biffen's suicide by self-poisoning is carefully accounted for by Gissing, as is Reardon's psychology in not committing suicide. Biffen's sad bachelorhood and will to die evince a denial of egoism, a refusal to perpetuate the self. Gissing describes Biffen as winning a battle against turmoil, self-serving, and delusion. His death wish comes just after he hears a thoughtless colleague go on about his own hopes for love and marriage. Biffen now, says Gissing:

knew the actual desire of death, the simple longing for extinction. One must go far in suffering before the innate will-to-live is thus truly overcome; weariness of bodily anguish may induce this perversion of the instincts; less often, that despair of suppressed emotion which had fallen upon Harold. Through the night he kept his thoughts fixed on death in its aspect of repose, of eternal oblivion. And herein he had found solace. . . . A few more days, and he was possessed by a calm of spirit such as he had never known. His resolve was taken, not in a moment of supreme conflict, but as the result of a subtle process by which his imagination had become in love with death. Turning from contemplation of life's one rapture, he looked with the same intensity of desire to a state that had neither fear nor hope. (*NGS*, 527–28)

Gissing clearly prefers Biffen's motives for suicide over Reardon's motives for living or Milvain's for getting on in life by dying to art. All three characters approximate types of men described and judged by Schopenhauer, whom Gissing had read and about whose work he wrote in an essay entitled "The Hope of Pessimism."[24] Milvain dangerously embodies a pragmatic egoism that undermines art, Schopenhauer's one route to optimism. Reardon behaves like the suicides imagined by Schopenhauer; he "wills life, and is dissatisfied merely with the conditions on which it has come to him."[25] Milvain is not really far off in expecting Reardon to kill himself; he only misjudges Reardon's kind of self-pity. And Biffen acts more like the Schopenhauerean man who with eyes open to human suffering denies the will to live. Schopenhauer would probably have condoned Biffen's will not to live, but not his suicide. Biffen's way may be the hope of pessimism, but it is still the way to dusty death. Gissing, however, was gloomier than Schopenhauer. All Gissing's characters are planted in the valley of the shadow of death, renamed "the valley of the shadow of books" and symbolized in *New Grub Street* by the reading room of the British Museum. All touch or are in some way associated with this room, the origin or repository for so many of their writings and strugglings and the bookish source of the formula for the effective poison that will kill Biffen. Gissing's literary London is above all else a place where people are spent in service to the word. Among the characters in its purview, only Biffen wholly refuses either to join the hectic dance of money and death or to await nasty oblivion. He resigns himself to a quieter kind of deadly withdrawal.

The extent of Gissing's sympathy for Biffen was in part a sign of the relaxing taboos against suicide in the 1890s. Biffen's self-destruction is Gissing's version of what *Blackwood's* had called the "universal appetite for calm" in the early 1880s. But it is also a protest against materialism, a statement of despair in a loveless world, a cry of doom over the death of writing as art, and a blow to bourgeois disdain for and fear of suicide. Little of this was lost on Gissing's Victorian reviewers, one of whom saw "the motive forces" of the whole book as: "Life, which suffers so much, and has no respite until death steps in to help; faith, which dies hard, after an agonizing struggle against circumstance; love, which gives all, and gains nothing in return."[26] Gissing used suicide to symbolize the pain inherent in the loss of such "motive forces" and in doing so would lead the way for a number of writers of the 1890s, the generation whom Yeats dubbed "tragic."

Another novel of 1891, Rudyard Kipling's *The Light That Failed*, also envisioned a bitter end for men who aspired to both art and love. Kipling's equivalent to Grub Street is the war-torn, imperialist Sudan, where his artist hero Dick Heldar and cohorts are vigorous and ambitious foreign correspondents. When Dick returns to England from the front, he finds his war pictures have made him popular, so much so that he begins to pander to public taste by subduing his gift for realism. But success breeds arrogance in Dick Heldar, an insecure man at best. Dick's early roots are in orphanhood and his early experiences in London have been bitter. Young and impoverished in the big city, he was once cheated of three pence he had been promised for carrying a man's bags. Bearing scars from such early wounds, Dick tries to make success compensatory, but Kipling will not let him off so easily. Dick's arrogance itself begins to fail as blindness from an old war-related injury sets in, along with bitterness and vulnerability. Dependent upon a cheating landlord and a scheming artist's model for his very existence, blind Dick makes one final gesture toward the days of comradeship and success. Alone, he goes back to Africa to seek out his old friends and this time is killed outright by a stray bullet. His is a fortuitous, sought-for end, an act of suicide. "Put me, I pray, in the forefront of the battle,"[27] he beseeches his friend Torpenhow, and Kipling closes by telling us that "his luck had held to the last, even to the crowning mercy of a kindly bullet through his head" (*WPRK*, 328).

Dick Heldar's attitudes toward life and death echo the rise and fall of Victorian optimism. While he is winning—working as a special war correspondent, selling his artwork, living well—Dick believes in himself. Even when he first knows blindness, he feels equal to life: "Dick knew," says Kipling, "in his heart of hearts that only a lingering sense of humour and no special virtue had kept him alive. Suicide, he had persuaded himself, would be a ludicrous insult to the gravity of the situation as well as a weak-kneed confession of fear" (*WPRK*, 268). Here Dick adopts a Carlylean stance against self-destruction; he girds himself against it and moves on. But when his situation becomes still graver, he dresses himself in a spotless uniform like an "untired man, master of himself, setting out on an expedition, well-pleased" (*WPRK*, 310) and courts death as his only alternative. Like Biffen, he succeeds in failing to live. Thus Dick confronts mortality with money and success and loses the confrontation, then pits willpower against death and also realizes defeat, and finally joins forces with death and commits suicide. By that time, "the arrogance of the man had disappeared, and in its place [had] settled despair" (*WPRK*, 218). Into the last volume of *The Light That Failed* marches the desperation of the late Victorian world, where suicide becomes preferable to a constant battle for recognition and even for existence.

It is not coincidental that Dick's blinding injury is sustained while Gordon is dying at Khartoum. Dick's fate signifies first the blindness and then the end of self-interested imperialism, an aggressive, combative course that might also have been suicidal from the start. The British attempt to master the world through talent and willpower would end like Dick's similar attempt to master loss—in a defeat whose only salvation lies in the acceptance of failure.[28] Moreover, here in Kipling's first novel, where imperialism betokens superiority in the art of dying, it also leads to the death of art. The Dick we lose is a talented, if deluded, man, and Kipling seems to be saying that cultural arrogance, like personal arrogance, is a weakness that prohibits cultural flowering. Dick accepts the standards of his culture and is sacrificed to them. On the other hand, so is Biffen, who refuses to accept them and also dies. And Dorian Gray, who thought he could toy with them, is consumed in the attempt. In all three of these important novels of 1891—*The Light That Failed*, *New Grub Street*, and *Dorian Gray*—a suicidal death of art inheres in the heart of falling darkness.

Art is not, however, the only "motive force" that keeps Dick Heldar alive for a time—love, too, motivates him. Unfortunately he also thinks of love as something he must control. Persistence and loyalty become his weapons in this contest, another he is doomed to lose. His choice in love is Maisie, a girl he has grown up with as an orphan who is now an emancipated "New Woman" and aspiring artist. With a mad infatuation that persists long beyond her disclaimers of love toward him, Dick pursues Maisie on and off through most of the book. He remains her friend by offering to help her with her painting, but he cannot win her deepest heart, even after he begins to go blind. Meanwhile their mutual struggle for dominance focusses in a competition to see who can paint a better representation of the figure of Melancholy from Thomson's *City of Dreadful Night*—a fitting emblem of a relationship which leads them both to despair. Dick's version will be his last work before total blindness descends, and it is destroyed by the model who poses for it and then tends to the blind artist. With the artifact Melancholy demolished, sightless Dick sets off for Africa and the death that will conquer real despair once and for all. He now woos Thanatos, not Eros.

In this fatal courtship, as in his final despair, Dick Heldar parallels other suicidal heroes of the 1890s—Jude Fawley, for example, in Hardy's *Jude the Obscure* (1895). After the disappointment of his bitter and foolish first marriage, Jude hears of his mother's suicide by drowning and tries to imitate her. Stepping onto a large frozen pond, he jumps up and down on the ice, trying to crack it and plunge to a frigid death. When the ice refuses to yield, he wonders why he has been spared. Possibly, says the narrator, "he was not a sufficiently dignified person for suicide. Peaceful death abhorred him as a subject."[29] Possibly, too, Jude thinks, he was meant to fulfill his original desire to be a student at Christminster, and he thrusts himself into the attempt. Jude thus counters the death-wish with a desire for learning and human betterment. In his first venture toward Christminster, he had mainly been thwarted by what he called "animal passion" (*JO*, 139) for his wife, Arabella. Inevitably, though, given his warmth toward women, Jude will once again be distracted, this time by Sue Bridehead, a highly complicated "New Woman" not unlike Maisie. As she tortures him endlessly in the name of what is right, Jude yields his whole life to Sue. And when, after many vacillations, many setbacks for them both, Sue turns her back on their long-term liaison, it is with suicidal self-mortification that she returns to her former husband. Suffering deeply from their separation and very ill, Jude determines to see Sue, "this time really to do for himself" (*JO*, 472). As he says to Arabella, "a fellow who had only two wishes left in the world, to see a particular woman and then to die, could neatly accomplish those two wishes at one stroke by taking this journey in the rain" (*JO*, 472). This journey and Sue's continued, painful ambivalence reward Jude with a lonely but willed death.

Both Kipling and Hardy resemble Freud in their belief that sexual energy is locked in painful, mortal combat with the death drive. Their heroes strive toward eros but are constantly restrained and pushed in the direction of death until they finally pursue death outright. In Jude's case even the children of his two unions are lost through suicide. Little Father Time, the son of Jude's marriage to Arabella, is certainly one of the most hopeless, death-embracing figures in literature. Convinced by rejection that there is "no laughable thing under the sun" (*JO*, 342), and further convinced by Sue in a weak moment that it is a "tragic thing to bring beings into the world" (*JO*, 382), young/old Father Time believes that "it would be better to be out of the world than in it" (*JO*, 406). With utter and desperate logic he proceeds to hang both of his younger siblings and then himself. His is the last resort in the struggle for survival. Commenting on this pitiful boy's terrible action, the attending doctor tells Jude that Father Time is a true child of the age, a boy "of a sort unknown in the last generation—the outcome of new views of life." He represents "the beginning of the coming universal wish not to live" (*JO*, 411).

The doctor's prediction invites speculation as to just what "new views of life" led to this coming universal wish. It is hard to believe that they are Jude's, for Jude holds out against failure and loss until the very end when he loses Sue, and even then calls for her on his deathbed. He possesses a kind of existential courage to be for the greater part of the book, constantly venturing himself against great odds in a world that eventually shows itself to be absurd. If Jude loses ambition, religious faith, love, and children—all "motive forces," everything—he endures, and not in the state of catatonia that some literary critics have attributed to him.[30] Jude is no spectre who escapes pain by dying to life. More the romantic than the Victorian Schopenhauerean, he lives his pain to the fullest, leaving life only when he is worn out by it. For Hardy, as for Kipling, failing was living. Sue speaks for her creator when she reassures Jude that "if you have failed, [it] is to your credit rather than your blame . . . . Every successful man is more or less a selfish man" (*JO*, 438). Nor are most of Sue's other "new views on life" deathlike, except in their influence on Father Time. At the agricultural show she expresses a hope in "Greek joyousness" (*JO*, 366) that parallels the openness in love she thinks she wants to have with Jude. What makes Sue self-destructive and a suicidal influence on Jude is her conservative streak—her puritanical self-sacrifice, her flight back to outworn marriage vows, her insecurity in her own beliefs. These lead to her own misery, to Phillotson's love-starved existence, and to Jude's bitter death. Thus Jude and Sue are "beforehand" (*JO*, 354) only in their views of marriage, not suicide. Only Father Time's premature despair is really "beforehand" in terms of self-destruction. His is a stunting, suicidal despair that makes real tragedy impossible—the "new" and uncurable "view of life." Heralding it may have been enough for Hardy—even enough to silence his voice as tragic novelist.

Not all of Hardy's contemporaries agreed with Hardy's prophetic physician in his diagnosis of the future. An anonymous reviewer for the *Illustrated London News* found the "horror of the infant pessimist . . . changed in a moment to ghastly farce by this inopportune generation of the 'advanced' doctor." He/she went on to say:

> We all know perfectly well that baby Schopenhauers are not coming into the world in shoals. Children whose lives, stunted by poverty or disease, have acquired a gravity beyond their years, may be found everywhere in the overcrowded centres of population; but such a portrait as little Jude Fawley, who advocates the annihilation of the species, and gives a practical example of it at a tender age, does not present itself as typical of a devouring philosophy.[31]

Nevertheless many late Victorians were deeply distressed by premature despair. Hopkins's leaden echo duplicated their feelings, finding that "wisdom [was] early to despair" and then resoundingly counselling: "Be beginning to despair, to despair / Despair, despair, despair, despair."[32] If Hopkins's other, golden echo answered that giving beauty back to God might end such deep sadness, Jesuit Hopkins himself knew hopelessness. In "Carrion Comfort," the poem's Hopkins-like narrator refuses to feed on Despair, opts not to "choose not to be," and yet desperately wrestles with his God. Although Hopkins won his contest, for others the intense agony he described often ended the other way, when faith as a motive force died "hard, after an agonizing struggle against circumstance."

Many late Victorians destroyed themselves in this struggle. One late-century novelist who vividly imagined their plight was Mary Augusta Ward. Niece of the theologically liberal Matthew Arnold and daughter of his Roman Catholic brother, Thomas, Ward fell heir both to Arnoldian earnestness and to the great religious controversies of her day. For most of her life, her own parents staunchly adhered to separate faiths: Julia Arnold remained Protestant and was allowed to bring up her daughters in that faith, while Thomas Arnold, twice converted to Roman Catholicism, wanted his sons raised as Catholics. Intellectually curious and marked by the pain of this split but loving family, Ward evolved, pondered, and revised her own liberal religious beliefs. Twice in her fiction she would return to the dilemma of deeply committed lovers who differ over religion. In 1888 in *Robert Elsmere*, her increasingly liberal Elsmere—much like Ward herself—becomes sorely at odds with his devout, evangelical wife. Eventually he wears himself out in self-sacrificial service to others in East End London. Then, in 1898 in *Helbeck of Bannisdale*, Ward presented a religious struggle so hopeless and tragic that it could be resolved only through the overt suicide of one of its two protagonists. Alan Helbeck and Laura Fountain are both powerless in the larger context of late nineteenth-century Britain. Helbeck's Roman Catholic family has no real outlet for its drive or talents. Its women have been self-denying; its men, without conventional education, have been cut off from careers in politics, the army, or the established church. Helbeck's one power is the power of conversion, and throughout the novel this power is aimed primarily at Laura. She, on the other hand, is equally firm of conviction and equally dispossessed. She adheres to a *passé* religion of feeling and Wordsworthian love of nature. The daughter of a Cambridge don, she is also imbued with his free-thinking skepticism but has not been properly educated as to the grounds of her disbelief. Ignorant of her dead father's rationale, she nonetheless remains loyal to his memory and torn between that memory and her love for Helbeck. Headstrong and heartstrong, she fights conversion and engages Helbeck in the battle they will both lose. Theirs, inevitably and ironically, becomes a battle to the death, terminating only with Laura's self-destruction.

Laura's suicide is both a sacrifice for the Catholic Helbeck and his sister and a romantic return to nature. Toward the end of the book, Laura's struggles with Helbeck intensify. She flees to Cambridge to her father's friends, returns to Bannisdale to tend Helbeck's sister—her dying stepmother—and then, back again near Helbeck, at last agrees to be converted and to marry him. A final pang of conscience, however, makes this impossible. Instead she gathers flowers from the bank of the swollen river Greet on Helbeck's estate and decks the bier of her stepmother. She then returns to the river and an Ophelia-like drowning, her body "beating against the gravelly bank, in a soft helplessness, her bright hair tangled among the drift of branch and leaf."[33] Helbeck believes her death an accident, just as she wished him to, for Laura does die partly to save Helbeck's illusions about her conversion. But her final surrender to him also stings; Helbeck cannot bring himself to enter the Protestant chapel in which she is buried. If Ward emphasizes Laura's compliance through her "soft helplessness" in the Greet—the river that Helbeck owns and where he wages "noble war" with salmon—she also emphasizes Laura's pyrrhic victory through the river. Both in her philosophy of nature and in her death, Laura comes closer to Bannisdale than does Helbeck. "The leaping river, the wide circuit of the fells . . . to them the girl gave back her soul, passionately resting in them. . . . The veil lifted between her and them. They became a sanctuary and a refuge with no exclusions, no conditions" (*HB*, 363–64). These offer Laura Fountain a confirmation of her ebullient nature far more than do Helbeck and his religion, and they help make her the new ghost of the Bannisdale lady, for whom she was once mistaken.

Laura's suicide is also an act of triumphant will, a deliberate, rational act on the part of a very emotional person. Early in the novel, Mr. Fountain tells Laura " 'you can't sacrifice your life.—It may be Christian . . . but it isn't sense' " (*HB*, 60). In Laura's case, however, although such an action is not Christian, it is the only sensible alternative available to a woman simultaneously loyal to father, self, and lover. Unlike Father Time's, Laura's suicide is tragic because it seems inevitable, the unavoidable exit from circumstances about which Laura is fully, truly cognizant. Laura is always stronger than her stepmother, and from the time of witnessing an industrial death from which "she recovered her power of action sooner than the men around her" (*HB*, 205), Laura has real presence of mind. Helbeck's assertions of will only steel her own. " 'There is,' " she tells him, " 'something in me that fears nothing—not even the breaking of both our hearts' " (*HB*, 257). That this fearlessness received the ultimate test of suicide gives Laura's story the tragic power of few Victorian novels. Laura knew of herself and Helbeck that "she must have room to breathe, without making her struggle for liberty a hideous struggle with him, and with love" (*HB*, 343). She chose to die, as her suicide note says, "Because death puts an *end*" (*HB*, 387).

Helbeck of Bannisdale instances Victorian concern with dilemmas, causes, nostalgia, and with the annihilation of eros through death of the self. It also reveals a sobering vision of life in 1898. Like so many Victorians, Ward looked two ways. Ward's sympathies lay with both protagonists—the conservative, landed, earnest Helbeck, whose world has eroded like his estate; and the lively, fresh Laura, who "might have made her Catholic respect her" (*HB*, 316). Ward seems to be saying that the best of the old is gone, that women without real education are doomed, that the new religions need intellectuals to apprehend them, and that energy and life now reside in the new cities. There rough men like Laura's cousin, Hubert, can carve out new lives, but there too steel mills devour workers without a thought for their children. Like many late Victorian novels, *Helbeck of Bannisdale* offers little hope. As in Charlotte Brontë's earlier *Shirley* (1849), which Ward admired, special religious interests, landed gentry, women, and workers all lose the struggle for significance and independence. In *Helbeck*, however, they also lose the struggle for existence.

Ward knew that her novel was tragic, and she treasured the notes of friends like George Wyndham who tried to decipher why its "crash is inevitable."[34] But for her new friend, Sir Leslie Stephen, Ward had a special copy bound, omitting the last chapter. She felt that Laura's death might "depress one who had known so much sorrow."[35] Yet Stephen might have best understood Laura's suicide. His own *Science of Ethics* (1882) had given a penetrating look at deaths like hers. If, said Stephen, one's "life could not serve others, and was only giving useless pain to his attendants," should one not be free to commit suicide? He went on to query:

> May we not say that he is acting on a superior moral principle, and that because he is clearly diminishing the sum of human misery? It is impossible to settle the case in concrete instances, because there is no fixed external test. The conduct may spring either from cowardice or from a loftier motive than the ordinary, and the merit of the action is therefore not determinable; but, assuming

the loftier motive, I can see no ground for disapproving the action which flows from it.[36]

Stephen's kind of arguing had become acceptable by 1898 when Ward published *Helbeck*. By then, the Victorian verdict on suicide was summarized in an 1897 paper from Oxford House: "The lenity of the law courts reflects the changed attitude of public opinion. Suicide is now regarded with sympathy rather than with abhorrence. It is spoken of as a 'misfortune' rather than a crime. Partly the change arises from a better understanding of the conditions of suicide; partly from that almost extravagant sympathy with wretchedness, as such, which characterizes an age at once selfish and sentimental."[37] Self-destruction had become one more way of dealing with loss, and in 1898 so very much seemed to be lost: the dominant Anglican faith; bourgeois morality; a settled sense of self, of love, of family; the power of the word; the hope of industrialism; the belief in progress; the empire. Even atheists and people in the vanguard of forward-looking political movements like Eleanor Marx, Karl Marx's spirited and dedicated socialist daughter, succumbed to suicide. Tussy Marx tested the atheist verse "If he be just who reigns on high, / Why should the Atheist fear to die?"[38] in 1898. On 31 March, she got up, washed, dressed herself in white, drank prussic acid, and lay down to die a death that recreated Emma Bovary's, whose story she had once translated into English. By 1898, many of Marx's contemporaries would not have found her actions sinful. That was the year when Perry-Coste's *Ethics of Suicide* asserted that "if it be still insisted that suicide *is* a sin of rebellion against those judgments of God which we are bound to endure humbly, then equally in kind—and in some cases even in degree—are obstetrics, fire insurance, and vaccination, acts of rebellion."[39]

In Marx's day, entropy or death undermined even the life force of individualists like Marx, who opted to die. Marx seemed only one of many. Strahan believed that suicides were legion, well under-represented by the statisticians who may have uncovered fewer than fifty percent of them;[40] while Gurnhill, a Christian Socialist, thought that anguished suicide notes reflected "the social experience of thousands."[41] And M. P. Shiel's story "The S. S." (1895) presented its detective hero, Prince Zaleski, with a case of apparent mass suicide and opened with the words: "To say that there are epidemics of suicide, is to give expression to what is now a mere commonplace of knowledge."[42] Zaleski solves the case by uncovering a murderous secret society that desires to exterminate diseased life, a kind of underground club of social Darwinists.

And so denial—inherent in hushing, covering up, overpowering, or displacing suicide—gave way to openness and then by the 1890s to exaggeration. Throughout their era, Victorians had mourned excessively for their dead, placing great value on public displays of sadness like funerals and mourning dress. And throughout their era, they had feared excessively for their murdered and cried strongly for justice in condemning their murderers. Now, at the end of that era, they placed suicide alongside natural death and murder and responded excessively to it, too. Masses of people did not die by their own hands, but the Victorians had finally exposed suicide and wished to overestimate its numbers and importance. By the end of Victoria's reign many wanted to believe in a "coming universal wish not to live."

NOTES

Introduction

1. Albert Camus, *The Myth of Sisyphus and Other Essays*, trans. Justin O'Brien (New York: Alfred A. Knopf, 1955).

2. Philippe Ariès, *The Hour of Our Death* (New York: Alfred A. Knopf, 1981), p. xvi.

Chapter I

1. H. Montgomery Hyde, *The Strange Death of Lord Castlereagh* (London: Heinemann, 1958), p. 20.

2. Ibid., pp. 22–23.

3. Lord Byron, *Don Juan*, ed. Leslie A. Marchand (Boston: Houghton Mifflin, 1958), p. 198.

4. Hyde, *The Strange Death*, p. 33.

5. *Annual Register and Chronicle* (London: Baldwin, Cradock and Joy, 1824), p. 82.

6. Ibid.

7. *London Times*, 24 June 1820, p. 3, col. 2.

8. Rev. Henry George Watkins, "Suicide: An Atrocious Offence against God and Man" (London: Cox and Son, 1818), p. 13.

9. Thomas DeQuincey, "On Suicide," *Collected Works*, 14 vols. ed. David Masson (Edinburgh: Black, 1890), vol. 8, p. 401.

10. *Catalogue of Parliamentary Reports and a Breviate of Their Contents* (London: Hansard, 1824), p. 416.

11. *Annual Register and Chronicle* (1824), p. 88.

12. Scottish law differed from the English. Although in Scotland there was considerable legal interest in the alterations in English law, Scottish juries could bring forth a verdict of "Not Proven" in both suicide and murder cases.

13. James Hogg, *The Private Memoirs and Confessions of a Justified Sinner* (1824; New York: W. W. Norton, 1970), p. 229.

14. In his well-known essay, "The Structure of *Wuthering Heights*," reprinted in *Wuthering Heights*, ed. William M. Sale, Jr. (New York: W. W. Norton, 1972), pp. 286–98, Charles Percy Sanger notes the same freedom in Emily Brontë's use of old and new inheritance law. *Wuthering Heights* was written in 1846.

15. All quotations from *Wuthering Heights* are from the 1847 edition, edited by William M. Sale, Jr. (New York: W. W. Norton, 1972), p. 153. References to *Wuthering Heights* hereafter appear in the text.

16. See S. E. Sprott, *The English Debate on Suicide from Donne to Hume* (La Salle, Ill.: Open Court, 1961), p. 97.

17. Q. D. Leavis, "A Fresh Approach to *Wuthering Heights*," in *Lectures in America* (New York: Pantheon, 1969), p. 146.

18. See *Man, Myth, and Magic*, ed. Richard Cavendish (New York: Marshall Cavendish Corp., 1970), p. 555; and *Examples of Printed Folk-lore Concerning the East Riding of Yorkshire, York, and Ainsty*, ed. Mrs. Gutch (London: Folk-Lore Society, 1901), 42, 48.

19. See Ephraim A. Jacob, *An Analytical Digest of the Law and Practice of England* (New York, 1880), vol. 3, pp. 3473–75.

20. See Edward Westermarck, *The Origin and Development of the Moral Ideas* (London: Macmillan, 1903), vol. 2, pp. 255–56.

21. Recent examples include Giles Mitchell in "Incest, Demonism, and Death in *Wuthering Heights*," *Literature and Psychology* 23 (1973): 29–30.

22. *Tedium vitae* is a subject favored by many of the Victorian commentators on suicide. See, for instance, Forbes Winslow's *The Anatomy of Suicide* (London: Henry Renshaw, 1840), chs. 4 and 8.

23. Philippa Prittie Jephson, "The Cross Roads," *Tinsley's Magazine* 34 (1886): 476.

24. James Cowles Prichard, *Treatise on Insanity and Other Disorders Affecting the Mind* (London: Sherwood, Gilbert and Piper, 1835).

25.———, *On the Different Forms of Insanity in Relation to Jurisprudence* (London: H. Ballière, 1842).

26. See Eric T. Carlson and Norman Dain, "The Meaning of Moral Insanity," *Bulletin of the History of Medicine* 36 (1962): 130–40.

27. Prichard, *Treatise*, pp. 6, 4.

28. Jean Etienne Dominique Esquirol, *Des Maladies Mentales* (Brussels: Meline, Cans et Compagnie, 1838).

29. See Dennis Leigh, *The Historical Development of British Psychiatry* (Oxford: Pergamon Press, 1961), p. 185.

30. See Carlson and Dain, "Moral Insanity," p. 135.

31. Winslow, *Anatomy*, p. vi.

32. Ibid., p. 36.

33. See Nigel Walker, *Crime and Insanity in England*, 2 vols. (Edinburgh: Edinburgh University Press, 1968 and 1973), vol. 1, p. 95.

34. Quoted in Alethea Hayter's *A Sultry Month* (London: Faber and Faber, 1965), p. 103.

35. Hayter, *A Sultry Month*, p. 114.

36. Ibid.

37. George R. Drysdale, *Elements of Social Science* (London: E. Truelove, 1854), p. 37.

38. "Suicide: Its Motives and Mysteries," *Irish Quarterly Review* 7 (1857): 50.

39. Thomas Mayo, *Croonian Lectures on Medical Testimony and Evidence in Cases of Lunacy* (London: John W. Parker & Son, 1853).

40. "On Suicide," *London Journal of Psychological Medicine* 11 (1858): 397.

41. Henry Maudsley, *Natural Causes and Supernatural Seemings* (London: Kegan Paul and Co., 1886), p. 116.

42. John Charles Bucknill, *The Psychology of Shakespeare* (London: Longman & Co., 1859).

43. Harriet Martineau, "Self-Murder," *Once a Week* (19 December 1859): 513.

44. William Carpenter, *Principles of Mental Physiology* (London: H. S. King, 1874), p. 666.

45. Henry Maudsley, *Pathology of Mind* (London: Macmillan, 1879), p. 332.

46. Ibid., p. 330.

47. James Davey, "On Suicide, in its Social Relations," *Journal of Psychological Medicine*, n.s. 4 (1878): 230–55.

48. Daniel Hack Tuke, ed., *A Dictionary of Psychological Medicine* (Philadelphia: Blakiston, 1892).

49. Olive Anderson, "Did Suicide Increase with Industrialization in Victorian England?" *Past and Present* 86 (1980): 167.

50. Henry Morselli, *Suicide: An Essay on Comparative Moral Statistics* (London: Kegan Paul, 1881), p. 3.

51. Ibid., p. 10.

52. Ibid.

53. Ibid., p. 354 (emphasis in original).

54. Ibid., p. 374.

55. William Wynn Westcott, *Suicide: Its History, Literature, Jurisprudence, Causation, and Prevention* (London: H. K. Lewis, 1885).

56. Ibid., p. 121.

57. G. H. Savage, "Constant Watching in Suicidal Cases," *Journal of Mental Science* (April 1884): 17–19.

58. Daniel Hack Tuke, *Chapters on the History of the Insane in the British Isles* (London: Kegan Paul, Trench, 1882), p. 455.

59. Ibid., p. 454.

60. S.A.K. Strahan, *Suicide and Insanity: A Physiological and Sociological Study* (London: Swan Sonnenschein, 1893).

61. Ibid., p. 31.

62. Henry Maudsley, "Suicide in Simple Melancholy," *Medical Magazine of London* 1 (1892): 46.

63. Ibid., p. 55.

Chapter II

1. Forbes Winslow, *The Anatomy of Suicide* (London: Henry Renshaw, 1840), p. 132. Attitudes like Winslow's persisted throughout the Victorian period. See also A. Wynter in *Curiosities of Toil*, 2 vols. (London, 1875), vol. 2, pp. 245–46, and William Wynn Westcott, *Suicide: Its History, Literature, Jurisprudence, Causation and Prevention, A Social Science Treatise* (London: H. K. Lewis, 1885), 141ff.

2. Edward Young, *Night Thoughts* (London, 1742–46), 5.442.

3. Robert Blair, *The Grave* (London: 1743), 2.403–4.

4. Thomas Hardy, *The Return of the Native*, ed. James Gindin (New York: W. W. Norton, 1969), p. 149.

5. Hanging in public was legal in England until 1868.

6. See Francis Steegmuller, *Flaubert and Madame Bovary* (New York: Vintage Books, 1957), pp. 20–21.

7. Rev. Solomon Piggott, *Suicide and Its Antidotes* (London: J. Robins & Co., 1824), pp. 130–31.

8. Thomas Carlyle, *Critical and Miscellaneous Essays* (London: Chapman and Hall, 1899), vol. 1, p. 218.

9. *Saturday Review*, (17 May 1856): 58.

10. *Handbook to the Gallery of British Paintings* (1857), p. 112; cited in *The Pre-Raphaelites* (London: The Tate Gallery/Penguin Books, 1984), p. 144.

11. Donald Smalley, ed., *Browning's Essay on Chatterton* (Cambridge: Harvard University Press, 1948), pp. 127–28.

12. "The Classic Land of Suicide," *The Psychological Journal* (1861); rpt. in *Littel's Living Age* 3.14 (1861): 195.

13. Ibid., p. 204.

14. Ibid., p. 196.

15. Emily Brontë, *The Complete Poems of Emily Jane Brontë*, ed. C. W. Hatfield (New York: Columbia University Press, 1941), p. 223.

16. In my discussion of romantic and Victorian will, I am indebted to John R. Reed, "Inherited Characteristics: Romantic to Victorian Will," *Studies in Romanticism* 17 (1978): 335–66.

17. George Henry Lewes, *The Life of Goethe* (New York: Frederick Ungar, 1965), p. 151.

18. Ibid., pp. 151–52.

19. Carlyle, *Critical and Miscellaneous Essays*, vol. 1, p. 223.

20. *The Collected Letters of Thomas and Jane Welsh Carlyle*, ed. Charles Richard Sanders and Kenneth J. Fielding (Durham, N.C.: Duke University Press, 1970), vol. 1, p. 378.

21. *Two Note Books of Thomas Carlyle*, ed. Charles Eliot Norton (1898; New York: Paul P. Appel, 1972), p. 56.

22. Wilhelm Dilthey, "*Sartor Resartus*: Philosophical Conflict, Positive and Negative Eras, and Personal Resolution," trans. Murray Baumgarten and Evelyn Kanes, in *Clio* 1 (June 1972): 54.

23. Thomas Carlyle, *Sartor Resartus*, ed. C. F. Harrold (New York: Odyssey Press, 1937), p. 146. All future references are from this edition and appear in my text.

24. *Correspondence between Goethe and Carlyle*, ed. Charles Eliot Norton (New York: Cooper Square, 1970), p. 7.

25. See Basil Willey, *Nineteenth Century Studies: Coleridge to Matthew Arnold* (1949; New York: Harper and Row, 1966), p. 102.

26. See George Levine, *The Boundaries of Fiction: Carlyle, Macaulay, Newman* (Princeton: Princeton University Press, 1968), p. 76.

27. Emery Neff, *Carlyle and Mill: An Introduction to Victorian Thought* (1926; New York: Octagon, 1964).

28. John Stuart Mill, *Autobiography*, ed. Currin V. Shields (New York: Bobbs Merrill, 1957), p. 90.

29. A. W. Levi, "The Mental Crisis of John Stuart Mill," *Psychoanalytic Review* 32 (January 1945): 86–101.

30. Gertrude Himmelfarb, *Victorian Minds* (New York: Alfred A. Knopf, 1968), ch. 4.

31. John Stuart Mill, *On Liberty* (New York: W. W. Norton, 1975), p. 95.

32. *John Stuart Mill: A Selection of His Works*, ed. John M. Robson (New York: Odyssey Press, 1966), p. 164.

33. Manuscripts quoted are from the Nightingale papers in the British Library (MS 43402, autobiography and other memoranda, 1845–1860), and quotations are by permission of the Department of Manuscripts and the Henry Bonham-Carter trust.

34. George Burrows, *Commentaries on the Causes, Forms, Symptoms and Treatment, Moral and Medical, of Insanity* (London: George Underwood, 1828), p. 426.

35. Cecil Woodham-Smith, *Florence Nightingale* (New York: McGraw-Hill, 1951), p. 341.

36. Florence Nightingale, MS45840, *Notes for Suggestions to the Searchers for Truth Among Artizans of England* (1860) 134, f. 178.

37. See F. B. Smith, *Florence Nightingale: Reputation and Power* (London: Croom Helm, 1982), p. 187.

38. Florence Nightingale, MS45837, f. 28.

39. ———, MS45848, f. 239.

40. ———, MS45848, f. 240.

41. Hunt was said to have used a female model, Annie Miller, for his Christ.

Chapter III

1. "Our Novels. The Sensation School," *Temple Bar* 29 (1870): 424.

2. *London Times*, 12 September 1839, p. 5, col. 2.

3. *Observer*, 15 September 1839, p. 1, col. 6.

4. Printed by T. Birt, 39 Great St. Andrews Street, Seven Dials.

5. Coroner's Inquest as reported in *The Weekly Dispatch*, 15 September 1839, p. 435, col. 4.

6. *London Times*, 12 September 1839, p. 5, col. 2.

7. "Copy of Verses," stanza 5, Noble Collection, Guildhall Library, London.

8. George Burrows, *Commentaries on the Causes, Forms, Symptoms and Treatment, Moral and Medical, of Insanity* (London: Thomas and George Underwood, 1828), p. 448.

9. Ibid., pp. 478–79.

10. Forbes Winslow, *The Anatomy of Suicide* (London: Henry Renshaw, 1840), p. 119.

11. "Facts on Suicide," from *Chambers Edinburgh Journal*, rpt. *Eclectic Museum* (November 1843): 395.

12. W. Dugdale, "Mischievous Literature," *The Bookseller* 1 July 1868.

13. *Observer*, 20 October 1839, p. 2, col. 1.

14. *The Weekly Dispatch*, 20 October 1839, p. 504, col. 2.

15. Ibid.

16. "Suicide: Its Motives and Mysteries," *Irish Quarterly Review* 7 (1857): 70.

17. Published by G. Gilbert, 2 Green-Arbour Court, Old Bailey.

18. Printed by T. Birt, 39 Great St. Andrews Street, Seven Dials. Courtesy of the Guildhall Library.

19. Baring Gould Collection, no. 154, British Library.

20. Charles Hindley, *Curiosities of Street Literature* (London: Reeves and Turner, 1871) p. 199.

21. Crampton Collection, vol. 2, p. 35, British Library.

22. Henry Dinsley, Printer, 57 High Street, St. Giles.

23. Charles Dickens, *The Christmas Books*, ed. Michael Slater, 2 vols. (Harmondsworth: Penguin, 1971), vol. 1, p. 158.

24. *London Times*, 20 April 1844.

25. *Hood's Magazine* (April 1844): 409–14. This same magazine carried Hood's own "Bridge of Sighs."

26. *London Times*, 23 October 1841.

27. Quoted in *Bloody Versicles: The Rhymes of Crime*, ed. Jonathan Goodman (Newton Abbot: David and Charles, 1971), p. 128.

28. G.W.M. Reynolds, *The Mysteries of London* (London: George Vickers, 1846), vol. 2, p. 347.

29. Ibid., p. 69.

30. Ibid.

31. For enlightening discussions of social melodrama see John G. Cawelti, *Adventure, Mystery and Romance: Formula Stories as Art and Popular Culture* (Chicago: University of Chicago Press, 1976); Louis James, "The Social Context of Early Victorian Fiction," in *The Yearbook of English Studies*, ed. G. K. Hunter and C. J. Rawson (Modern Humanities Research Association, 1981), pp. 87–101; and Anne Humpherys, "The Geometry

of the Modern City: G.W.M. Reynolds and *The Mysteries of London*," *Browning Institute Studies* 11 (1983): 69–80.

32. See Martha Vicinus, " 'Helpless and Unfriended': Nineteenth-Century Domestic Melodrama," *New Literary History* 13 (Autumn 1981): 127–43.

33. Quoted in Kathleen Tillotson, "The Lighter Reading of the Eighteen-Sixties," an introduction to Wilkie Collins's *The Woman in White* (Boston: Houghton Mifflin, 1969), p. xvi.

34. Ulrich Knoepflmacher, "The Counterworld of Victorian Fiction and *The Woman in White*," in *The Worlds of Victorian Fiction*, ed. Jerome H. Buckley (Cambridge: Harvard University Press, 1975), p. 352.

35. *The Works of Wilkie Collins*, 30 vols. (New York: Peter Fenelon Collier, ca. 1900), vol. 8, preface.

36. Quoted in Richard Stang, *The Theory of the Novel in England, 1850–1870* (New York: Columbia University Press, 1959), p. 200.

37. Wilkie Collins, *No Name* (New York: Stein and Day, 1967), preface.

38. Collins, *Works*, vol. 5, p. 3.

39. Ibid., vol. 27, pp. 5–6.

40. Ibid., vol. 5, p. 535.

41. Ibid., p. 558.

42. Ibid., vol. 29, p. 191.

43. Ibid., p. 309.

44. Ibid., p. 501.

45. See especially Winslow, *Anatomy*; William Wynn Westcott, *Suicide: Its History, Literature, Jurisprudence, Causation and Prevention. A Social Science Treatise* (London: H. K. Lewis, 1885); and Henry Morselli, *Suicide: An Essay in Comparative Moral Statistics* (London: Kegan Paul, 1881).

46. Anthony Trollope, *The Way We Live Now*, ed. Robert Tracy (New York: Bobbs Merrill, 1974), p. 65.

47. *London Times*, 1 March 1861.

48. J. N. Radcliffe, "The Prevalence of Suicide in England," Transactions of the *National Association for the Promotion of Social Sciences* (1862), p. 472.

Chapter IV

1. Cited by Kemper Fullerton, "Calvinism and Capitalism: An Explanation of the Weber Thesis," in *Protestantism and Capitalism*, ed. Robert W. Green (Boston: D. C. Heath, 1959), p. 19.

2. John Henry Newman, *Parochial and Plain Sermons* (London: Rivington, 1871), vol. 7, p. 159.

3. *The Complete Works of John Ruskin*, 39 vols. ed. E. T. Cook and Alexander Wedderburn (London: George Allen, 1905), vol. 17, p. 105.

4. Samuel Smiles, *Self-Help* (Boston: Ticknor and Fields, 1860), p. 263.

5. Ibid., p. 289.

6. "Suicide," *Blackwood's* January–June 1880: 133.

7. "Suicide," *Chambers's* 10 May 1884: 295.

8. *Selected Poems of Thomas Hood*, ed. John Clubbe (Cambridge: Harvard University Press, 1970), p. 212. Subsequent references to Hood will be cited by line number and included in my text.

9. *Annual Register* (London: Rivington, 1857), p. 35.

10. Dr. Moore, "Chagrin and Suicide," *Hogg's Instructor* 8 (1852): 60–61.

11. *The Standard*, 13 March 1856: p. 3, col. 3.

12. "Suicide: Its Motives and Mysteries," *Irish Quarterly Review* 7 (1857), p. 49.

13. *Annual Register* (London: Rivington, 1857), p. 242.

14. P. D. Edwards, "Trollope Changes His Mind: The Death of Melmotte in *The Way We Live Now*," *Nineteenth Century Fiction* 18 (June 1963): 89–91.

15. Anthony Trollope, *The Way We Live Now*, ed. Robert Tracy (New York: Bobbs Merrill, 1974), p. 657. Subsequent references to this novel will be to this edition and will be included in the text.

16. Charles Dickens, *Little Dorrit*, ed. R. D. McMaster (New York: Odyssey Press, 1969), p. 236. Subsequent references to this novel will be to this edition and will be included in the text.

17. Thomas Carlyle, *Latter-Day Pamphlets* (New York: AMS Press, 1969), p. 262.

18. W. S. Gilbert, "A Discontented Sugar Broker," in *The Bab Ballads*, ed. James Ellis (Cambridge: Harvard University Press, 1970), p. 133. Subsequent references to this ballad, originally published in *Fun* in 1867, will also be to this edition.

19. S.A.K. Strahan, *Suicide and Insanity: A Physiological and Sociological Study* (London: Swan Sonnenschein, 1893), p. 83.

20. Emile Durkheim, *Suicide: A Study in Sociology*, trans. John A. Spaulding and George Simson (New York: Macmillan, 1951), p. 253.

21. Strahan, *Suicide and Insanity*, p. 58.

22. See ch. 1, p. 27 of this study, and Durkheim, *Suicide*, ch. 4.

23. Strahan, *Suicide and Insanity*, p. 41.

24. William Wynn Westcott, *Suicide: Its History, Literature, Jurisprudence, Causation, and Prevention* (London: H. K. Lewis, 1885), p. 5.

25. See David G. Tucker, "The Reception of *A Tale of Two Cities*, Part I," *Dickens Studies Newsletter* 10 (March 1979): 10.

26. Charles Dickens, *A Tale of Two Cities*, ed. George Woodlock (Harmondsworth: Penguin, 1985), p. 115. Subsequent references are to this edition and appear in the text.

27. John Kucich, *Excess and Restraint in The Novels of Charles Dickens* (Athens: University of Georgia Press, 1981), p. 119.

28. Garrett Stewart, *Death Sentences* (Cambridge: Harvard University Press, 1984), p. 97.

29. See Forbes Winslow's *Anatomy of Suicide* (London, 1840); and A. Wynter's *Curiosities of Toil* (London, 1875), 254 ff.

30. Winslow, *Anatomy*, p. 333.

31. Ibid.

32. *The Poems of Tennyson*, ed. Christopher Ricks (London: Longmans, 1969), p. 1041, 1.9–12. Subsequent references to *Maud* are by part and line number and appear in the text.

33. Strahan, *Suicide and Insanity*, p. 24.

34. See Matthew Lalumia, "Realism and Anti-aristocratic Sentiment in Victorian Depictions of the Crimean War," *Victorian Studies* 27 (Autumn 1983): 25–51.

35. J. S. Bratton, *The Victorian Popular Ballad* (Totowa, N.J.: Rowman and Littlefield, 1975), p. 68.

36. Frederick Langbridge, ed., *Ballads of the Brave*, 4th ed. (London: Methuen, 1911), p. 184.

37. Louise De la Ramée, *Under Two Flags* (New York: A. L. Burt, 1906?), pp. 401–2. Subsequent references to *Under Two Flags* are to this edition and appear in the text.

38. Data here are drawn from W. H. Millar, "Statistics of Deaths by Suicide among

Her Majesty's British Troops Serving at Home and Abroad during the Ten Years 1862–71," *Journal of the Royal Statistical Society* 37 (1874): 187–92.

39. As quoted in Millar, "Statistics of Death," p. 191. Mouat's remark represents his response to Millar's paper.

40. As quoted in Millar, "Statistics of Death," p. 192, also in response to Millar.

41. See H.E.L. Mellersh, *FitzRoy of the Beagle* (New York: Mason and Libscomb, 1968), p. 135.

42. Joseph Conrad, *Lord Jim* ed. Cedric Watts and Robert Hampson (Harmondsworth: Penguin, 1985), p. 48. Subsequent references are to this edition and are included in the text.

Chapter V

1. See S. E. Sprott, *The English Debate on Suicide from Donne to Hume* (LaSalle, Ill: Open Court, 1961).

2. Alexander Pope, "Elegy to the Memory of an Unfortunate Lady," in *The Rape of the Lock and Other Poems*, ed. G. Tillotson (New Haven: Yale University Press, 1954), pp. 332-33.

3. Theophilus Cibber, *The Lives of the Poets of Great Britain and Ireland*, 5 vols. (1753; Hildesheim: Verlag Georg Olms, 1968), vol. 5, p. 13.

4. George Clayton, *The Dreadful Sin of Suicide* (London: Black, Parry, and Kingsbury, 1812), p. 49.

5. Ibid., p. 54.

6. Reverend Solomon Piggott, *Suicide and Its Antidotes* (London: J. Robins & Co., 1824), pp. 218-19.

7. Forbes Winslow, *The Anatomy of Suicide* (London: Henry Renshaw, 1840), p. 1.

8. Ibid., p. 2.

9. Ibid., p. 5.

10. Frank Turner, *The Greek Heritage in Victorian Britain* (New Haven: Yale University Press, 1981), p. xii.

11. S.A.K. Strahan, *Suicide and Insanity: A Physiological and Sociological Study* (London: Swan Sonnenschein, 1893), p. 1.

12. Elizabeth Barrett Browning, *Aurora Leigh* ed. Gardner B. Taplin (Chicago: Academy, Ltd., 1979), p. 163.

13. *The Poems of Matthew Arnold*, ed. Kenneth Allott (New York: Barnes and Noble, 1965), p. 141. Unless otherwise noted, subsequent references to Arnold's poetry are by line numbers or by act and line number and appear in the text.

14. Arnold, *Poems*, p. 591.

15. David Sonstroem, "Abandon the Day: FitzGerald's *Rubáiyát of Omar Khayyám*," *Victorian Newsletter* 36 (Fall 1969): 13.

16. Shairp's letter to Clough is quoted in C. B. Tinker and H. F. Lowry, *The Poetry of Matthew Arnold: A Commentary* (London: 1940), p. 287.

17. Tinker and Lowry, *Poetry*, p. 287.

18. *The Letters of Matthew Arnold to Arthur Hugh Clough*, ed. H.F. Lowry (London: Oxford University Press, 1932), p. 124.

19. As quoted in Tinker and Lowry, *Poetry*, p. 288.

20. Arnold, *Poems*, p. 592.

21. Dwight Culler, *Imaginative Reason: The Poetry of Matthew Arnold* (New Haven: Yale University Press, 1966), p. 174.

22. Arnold, *Poems*, p. 164.

23. Antonin Artaud, *Artaud Anthology*, ed. Jack Hirshman (San Francisco: City Lights Books, 1965), p. 56.

24. Lowry, *Letters*, p. 68.

25. Quoted by Sir Charles Tennyson in *Alfred Tennyson* (London: Macmillan, 1968), p. 286.

26. Sir Charles Tennyson, *Alfred Lord Tennyson: A Memoir by His Son*, 2 vols. (New York: Macmillan, 1897), vol. 2, p. 35.

27. *The Poems of Tennyson*, ed. Christopher Ricks (London: Longmans, 1969), p. 1213. Subesequent references to "Lucretius" are by line number and appear in the text.

28. Richard Jebb, "On Mr. Tennyson's 'Lucretius'," *Macmillan's* June 1868: 103.

29. See Edgar F. Shannon, "The Publication of Tennyson's 'Lucretius'," *Studies in Bibliography* 34 (1981): 146–86.

30. Thomas Cooper, *The Purgatory of Suicides: A Prison-Rhyme* (London: J. Watson, 1851), 9.45. Subsequent references are to book and line numbers.

31. "Suicide," *Chambers's* 10 May 1884: 293.

32. Strahan, *Suicide and Insanity*, p. 25.

33. George Meredith, "Empedocles," *Anti-Jacobin* 12 December 1891; rpt. in *The Poems of George Meredith*, ed. Phyllis B. Bartlett (New Haven: Yale University Press, 1978), p. 544.

34. Robert Browning, *The Complete Poetical Works of Browning* (Cambridge: Riverside Press, 1895), p. 767. Subsequent references are to page numbers.

35. See Mark Siegchrist, *Rough in Brutal Print: The Legal Sources of Browning's "Red Cotton Night-Cap Country"* (Columbus: Ohio State University Press, 1981), p. 16.

36. Ibid., ch. 5.

37. Jerome Buckley, *The Victorian Temper* (1951; New York: Vintage Press, 1964), p. 13.

38. As quoted in *Browning: The Critical Heritage*, ed. Boyd Litzinger and Donald Smalley (New York: Barnes and Noble, 1970), p. 378.

39. See Siegchrist, *Rough in Brutal Print*, p. 14.

40. Walter Pater, *Imaginary Portraits*, ed. Eugene J. Brzenk (New York: Harper and Row, 1964), p. 130. Subsequent references to "Sebastian van Storck" are to this edition.

41. Walter Pater, *Plato and Platonism* (London: Macmillan, 1928), p. 33.

42. Ulrich C. Knoepflmacher, "Historicism as Fiction: Motion and Rest in the Stories of Walter Pater," *Modern Fiction Studies* 9 (Summer 1963): 142.

43. Ulrich C. Knoepflmacher, *Religious Humanism and the Victorian Novel: George Eliot, Walter Pater, and Samuel Butler* (Princeton: Princeton University Press, 1964), p. 220.

44. Walter Pater, *Marius the Epicurean* (New York: Macmillan, 1926), p. 183.

45. George Orwell, *1984* (New York: Harcourt, Brace, and World, 1949), p. 251.

46. Julius Hare, *Guesses at Truth*, 2d ed., 2d ser. (London, 1848), p. 71.

47. A. P. Stanley, as quoted in Duncan Forbes, *The Liberal Anglican Idea of History* (Cambridge: Cambridge University Press, 1952), pp. 191–92.

48. Sir Henry Maine, *Ancient Law* (Oxford: Oxford University Press, 1954), p. 18.

49. See Sir James Frazer's *Golden Bough*, 3rd ed., 12 vols. (London: Macmillan, 1907–15), and Edward Westermarck's *Origin and Development of the Moral Ideas*, 2 vols. (London: Macmillan, 1903).

50. C. A. Bayley, "From Ritual to Ceremony," in *Mirrors of Morality: Studies in the Social History of Death*, ed. Joachim Whaley (London: Europa Publications, 1981), p. 173.

51. See, for example, "Excess of Widows over Widowers," *Westminster Review* 131 (1889): 502–05.

52. Piggott, *Suicide and Its Antidotes*, pp. 150-51.

53. Maine, *Ancient Law*, p. 213.

54. Strahan, *Suicide and Insanity*, p. 2.

55. Frazer, *Golden Bough*, vol. 4, p. 141.

56. Westermarck, *Origin and Development*, p. 242.

57. Ibid., p. 261.

58. Ibid., pp. 263–64.

59. Frazer, *Golden Bough*, vol. 1, p. 181.

Chapter VI

1. See Wolfgang Kayser, *The Grotesque in Art and Literature* (New York: McGraw Hill, 1966).

2. Mary Shelley, *Frankenstein*, ed. James Rieger (New York: Bobbs-Merrill, 1974), p. 72.

3. Quoted in Robert Rogers, *A Psychoanalytical Study of the Double in Literature* (Detroit: Wayne State University Press, 1970), p. 3.

4. *Varney the Vampire, or The Feast of Blood*, 3 vols. (New York: Arno Press, 1970), vol. 3, p. 274.

5. Ibid., vol. 3, p. 868.

6. *The Poems of Matthew Arnold*, ed. Kenneth Allott (New York: Barnes and Noble, 1965), p. 591.

7. *Varney the Vampire*, vol. 3, p. 2.

8. Ibid.

9. Michael Howell and Peter Ford, *The True History of the Elephant Man* (Harmondsworth: Penguin, 1980), p. 129.

10. Lady Geraldine Somerset, 22 May 1887, cited in Howell and Ford, *True History*, p. 129.

11. Howell and Ford, *True History*, p. 189.

12. Ibid., p. 210.

13. Ibid.

14. Peter Brooks, *Reading for the Plot: Design and Intention in Narrative* (New York: Knopf, 1984), p. 284.

15. Charles Dickens, *The Old Curiosity Shop*, ed. Angus Easson (Harmondsworth: Penguin, 1972), p. 65. Subsequent references appear in the text.

16. See Joan D. Winslow, "*The Old Curiosity Shop*: The Meaning of Nell's Fate," *The Dickensian* 72 (Autumn 1981): 162–67, and John Kucich, "Death Worship among the Victorians: *The Old Curiosity Shop*," *PMLA* 95 (January 1980): 58–72.

17. Charles Dickens, *Nicholas Nickleby*, ed. Michael Slater (Harmondsworth: Penguin, 1978), p. 906.

18. Joseph Sheridan Le Fanu, *The Purcell Papers* (Sauk City, Wis.: Arkham House, 1975), p. 26. Subsequent references appear in the text.

19. See Julia Briggs, *Night Visitors: The Rise and Fall of the English Ghost Story* (London: Faber, 1977), p. 51.

20. Joseph Sheridan Le Fanu, *Ghost Stories and Tales of Mystery*, intro. Devendra P. Varma (New York: Arno Press, 1977), p. 60. Subsequent references to "The Watcher" appear in the text.

21. Joseph Sheridan Le Fanu, *Uncle Silas: A Tale of Bartram-Haugh* (Oxford: Oxford University Press, 1981), pp. 193–94. Subsequent references appear in the text.

22. Patrick Brantlinger, "What is 'Sensational' about the 'Sensation Novel'?" *Nineteenth Century Fiction* 37 (June 1982): 21.

23. Joseph Sheridan Le Fanu, *In a Glass Darkly*, intro. Devendra P. Varma, vol. 1 (New York: Arno Press, 1977), p. 275.

24. Ibid., p. 80.

25. Jack Sullivan, *Elegant Nightmares: The English Ghost Story from Le Fanu to Blackwood* (Athens, Ohio: Ohio University Press, 1978), p. 14.

26. Matthew Arnold, *Dissent and Dogma*, ed. R. H. Super (Ann Arbor: University of Michigan Press: 1968), p. 112.

27. Thomas Carylle, *Sartor Resartus*, ed. Charles Frederick Harrold (New York: Odyssey Press, 1937), p. 165.

28. Tzvetan Todorov, *The Fantastic*, trans. Richard Howard (Cleveland: Case Western Reserve, 1973), p. 25.

29. See Rogers, *A Psychoanalytic Study*, pp. 14–15.

30. Otto Rank, *Beyond Psychology* (New York: Dover, 1941), pp. 71–76.

31. Robert Louis Stevenson, *The Strange Case of Dr. Jekyll and Mr. Hyde and Other Stories*, ed. Jenni Calder (Harmondsworth: Penguin Books, 1979), p. 32. Subsequent references appear in the text.

32. "Lay Morals," *The Works of Robert Louis Stevenson*, Vailima Edition, 26 vols., ed. Lloyd Osbourne (London: William Heinemann, 1923), vol. 24, p. 208.

33. John Addington Symonds, as quoted in John Alexander Steuart, *Robert Louis Stevenson: A Critical Biography*, 2 vols. (Boston: Little Brown, 1924), vol. 2, p. 83.

34. Mentioned in George S. Hellman, *The True Stevenson: A Study in Clarification* (Boston: Little Brown, 1925), p. 160.

35. *The Poems of Tennyson*, ed. Christopher Ricks (London: Longmans, 1969), p. 1581. Subsequent references to "Balin and Balin" are cited by line numbers in the text.

36. Rank, *Beyond Psychology*, p. 84.

37. Oscar Wilde, *The Picture of Dorian Gray*, ed. Peter Ackroyd (Harmondsworth: Penguin Books, Ltd., 1982), p. 26. Subsequent references appear in the text.

38. *Daily Chronicle* 30 June 1890, p. 7.

39. *Punch* 19 July 1890: 25.

40. Matthew Arnold, *Culture and Anarchy*, in *Prose of the Victorian Period*, ed. William E. Buckler (Boston: Houghton Mifflin, 1958), p. 481.

Chapter VII

1. See such fine recent studies as Nina Auerbach's *Woman and the Demon* (Cambridge: Harvard University Press, 1982), and Sally Mitchell's *The Fallen Angel* (Bowling Green: Bowling Green University Popular Press, 1981).

2. See especially J. N. Radcliffe's "On the Prevalence of Suicide in England," *Transactions of the National Association for the Promotion of Social Science* (London, 1862), p. 465.

3. See Elaine Showalter, *The Female Malady* (New York: Pantheon Books, 1985).

4. See George Henry Lewes, "Suicide in Life and Literature," *Westminster Review* July 1857: 52–78.

5. Ibid., p. 71.

6. "Suicide," *Blackwood's* June 1880: 727.

7. Harriet Martineau, "Self-Murder," *Once A Week* 17 December 1859, p. 511.

8. S.A.K. Strahan, *Suicide and Insanity: A Physiological and Sociological Study* (London: Swan Sonnenschein, 1893), p. 179.

9. Havelock Ellis, *Man and Woman* (London: Walter Scott, Ltd., 1894), p. 335.

10. Frances Power Cobbe, "Criminals, Idiots, Women, and Minors," *Fraser's Magazine* December 1868: 789.

11. For a recent examination of such diminishment see Beth Ann Bassein, *Women and Death* (Westport, Conn.: Greenwood Press, 1984), ch. 1.

12. J. W. Horsley, *Jottings from Jail* (London: T. Fisher Unwin, 1887), p. 256.

13. Ibid., p. 241.

14. John Stuart Mill, *On the Subjection of Women* (London: Longmans, Green, Reader, and Dyer, 1869), p. 27.

15. Forbes Winslow, "Recent Trials in Lunacy," *Journal of Psychological Medicine and Mental Pathology* 7 (1854): 623.

16. Charles Kingsley, "Tennyson," *Fraser's Magazine* September 1850: 250.

17. Anna Jameson, *Characteristics of Women* (London: George Bell and Sons, 1889), p. 276.

18. Charlotte Brontë, *The Professor* (London: J. W. Dent, 1969), p. 226.

19. See Auerbach, *Woman and the Demon*, ch. 1.

20. John R. de C. Wise, "Belles Lettres," *Westminster Review* 84 (1865): 568.

21. Edward Burne-Jones, *Burne-Jones Talking*, ed. Mary Lago (Columbia: University of Missouri Press, 1981), p. 11.

22. Cesare Lombroso, *The Female Offender*, intro. W. Douglas Morris (New York: Appleton, 1895), 150–52.

23. Mill, *Subjection*, p. 77.

24. Ibid., pp. 64–65.

25. Frances Power Cobbe, "The Final Cause of Women," in *Woman's Work and Woman's Culture*, ed. Josephine E. Butler (London: Macmillan, 1869), p. 9.

26. Oscar Wilde, *The First Collected Edition of the Works of Oscar Wilde*, ed. Robert Ross, 15 vols. (1908–22; London: Methuen, 1969), *The Importance of Being Earnest*, p. 50.

27. See Showalter, *Female Malady*, introduction and ch. 3.

28. "The Suicide," in *Forget-Me-Not*, ed. Frederic Shoberl (London: R. Ackermann, 1827), pp. 204–06.

29. Thomas DeQuincey, "On Suicide," *Collected Works*, 14 vols., ed. David Masson (Edinburgh: Black, 1890), vol. 8, p. 399.

30. See Mitchell, *Fallen Angel*, p. x.

31. Charles Dickens, *Miscellaneous Papers* (London: Chapman and Hall, 1911), p. 408.

32. Ibid., p. 395.

33. William Acton, *Prostitution Considered in Its Moral, Social and Sanitary Aspects* (1870; London: Frank Cass and Co., 1972), p. 38.

34. William Bell Scott, "Rosabell," in *Autobiographical Notes of the Life of William Bell Scott*, ed. W. Minto, 2 vols. (New York: Harper, 1892), vol. 1, p. 151.

35. John Armstrong, "Female Penitentiaries," *Quarterly Review* 83 (1848): 375–76.

36. Elizabeth Barrett Browning, *Aurora Leigh*, ed. Gardner B. Taplin (1864; Chicago: Academy Chicago Limited, 1979), p. 112. Subsequent references appear in the text by page number.

37. *The Works of George Meredith*, 29 vols. (New York: Scribner's, 1910), vol. 5, p. 98. Subsequent references are to volume five and appear in the text.

38. See *The Standard Edition of the Complete Psychological Works*, ed. James Strachey, et al., 24 vols. (London: Hogarth Press, 1953–74), vol. 18, 162 n.

39. Charles Dickens, *David Copperfield* (London: Oxford University Press, 1981), p. 581.

40. ———, *Oliver Twist* (London: Oxford University Press, 1966), p. 354.

41. ———, "Wapping Workhouse," in *The Uncommercial Traveller* (London: Chapman and Hall, 1911), p. 22.

42. *Selected Poems of Thomas Hood*, ed. John Clubbe (Cambridge: Harvard University Press, 1970), p. 392. Subsequent references are by line number and are incorporated into the text.

43. J. W. Horsley, "Suicide," *Fortnightly Review* 35 (1881): 509.

44. Showalter, *Female Malady*, p. 92.

45. Provenance courtesy the Delaware Art Museum, Wilmington, Delaware.

46. See Martin Meisel's *Realizations: Narrative, Pictorial, and Theatrical Arts in Nineteenth-Century England* (Princeton: Princeton University Press, 1983), p. 140.

47. G.W.M. Reynolds, *The Mysteries of London* (London: John Dicks, 1846), vol. 2, p. 69.

48. See Hans Peter Duerr, *Dreamtime* (New York: Basil Blackwell's, 1985).

49. Ellis, *Man and Woman*, p. 334.

50. People "found drowned" were not in fact counted as suicides. See R. Thompson Jopling, "Statistics of Suicide," *Assurance Magazine* 2 (1851): 39.

51. See *The Brontës: Life and Letters*, ed. Clement Shorter, 19 vols. (New York: Scribners, 1908), vol. 2, p. 264.

52. Lady Blessington, *The Governess* (Philadelphia: Lea and Blanchard, 1839), p. 60.

53. Eliza Meteyard, "Lucy Dean: the Noble Needlewoman," *Eliza Cook's Journal* 16 March–April 1850: 312–95.

54. *The Complete Plays of Gilbert and Sullivan* (New York: Garden City, 1938), p. 356.

55. Harriet Cope, *Suicide* (London: Bryer, 1815).

56. For access to Ann Jewett's letter I am grateful to my friend Sarah Van Camp, a descendant of the Jewett family.

57. Auerbach, *Woman and the Demon*, p. 94.

58. William Makepeace Thackeray, *Letters and Private Papers of William Makepeace Thackeray, 1817–1840*, ed. Gordon N. Ray, 4 vols. (Cambridge: Harvard University Press, 1945), vol. 1, p. 483.

59. Ibid.

60. Ibid., p. 473.

61. Ibid., vol. 2, p. 440.

62. Quoted in Oswald Doughty, *A Victorian Romantic: Dante Gabriel Rossetti* (London: Oxford University Press, 1960), p. 269.

63. In *Dante Gabriel Rossetti: Family Letters and a Memoir*, 2 vols., ed. W.M. Rossetti, (London, 1895), vol. 1, p. 177.

64. See Sandra M. Donaldson's " 'Ophelia' in Elizabeth Siddal Rossetti's Poem 'A Year and a Day'," *Journal of Pre-Raphaelite Studies* 2 (November 1981): 126–33.

Chapter VIII

1. William Knighton, "Suicidal Mania," *Contemporary Review* 39 (1881): 82.

2. Havelock Ellis, *Dance of Life* (London: Constable, 1923), p. 199.

3. John Ruskin, *The Storm-Cloud of the Nineteenth Century*, *Works*, Library Edition,

39 vols., ed. E. T. Cook and Alexander Wedderburn (London: Allen, 1903–12), vol. 34, pp. 78–79.

4. Arthur Balfour, *The Foundations of Belief* (London: Longmans, Green and Co., 1895), p. 30.

5. Francis Adams, *A Child of the Age* (London: John Lane, 1894), p. 212.

6. T. O. Bonser, *The Right to Die* (London: Freethought, 1885), p. 8.

7. W. Knighton, *Suicidal Mania*, p. 81.

8. [Frederick Marshall] "Suicide," *Blackwood's* June 1880: 719–35.

9. Marshall, "Suicide," p. 720.

10. Marshall, "Suicide," p. 725.

11. For example, in Volume 1 (April and May 1877) appeared "The Influence upon Morality of a Decline in Religious Belief," a symposium that opened and closed with remarks by James Fitzjames Stephen.

12. Rpt. in *Current Discussion*, ed. Edward L. Burlingame (New York: Putnam's, 1878), vol. 2, p. 332.

13. L. S. Bevington, "Modern Atheism and Mr. Mallock," *Nineteenth Century* December 1879: 1001.

14. Bevington, "Modern Atheism," p. 1015.

15. Quoted by Christopher Ricks in *The Poems of Tennyson* (London: Longmans, 1969), p. 1299.

16. Sir Charles Tennyson, *Alfred Tennyson* (New York: Macmillan, 1949), pp. 460–61.

17. *The Poetical Works of James Thomson*, ed. Bertram Dobell, 2 vols. (London: Reeves and Turner, 1895), vol. 1, p. 129. Subsequent references appear in the text by section and line number.

18. Reverend J. Gurnhill, *The Morals of Suicide* (London: Longmans, Green and Co., 1900), p. 180.

19. Olive Anderson points out the erroneousness of the habit of arguing from London that was *sui generis* in terms of suicide in "Did Suicide Increase with Industrialization in Victorian England?" *Past and Present* 86 (February 1980): 155.

20. Marshall, "Suicide," p. 725.

21. W. R. Lethaby, "Of Beautiful Cities," *Art and Life, and the Building and Decoration of Cities* (London: Rivington, Percival and Co., 1897), p. 99.

22. Jack London, "Suicide," in *The People of the Abyss* (New York: Macmillan, 1903), pp. 23–73.

23. George Gissing, *New Grub Street*, ed., Bernard Bergonzi (Harmondsworth: Penguin, 1983), p. 36. Subsequent references are to this edition and appear in the text.

24. See Pierre Coustillas, "Pessimism in *New Grub Street*: Its Nature and Manifestations," *Cahiers Victoriens et Edouardiens* 11 (1980): 45–64.

25. Arthur Schopenhauer, *The World As Will and Representation*, trans. E.F.J. Payne, 2 vols. (Indian Hills, Colorado: Falcon's Wing Press, 1958), vol. 1, p. 398.

26. *Whitehall Review* 18 April 1891: 19.

27. *The Writings in Prose and Verse of Rudyard Kipling*, 35 vols. (New York: Charles Scribner's Sons, 1917), vol. 9, p. 329. Subsequent references are also to this volume.

28. My insights into the question of failure in Kipling's novel have been strengthened by conversations with Robert Caserio whose work on the subject recently appeared as an essay entitled "Kipling in the Light of Failure" in *Grand Street* 5 (Summer 1986): 129–212.

29. Thomas Hardy, *Jude the Obscure*, ed. C. H. Sisson (Harmondsworth: Penguin, 1981), p. 117. Subsequent references are to this edition and appear in the text.

30. See Laurence J. Starzyk, "The Coming Universal Wish Not to Live in Hardy's 'Modern' Novels," *Nineteenth Century Fiction* 26 (March 1972): 419–35. A nearly opposing view, closer to mine, is taken by Richard Benvenuto in "Modes of Perception: The Will to Live in *Jude the Obscure*," *Studies in the Novel* 2 (Spring 1970): 31–41.

31. *Illustrated London News* 11 January 1896; reprinted in *Thomas Hardy: The Critical Heritage*, ed. R. G. Cox (New York: Barnes and Noble, 1970), p. 275.

32. "The Leaden Echo and the Golden Echo," *The Poems of Gerard Manley Hopkins*, 4th ed., W. H. Gardner and N. H. Mackenzie, eds. (London: Oxford University Press, 1967). p. 91.

33. Mary Augusta Ward, *Helbeck of Bannisdale*, intro. Brian Worthington (Harmondsworth: Penguin, 1983), p. 385. Subsequent references are to this edition and appear in the text.

34. Mrs. Humphrey Ward, *A Writer's Recollections*, 2 vols. (New York: Harper Brothers, 1918), vol. 2, p. 185.

35. Ibid., p. 184.

36. Leslie Stephen, *The Science of Ethics* (London: Smith, Elder, 1882), p. 392.

37. H. H. Henson, *Suicide* (London: Oxford House, 1897), p. 67.

38. Quoted in Susan Budd, "The Loss of Faith in England, 1850–1950," *Past and Present* 36 (1967): 120.

39. F. H. Perry-Coste, *The Ethics of Suicide* (London: The University Press, Ltd., 1898), p. 9.

40. S.A.K. Strahan, *Suicide and Insanity: A Physiological and Sociological Study* (London: Swan Sonnenschein, 1893), p. 185.

41. Gurnhill, *Morals of Suicide*, p. 125.

42. M. P. Shiel, *Prince Zaleski* (London: John Lane, 1895), p. 100.

INDEX

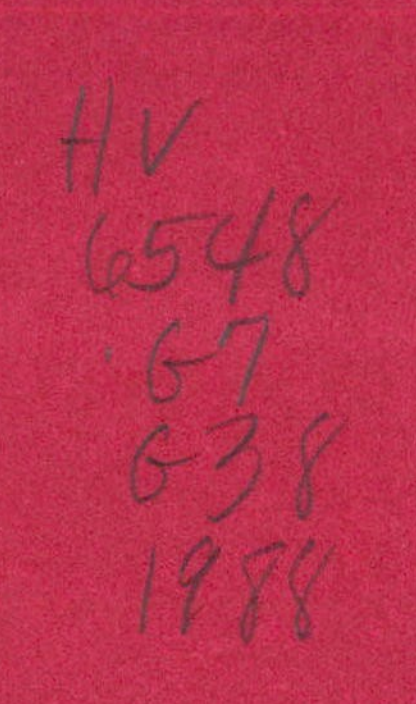